'We Made Our Own Fun!'

In a golden era called yesteryear, money didn't buy fun, and having a good time often took a good imagination. The stories in this book were shared by readers of *Reminisce*, who can remember a time when kids never said, "I'm bored", and even adults could "play" for a song.

REMINISCE BOOKS

OH, WHAT FUN WE HAD! Whether it was dressing "down" like little girls with lollies, as these young ladies had a ball doing, or gathering around the family piano, it seems yesteryear amusements came in endless supply.

Editor: Bettina Miller
Contributing Editor: Clancy Strock
Assistant Editors: Deb Mulvey, John Schroeder, Kristine Krueger, Michael Martin, Mike Beno
Art Director: Maribeth Greinke
Art Associates: Stephanie Marchese, Vicky Wilimitis, Linda Dzik, Nancy Krueger, Sue Myers, Bonnie Ziolecki
Photo Coordination: Trudi Bellin
Editorial Assistants: Blanche Comiskey, Joe Kertzman, Jack Kertzman
Production Assistant: Judy Pope
Publisher: Roy J. Reiman

© 1995 Reiman Publications, L.P.
5400 S. 60th St., Greendale WI 53129

Reminisce Books
International Standard Book Number: 0-89821-155-7
Library of Congress Catalog Number: 95-72529
All rights reserved. Printed in U.S.A.

Photos on the cover and this page: J.C. Allen and Son

For additional copies of this book or information on other books, write: Reminisce Books, P.O. Box 990, Greendale WI 53129. **Credit card orders call toll-free 1-800/558-1013.**

Contents

HOW'S THE WEATHER UP THERE? A few pieces of lumber and a handful of nails were all it took to bring a smile at a Sunday school picnic in Old Zionsville, Pennsylvania. Fun was simple and easy to find in the good old days. Join us and see!

Prologue

By Clancy Strock, Contributing Editor, Reminisce Magazine

THERE SAT my 1-year-old firstborn on the floor of her room, a little queen surrounded by treasure bestowed upon her by adoring grandparents, aunts, uncles, neighbors and parents.

Her bounty included colorful balls, a half dozen rattles, things that jingled and things that tinkled, things to pound on, push or pull, things that woofed and things that chirped. But what was she actually *playing* with? A discarded set of plastic measuring cups and a dented pie tin!

She had discovered a great truth—it doesn't take a lot of money to have fun. Each person's imagination is the greatest toy store of all. It's open 24 hours a day, and the price is always right.

Sometimes we forget that piece of wisdom, but then remember it in a hurry when hard times strike.

The stories you are about to read in this book are mainly about having *fun on the cheap.* Those of us who lived through the bleak decade of the '30s and the sparse wartime years are experts on having fun for little or no money. And now we're relearning it during our retirement years. The nice part is that fun isn't measured by how much money you spend. The only measure is…uh, how much *fun* you have.

During the hot summer months in those days before air-conditioning, we'd seek relief from the scalding, dead-calm night by "going for a drive". We had no destination, and there was nothing within 15 miles that we hadn't seen hundreds of other times. No matter. It just felt good to bask in the breeze that blew in the open windows regardless of how hot it was.

As I'm sure you recall, those were the days when the front windows had little wing windows that could be cracked forward to move more air into the car. Hey, Detroit…why did you take them away from us?

The Panther Panic

I recall one of those summers when Dad had more fun without investing a dime…and was never able to tell anyone about it! It started a few days after a traveling circus departed town and the local newspaper began carrying reports that a black panther had been spotted by several people. Three farmers reported livestock missing and footprints "as big as a dinner plate" left by the critter.

The circus denied losing any animals, and certainly not a black panther. But everyone knew circus people weren't always the most honest folks to pass through town.

Then Dad had an idea, and you could almost see the little

BUSY LITTLE HANDS found plenty to do with a piece of string and plain wooden beads. Maybe it'll be a "diamond necklace" to wear to the ball!

light bulb blazing above his head. He took a discarded round washtub and drilled a small hole dead center in the bottom. Then he took a length of clothesline, coated it with rosin he borrowed from my sister, the violinist, and threaded it through the hole. When he sawed the clothesline back and forth, you didn't need much imagination to hear a black panther roaring.

That night, there wasn't a breath of air stirring when he took the washtub to high ground at the edge of the farm and gave a stirring half-hour "black panther concert". It was heard for miles around.

The next day's newspaper was filled with reports of the marauding beast. Farmers told of mutilated livestock. Dozens of sober citizens had "narrowly escaped" from the brute. People were advised to keep their children and pets indoors. The panther was everywhere!

Dad was ready to set out for another go at it the next night when a caravan of fearless, armed neighbors arrived to recruit him for a black panther hunt. They said they knew how to go about it from reading *National Geographic.* They'd surround the area where the panther seemed to be hiding and send in "beaters" to drive it toward the riflemen. (All they lacked were elephants!)

That was the point when Mom put her foot down on Dad's shenanigans. Firmly. The black panther was heard no more.

Sunday night in our home was another exciting event—and the most enjoyable time of the week. That was the night to shell popcorn (we grew our own) and laboriously extract the meat from black walnuts while Dad made fudge.

It was Dad's fudge-making that furnished the excitement…mainly because week after week, year after year, the results remained unpredictable.

There were nights when we gathered around and ate his fudge from the pan with a spoon, and other nights when a hammer and chisel would have been useful! And some nights, the fudge could have won a blue ribbon at the county fair. But you never knew...

Never mind. We'd take the popcorn and fudge into the living room and settle down for a good night's entertainment on the radio. It kicked off with Jack Benny and Mary Livingston, with a cast including Kenny Baker, the Irish tenor, raspy-voiced Andy Devine, Don Wilson, and comical Phil Harris and his orchestra.

An hour later came the Chase and Sanborn program with ↻

Don Ameche, Dorothy Lamour, Edgar Bergen and Charlie McCarthy and guests such as W.C. Fields.

Next was *Manhattan Merry-Go-Round* (with one of the most upbeat theme songs ever written), and later in the evening came *The Hour of Charm* with Phil Spitalny's All-Girl Orchestra (remember "Evelyn and her Magic Violin?").

What a night! Dare I use the term "wholesome, cheap family entertainment", or does that make me hopelessly square?

Pleasure by the Page

For day-in, day-out cheap pleasure, though, I'd have to put magazines at the top of the list. That was the era of *great* magazines, and our family subscribed to several of them.

The Saturday Evening Post was the one that set the pace. Its articles on current affairs were probing and enlightening. Its biographies of newsmakers brought the famous and powerful right into your home for a visit. And there always was a mystery serial that left you panting for the next installment.

My favorite author of those cliff-hangers was Clarence Buddington Kelland. I also looked forward to the comical misadventures of Alexander Botts, the inept but successful salesman for the mythical Earthworm Tractor Company.

The *Post's* cartoons were unmatched, too. Mostly they were in the back pages of the magazine, so that's where I started with every new issue, leafing from back to front. And that's how I still read magazines to this day.

And there were Norman Rockwell's magnificent *Post* covers that again and again reminded America of the good in a world that was temporarily lacking in cheer.

We also took *American* magazine and *Collier's*, general-interest magazines that also published some of the best authors of the era. Mom subscribed to *Woman's Home Companion* and Dad, a farmer, was a faithful *Country Gentleman* reader.

LIFE was a whole new concept in magazines, featuring page after page of marvelous photography from all over the world. And we often picked up a copy of *Look*, a hybrid that was part *LIFE* and part the forerunner of today's *People*.

"MR. FUN" HIMSELF. Clancy Strock recalls when "cheap thrills" meant good clean fun.

At the barbershop, I'd sometimes find a copy of *Liberty,* a news magazine famous for its taunting "Reading time, 3 mins. 20 secs." challenge at the start of every story.

Magazines weren't that much of a luxury, even in the Depression. The total cost per month was, I'm sure, less than $1.60, remembering that two of the magazines were monthly and another was bimonthly. We read a lot. And we also learned a lot more, for example, than if we'd watched television for 6 hours a day.

Tornado Gave New Twist on Toys

It was during one of those cruel summers that a baby tornado came along and destroyed a shed in which we kept our farm implements. Lumber and corrugated sheet metal were scattered everywhere.

Those were the days when roofing nails used to nail down the corrugated panels had lead washers designed to thwart leaking during rainstorms. Opportunity knocked!

I spent 2 weeks poking through the wreckage to salvage those little lead washers. Eventually, I had amassed more than 10 pounds of lead.

Our minister's son owned dozens of those metal molds used to cast lead soldiers and Indians, so we worked out a deal. I provided the lead and he furnished the molds. We split the output and each ended up with a large troop of soldiers and a horde of Indians. There were foot soldiers and mounted cavalry, as well as rampaging redskins, some with bows and arrows and others brandishing tomahawks and spears while astride their ponies. They brought me hundreds of hours of pleasure and didn't cost a cent.

Meanwhile, Indy 500 drivers such as Wilbur Shaw, Floyd Roberts and Louis Meyer made headlines by topping the 100-mph barrier at the Indianapolis raceway.

One hundred miles per hour! Uncle Willard had a Studebaker that he claimed could do 70, but his reputation for accuracy was shaky. The mind boggled at the idea of traveling 100.

Soon boys began building their own Indy racers, powered not by Offenhauser engines but by feet and a helping push down a steep hill. They scavenged the necessary materials from garages, basements and even the city dump.

Before long, communities were holding sanctioned "Soap Box Derby" contests, and the winners went to a national competition in Akron, Ohio.

Boys weren't the only ones who made

YUM, YUM. Norma Hurt of Riverton, Illinois and her big sis had fun forming mud cakes in an old Prince Albert tin. Both grew up to own restaurant/catering businesses. "I guess you could say we started from the ground up," laughs Norma.

their own toys. I remember when my sister, Mary, roamed the fencerows and ditches to gather milkweed pods. She laboriously extracted the floss and used it to stuff a mattress for her doll cradle.

She also made necklaces and bracelets from looped-together dandelion stems and whipped up tasty salads for her doll family from weeds and wildflowers. With Mom's help, she learned how to sew doll clothes, too.

Mary and I also originated the very *first* "Friends and Family" phone plan. It came about after our old "tulip-horn" battery-powered radio was replaced by a new Silvertone Superheterodyne 12-tube console. Dad let me dismantle the old relic and showed me how the headphones and speaker could be hitched up with a piece of electrical wire and turned into a crude telephone system.

Soon Mary and I had a far-flung communications network that stretched all the way from the chicken house to the

---

> ## "Never mind if you didn't have a dime for one of the kites sold at Woolworth's..."

---

barn...at least 80 feet! And just like a certain long-distance company today, we insisted that all our friends and family try out our new marvel.

Look at all the fun we were having...and all for free! Never mind if you didn't have a dime for one of the kites sold at Woolworth's. You could make your own with just two thin sticks, a sheet of newspaper and some flour-and-water paste. Then you raided Mom's ragbag for enough scraps of cloth to make a serviceable tail.

I'll admit these homemade kites didn't hold up too well, but usually the only repair you needed was another piece of newspaper.

My own flights of fancy took a different turn after some barnstorming aviators came to town. The grand finale was a thrilling parachute jump. Their little biplane climbed higher and higher as we strained to watch it. Everyone gasped when a tiny figure leaped out. It fell and fell as we held our breaths until the chute opened. The crowd oohed and the parachutist drifted down to land in a nearby field.

Oh, to be a parachute jumper! As soon as I got home, I recruited one of the lead soldiers from my toy army and assigned him to parachute duty. Perhaps he was the world's first paratrooper.

The chute was constructed from a square of cloth cut from an old feed sack and four pieces of string that were tied to the soldier. I carefully folded the chute into a tidy bundle with the paratrooper tucked inside, and fired him aloft with the slingshot...up higher than the peak of the barn. When things worked right, the chute unrolled and the soldier drifted back to earth. But the failure rate was high.

The Roaring Twenties, a time when *everyone* seemed to have plenty of money, were nothing but a memory for the grown-ups when I was young. Who could afford the expensive entertainment of that era?

Perhaps it's true that "misery loves company". At any rate, the '30s saw a lot more at-home socializing, as I remember it. Families became closer again. We rediscovered the sim-

ple pleasures of creating our own entertainment. Mom and Dad got together with friends to play pinochle and rummy. The new game of Monopoly was an instant hit. (People who didn't know where their next meal was coming from could become investment tycoons for an evening.) Often folks just got together for an evening of conversation.

"Lazy Susan Golf"

An ingenious friend of our family built a remarkable indoor putt-putt golf course that required moving the table out of the dining room. The six holes were on a sort of giant lazy Susan covered with green felt. The golf hole was in the center. You putted across a 6-foot ramp onto the lazy Susan, played the hole, then rotated the contraption a one-sixth turn to be ready for the next challenge.

They had to eat in the kitchen, but they sure didn't lack for company on weekends!

That's what this book is all about—how folks *had fun together*. Lacking money, they made much of their own amusement. Families really did gather around the piano to sing. They played games together, or just sat and talked and laughed.

Norman Rockwell's *Saturday Evening Post* covers had it exactly right. And looking back, I realize now that the most fun of all was simply *being together.* ❧

Harold M. Lambert

COOLING WATERS. A drive to the country in the old Model T, a picnic lunch and a thermos of lemonade was the perfect remedy for relief on a sultry summer day. No bathhouse? No problem. Just bring along a tarp and you had instant privacy for changing into that "revealing" swimsuit. Best of all, there were no crowds to fight in the good old days.

Chapter One
In the Good Old Summertime

Cooling off took a little more effort...but it was a lot more fun.

Electric refrigerators are a marvelous invention, but they did steal one special summer pleasure from us. We just don't need to "go out for ice cream" much anymore. And I miss that.

What did you do after a band concert on a hot July evening? Of course! You stopped on the way home to buy an ice cream cone. What did you do on Saturday night after the stores closed? Well, our family went to Dondero's, a soda fountain/candy store/newsstand and got an ice cream cone...then headed to the ice plant to pick up a 50-pound block that sat on the running board of the car as we hurried home. Or we went to the A&S Dairy store, which made the best chocolate ice cream in town.

During the '30s, the man who owned the ice plant, Earl Prince, built a place that specialized in ice cream, milk shakes and malts. The little building was made from stone and looked like a miniature castle, complete with turrets and battlements on top.

Naturally he called it a "Prince Castle". It was so successful that he eventually built a whole chain of them. There was a serious debate in town, however, as to whether the best malts were made by the Dondero boys or Mr. Prince. But no one disputed that the Prince Castle triple-dip cones were the best!

Another great treat on a hot summer evening was to stop in at the A&W Root Beer stand on the east edge of town. Those huge frost-covered mugs with creamy root beer foaming over the sides just got better and better as the temperature rose.

The Whole Family Came Along

Back then, we had outdoor band concerts, circus parades, tent revival meetings, Chautauquas, creeks to swim in, beaches to explore, baseball games to be played, trees to be climbed and woodsy trails to be explored, and we always anticipated the annual "threshing ring" picnic.

There were two dozen or more families in our ring who all helped each other out during threshing season. When it was over, everyone got together for a monstrous picnic at Lawrence Park, an island in the middle of the Rock River. Each family brought a big dish—baked beans, potato salad, the legendary "covered hot dish" or perhaps a cake—and the man who owned the threshing machine provided ice cream and soft drinks.

This was also the time of year when fireflies made the night sparkle. I've never known what practical purpose fireflies serve in Mother Nature's grand scheme. Perhaps it is nothing more than providing children with an incentive to run off their excess energy before bedtime. It takes a heap of running to collect enough fireflies to fill a mason-jar lantern.

When I had children of my own, we discovered the pleasures of family camping before it got as popular as it is now. Sometimes we had an entire campsite to ourselves in the middle of a national forest or state park, far away from the clatter and clutter of "civilization". Can there be anything better than a watermelon that's spent the afternoon chilling in a sparkling North Carolina mountain stream? Or a hair-raising encounter with a wandering bear while toasting marshmallows over a campfire in northern Minnesota?

Few memories are as sweet as our summer memories, as you'll discover on the pages that follow.

—*Clancy Strock*

Rockaway Beach Was Mother's Riviera

By Judi Barrett, Port Richey, Florida

WE USED TO spend summers on Rockaway Beach, at the southern tip of Long Island, with fellow Irish-Americans from the Bronx and Queens (the Brooklynites preferred Coney Island).

Every March, Mother and her sister drove out to make the arrangements, and even in the bone-chilling wind, Mom would walk the boardwalk, recalling childhood summers. For her, going to Rockaway Beach was like coming home.

With everything looking so bleak, it seemed amazing that the shack-like bungalows had survived another winter. "God forbid anything should happen here," Mother would say. "It's the nearest thing to Heaven in my eyes."

We rented in an area nestled between 116th and 98th streets from the ocean to the bay. Affectionately called "Irish-Town", it was made up of old houses and bungalows and a quaint bar-and-grill here and there.

Mother's favorite bungalow was anything with a porch. Hot water was not a necessity, but there *had* to be a porch. From there, she could sit in a rocking chair facing the common courtyard and talk to neighbors, watching everyone come and go.

Relieved to have the arrangements finalized, Mother could begin looking forward to Memorial Day, the official start of summer.

We're Here!

Many took the Long Island Railroad from Queens, and as soon as the train creaked along the trestle over Jamaica Bay and screeched to a stop, vacationers descended the station stairs and began swarming to rented dwellings.

We always drove our old car in from the Bronx and breathed a sigh of relief that we'd made it to Broad Channel. Once across the Rockaway Bridge, we felt the dampness and got our first whiff of the salt air.

"Doesn't this smell wonderful?" Mother would say. We agreed, holding our noses.

As other families arrived, the little houses were spruced up with fresh coats of paint. New curtains were hung, and the mattresses were carried outdoors to air in the sun.

That evening after everyone was settled, kitchen tables were moved outside for potluck dinners. Mother was in her glory at these parties, catching up on the winter's news. "You look wonderful…God love you—you never change…That's a shame you got that

---

"The courtyards were alive with laughter…"

---

old gout again…Looks like there'll be another little Catholic coming soon!"

The courtyards were alive with laughter and Irish ballads. The neighbor across from us was a proud little Irish woman who thought she fooled everyone with the teacup in her lap.

As the party progressed, though, she would sing the loudest and forget the words. "God love her and that wonderful tea she drinks," Mother laughed.

The next morning, the courtyard bustled with adults carrying umbrellas and wooden beach chairs toward the boardwalk, with the kids in tow. It was a real feat to walk the length of the boardwalk without getting a splinter.

On the beach, green, orange and yellow striped umbrellas sprouted across the sand. Housecoats, underwear and shirts hung from the metal spikes, serving as markers so their owners could find their way back after swimming.

Positioning those wooden beach chairs in the sand was a tricky task so as not to sit down and be crushed up like an accordion. (This guaranteed a big chuckle from my mother.)

Lagging behind Mother to the ocean, the first twinges of icy water turned our toes blue. We waded in slowly so we wouldn't feel the waves' full force all at once, but Mother dove right into the crest. "Come on in—it's wonderful," she urged. "Don't ever be afraid of God's beautiful ocean."

At noon, bells from the nearby convent signaled it was time for the Angelus. All Catholics, including even the lifeguards, rose and bowed their heads to pray. Even some non-Catholics stood out of respect.

People Watching

Mother was the beach's unofficial lifeguard, scanning the ocean for swimmers in trouble or shifting sandbars. She could sense when a sandbar was going to move and alerted everyone even before the real lifeguards did.

She was just as sharp observing people on the beach. "Boy, look at her… some shape on that one." Or, "Gee, I thought *I* was fat!

"Look at that guy eyeing the young girl!" she'd point. "The old fool. Well, I guess he isn't dead yet."

As we sat there, I often teased Mother about seeing what was on "the other side of the horizon".

"To tell you the God's honest truth, I'm happiest here," she'd reply. "This is my Riviera."

"But Ma—don't you ever get tired of sand in the bed, the cold showers, jellyfish, the outhouse?"

"No," she'd answer. "I love it all. Where else can you have the beach, wonderful neighbors, fireworks, an amusement park…and a link to our heritage!" she continued.

"Irish singing and dancing Saturday nights, the smell of fresh-baked Irish soda bread Sunday mornings after Mass, and the legacy of my grandparents who strolled this same boardwalk!

"There's no place in the world that compares to where we are right now," Mother would say.

And I had to agree. ☘

AT THE "RIVIERA". Judi Barrett (left, holding a girl from the courtyard) and her mother (seated next to her) relax with friends at Rockaway Beach in 1960. Taken the year she passed away, this was her mother's last summer at the place she considered "the nearest thing to Heaven".

MAIN STREET OF FUN. Surf Avenue at Coney Island was the main street of the popular amusement park, featuring interesting sideshow attractions and lots of food.

SOUVENIR SNAP. A fun day at Coney Island in '43 ended with a keepsake photo for Jean Carroll of Carlsbad, California (right) and friend Josie.

Rides, Food Filled Day At Coney Island

A DAY at Coney Island and Steeplechase Park was the ultimate summer adventure for my friend Helen and me.

As we got off the trolley with my parents, we heard a calliope chiming in the distance. Directly ahead, exquisitely carved horses on a huge, brightly colored carousel danced up and down in time to the music. Riders could reach for the iron rings held by the carousel operator, trying for the one brass ring that would win a free ride.

"Freak shows" of sword swallowers, fire eaters, the alligator man and tattooed lady lined the main streets, and each concessionaire boasted of their own favorite.

The air was filled with the aroma of Nathan's hot dogs, Shatskin's knishes, hot buttered corn and french fries. We always bought Willie's custard for dessert: vanilla, chocolate, strawberry, banana or pistachio with juicy green nuts.

Strolling along the boardwalk, we watched in awe as pink, yellow and blue sugar was poured into spinning metal containers and trans-formed into cotton candy. We stuffed puffy handfuls into our mouths, letting it melt on our tongues.

My parents waited patiently on the boardwalk while Helen and I entered Steeplechase Park through the spinning barrel rides.

Shaking with fright, trying to keep our balance, we'd tumble and fall. We were carried up the sides of the barrel and dropped down again before finally tumbling out the other side, where we'd look up woozily to see a giant cutout of a red-haired clown with a huge red mouth and a white toothy grin.

SANDY SHADE. Her parents, James and Ruth Nelson, found romance and a little relief from the summer sun at Myrtle Beach, South Carolina in 1927, says Carolyn McDonald of Alexandria, Virginia.

We also enjoyed the steeplechase ride, six mechanical horses on metal rails, and the Hall of Mirrors, which could distort our bodies into a squat shape with pointed head, puffy cheeks and toothpick-thin legs.

In the TV rooms, people shook their heads in disbelief as they watched a live Brooklyn Dodgers game from Ebbetts Field.

Before entering the Roulette Wheel, we had to remove our sneakers. With the wheel in motion, centrifugal force held us to the top like a magnet as the wheel spun. As it slowed, people slipped off one by one and dropped to the "well" at the bottom. The ride ended with a tangle of bodies and the odor of feet and sweat, but the accidental pokes, punches and scratches were all part of the fun.

All too soon, the wonderful day was drawing to a close. The salty sea air mingled with the coconut scent of suntan oil as people pushed and shoved to get home before dark. The mechanical laughing lady giggled *good-bye*...signaling the end of a magical day.

—*Judith Heller*
Brooklyn, New York

Ventures to a Boardwalk Wonderland

By Joseph Barbella
Havertown, Pennsylvania

MY DAD just loved the shore and couldn't wait for Sunday mornings when we'd head for Atlantic City. (Mom probably couldn't wait either, as she always stayed home and enjoyed a relaxing day without us around.)

At 5 a.m., Dad would wake my brother and me with a big grin on his face. We'd pack lunches, grab swimsuits and towels and put everything in a shopping bag. Then we'd catch a trolley to the ferry crossing the Delaware River, and take that to the crowded train station.

I thought the train ride was very exciting. I glued myself to the window, watching farms and small towns whiz by and waving to truck drivers at crossroads. The New Jersey countryside looked so bright and clean on those mornings.

Eventually we'd see small lakes and bays dotted with colorful fishing boats. The ocean was getting closer. Then Atlantic City came into view, and we were there. In 1935, it was a real wonderland—full of free attractions, surprises and great stores from one end of the boardwalk to the other.

ON THE BOARDWALK IN ATLANTIC CITY...the old song sings the praises of the great recreation spot, and it was true, agrees Joseph Barbella.

Our first stop was the public bathhouse, where Dad rented lockers for 15¢. We'd change into our swimsuits and make a mad dash for the ocean. Dad's favorite spot on the beach was in front of Convention Hall, so we'd always know where to go if we got lost.

By noon, we'd be showered and back on the boardwalk to enjoy attractions like the mechanical "chef" lifting spaghetti from a pot of boiling water, raising his eyebrows and smiling. A large "Mr. Peanut" mannequin tipped his top hat and pointed his cane to a store entrance.

A giant racetrack billboard featured lighted miniature horses. When *They're off!* would light up, we picked the horse we hoped would win. There were no prizes—it was free fun for everyone.

The penny arcade was a world of fun all itself. With a dollar from Dad, I could play for hours—pinball, rifle targets, Skee-Ball and guessing games. My favorite was the motion picture machines. What a thrill to see Tom Mix, Rudy Vallee, Mae West and even belly dancers flip by as I cranked the handle!

I saved my last penny for the "gypsy fortune teller" machine but avoided her eyes as she moved her head, nodded and pointed to a row of cards on her lap. When the message dropped from the machine, I stuffed it into my pocket. Even though it was usually good news, I didn't feel safe enough to read it until we were riding the train back home! ✤

BEACH BUMETTE. It seems Marion Gilson Blaetz of Pemberton, New Jersey spent most of her young life on the beach. She played in the Atlantic City sand (below) in 1919 at age 11, then 8 years later posed with friends (center in photo at left) at Ocean City, New Jersey. It was 1927 by then, and swimsuits were "skimpy" in the Roaring '20s.

Surf... Sand... Sun and Suits Through the Century

OLD-TIME SUNSCREEN. There wasn't much danger of a sunburn as these ladies (above) cavorted in the surf at Long Island, New York in 1899. And those neck-to-knee costumes didn't seem to stop them from having fun.

FLAG-WAVING WAVE MAIDEN. Just because turn-of-the-century swimsuits were all-encompassing doesn't mean they couldn't be colorful, as this bathing beauty's flag suit (above) shows. And, yes, those are high-buttoned bathing shoes.

HEY SAILOR, GET WET! It was the summer of 1943 when a roving photographer from the *Milwaukee Journal* captured this sunny scene at Bradford Beach on Lake Michigan in Milwaukee, Wisconsin. Rosemary Greinke of Milwaukee shared the photo.

Mom Found Creative Way To Keep Daughters Cool

SUMMERS in St. Louis, Missouri were hot and muggy. When my sister and I were small, Mom would sit us in old washtubs filled with water to cool us off.

As we grew older, Mom had an even better idea. Our house had an outside stairwell leading to the basement, with a metal plate on the door to protect it from snow. Mom piled old rugs inside the basement door and filled the well with about 2 feet of water. It kept us cool for hours.

When swim time was over, Mom removed the rugs. Brooms in hand, my sister and I helped sweep the water down the basement drain. We had the cleanest basement in town!

—Betty Reifeiss
Santa Maria, California

TUBBIES. Great minds think alike when it comes to cooling down. Phyllis Boyce of Menasha, Wisconsin says her husband, Emmett (far left), his sister and cousins went tubbing in 1931, as did Ken Walker of Souderton, Pennsylvania and his sisters (above).

COOL IDEA. Bank manager Dan McLeod, Violet Johnson's father (second from left), munches on an impromptu picnic lunch provided by his friend Milton Gair (in center of photo) after the bank installed air-conditioning.

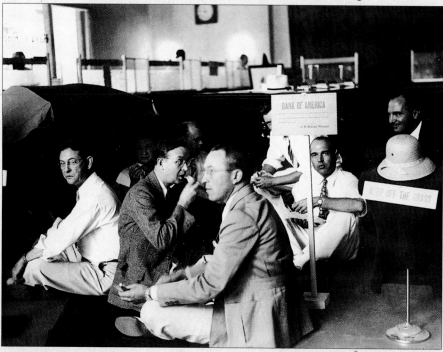

Bank on It: Lobby Was Coolest Spot in Town

IN THE EARLY 1930s, the Bank of America branch that my father managed was one of the first establishments in Redlands, California to get air-conditioning. Dad's friend Milton Gair, a practical joker, decided to take advantage of this newfangled installation.

One hot summer day, Mr. Gair came to the bank at noon and proceeded to spread a blanket right in the middle of the lobby, oblivious to the gawking customers. As the photo (left) shows, he'd decided to have a picnic at the coolest spot in town!

Mr. Gair invited Dad and several others to join him for sandwiches, potato chips and cookies. He even brought a jar of "ants" and a sign that said "Please keep off the grass". The "luncheon" made the local paper the next day.

—Violet Johnson
Fullerton, California

Farm Boys Savored Trips to Swimming Hole

ON HOT SUMMER DAYS, we farm boys yearned for a dip in our swimming hole. As soon as milking was done, the other boys in the neighborhood would come over. We'd pile into two or three

Model A Fords and drive off to Sucker Creek.

Behind a big clump of bushes, we'd slip out of our clothes and into our swim trunks. It was one big splash after another as we dived off the grassy bank into the cool refreshing water. We had a diving board, too—a long plank shoved into a hole we'd dug into the bank and cemented with wet mud.

Sometimes we went swimming on the spur of the moment and had no time to run home for our trunks. When our screaming and yelling attracted neighborhood girls, we'd tell them to stay away because we were skinny-dipping.

"Then you stay under water!" they'd yell back—and we did.

At dusk, the mosquitoes closed in on us in swarms. They just about ate us alive. We'd hurry into our underwear and run for the cars half-dressed, flailing at the mosquitoes while clutching shirt and pants in one hand, shoes and socks in the other. I can still see one of the boys sprinting naked for the car, swinging at mosquitoes the whole way, just as if it was yesterday.

On the way home, we stopped at the ice cream stand in town for a double- or triple-dip cone. It was the perfect end to a refreshing day. —*Bob Witkovsky*
Bay City, Michigan

Grapevines Offered Taste of High Adventure

OUR WOODS were full of grapevines that reached to the tops of the trees. The best ones for swinging grew along the creek banks.

We tested the vine's strength by jumping about a foot off the ground and pulling on it. If it was the least bit loose, it would come down a little or even all the way. When we found one that passed the test, we cut it off at ground level with a pocketknife.

We had to get a good running start, or the vine wouldn't take us out far enough to swing all the way back. This often happened to my brother, who wasn't heavy enough to get good momentum. After a few feeble swings, he'd be dangling about 3 feet or so over the middle of the creek. None of us could reach him, so he had no choice but to drop into the water.

Sometimes, even a tested vine would drop a foot or so at the far arc of the swing. You'd hear small branches snapping above and feel a jerky bounce as

OL' SWIMMIN' HOLE was the best place of all for a summer dip, with nature for a dressing room.

Harold M. Lambert

the vine dropped a foot or more. A couple of times, the whole thing came down, but none of us broke a leg or anything. Pure luck, I guess.

Swinging over the creek was a real sport. It was high adventure for a 10-year-old, never knowing whether you could hold on long enough to get back where you started. —*Norm Hasenfang*
Montpelier, Virginia

Grandma Was the Best Fishing Buddy

THE BEST PART of visits to my grandparents' farm in Iowa was fishing with Grandma.

John E. Spangler

I'd pester her until she agreed to go, then fly into the backyard with a spade to dig for worms, which I stashed in a coffee can filled with a little dirt. When I presented the can to Grandma, she'd hunt up the cane poles, get an old milk bucket to hold our catch and ask my uncle to drive us to the river.

Grandma and I would sit side by side on a grassy bank while I baited the hooks. We threw out our lines and watched the cork bobbers jiggle as they drifted downstream. We talked about nothing and everything. She was always kind and gentle.

And what wild excitement when the cork went way down under the water! We'd jerk the line and pull it in quick. The barbed stingers on the bullheads and catfish made them devils to get off the hook, so that was Grandma's job. We usually caught seven or eight dandies.

On the drive back home, I understood why dogs like to ride with their noses out the window, ears flapping in the breeze. I felt the same exhilaration standing up in the back of my uncle's narrow truck bed, nose to the wind, hair blowing straight back…another glorious childhood day.

—*Colleen Germain*
Madison, Wisconsin

OL' FISHIN' HOLE. The swimming hole could be turned into the fishing hole with just an old cane pole and a can of worms.

Boy Scouts Were Real Troopers

By Robert DeBuhr, Rainier, Oregon

BEING A BOY SCOUT during the Depression wasn't glamorous. Few could afford new uniforms, so we conducted an annual drive to collect old ones.

New members earned an old uniform by opening a savings account with at least $1. Our mothers patched them, then scrubbed them with homemade soap. The lye bleached out so much of the khaki color that a few skinny kids standing at attention could pass for a picket fence!

We prized those uniforms, and often wore old school clothes on hikes to keep the uniforms clean. (On one hike, as we lay sprawled along a trail for a rest, a forest ranger rushed up and asked if there were any survivors.)

Scouts couldn't expect much financial help from their parents, so they earned the 50¢ membership fee and nickel-a-week dues in various ways. Some of us raised pigs, cows, chickens, garlic and onions, while others sold fertilizer.

One patrol cleaned up rice after weddings at a local church. They didn't make much money, but they enjoyed rice pudding on every camping trip.

Boys had to be 12 to join in those days, and older if the troop was between scoutmasters. Adult scoutmasters rotated through our troop fast, and no wonder. Taking us camping up a mountain trail took a lot of will and strength.

Our packs bulged with quart jars of home-canned meat, fruits and vegetables, bottles of milk, sacks of flour and potatoes. We took an iron skillet and Dutch oven, too. (After one of our longer hikes, the Hyena Patrol asked to change its name to the Hernia Patrol.)

We learned to cut down weight by cooking on rocks, sticks and coals. As we dug a blackened spud out of the coals one day, I recall a new recruit saying, "Now I know why you pray before you eat."

In the summer, we learned to build coolers rather than add another 50-pound chunk of ice to our packs. One patrol solved the refrigeration problem by bringing live chickens to camp. They enjoyed fresh eggs all week, then treated the whole troop to chicken dinner on Sunday.

HE'S PREPARED! Robert DeBuhr shared this photo showing what the well-dressed (and well-prepared) Boy Scout looked like in the mid-1920s. Anyone remember the leggings and button shoes?

Girl Scouts Made Camp In Farmer's Cow Pasture

THE GIRL SCOUT CAMP I went to for 4 years in the mid-'20s wasn't traditional, but it made for some fond memories. Each summer, we rented a farmer's cow pasture along the shores of a Wisconsin lake.

Many of our activities reflected military style and everyone took turns at different jobs. We woke to *Reveille* and ended the day with *Taps*, and everyone had a mess kit for meals, which we cooked over an open fire.

A favorite assignment was walking to town for supplies. (Once I was carrying a watermelon and dropped it. The melon broke into several pieces and we had to go back and buy another one.)

The worst duty was going to the beach and bringing back pails of water for drinking and cooking.

Every night we built a bonfire, sang by ukulele, roasted marshmallows and performed skits. Sometimes we hiked to town for a movie and chocolate marshmallow sundaes at the drugstore afterward.

On the last day, a Sunday, we attended church in town. The highlight of the service was being asked to perform as the choir. Then it was back to camp for lunch, the eager wait for our families, and one last swim before returning the pasture to the cows. —*Nora Myers, Kansasville, Wisconsin*

TENTING IN THE PASTURE. It wasn't anything fancy, but Nora Myers (left) and her Girl Scout buddies (below) enjoyed camp nonetheless. They rented a cow pasture! It was on the shores of a nice lake, though, and town, with supplies and church, was a pleasant walk away.

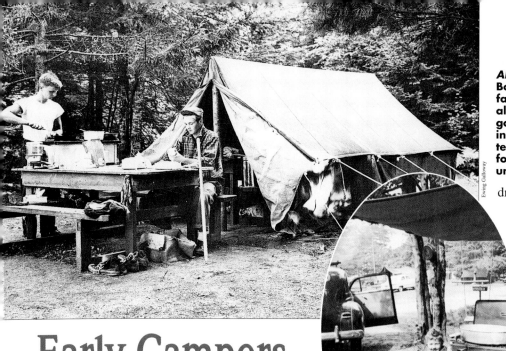

ALL THE COMFORTS. When Rita Boehm (below in 1952) and her family went camping, they took along enough stuff to keep them going for a week. Like the campers in the photo at left, they had a big tent, cots, stoves and hampers of food. It was all pretty comfortable, until it rained.

Early Campers Roughed It

By Rita Boehm, Mesa, Arizona

THE FIRST TENT we used for camping was Grandmother's. It looked like Civil War army surplus, with heavy hardwood poles, metal stakes and no fewer than a dozen ropes.

Our other gear included a red metal Coca-Cola ice chest, food for a week, clothes, bedding and wood-frame army cots. (Dad packed all this so expertly into the trunk and backseat that when we pulled out of the driveway, no one had a clue we were going camping.)

One evening, my sister and I were playing with friends when our campground fell silent. Everyone's attention was drawn to a car that had just pulled in with a strange box-like object in tow. We discovered the "box" held a full-size bed—possibly one of the first travel trailers.

The rest of us didn't sleep in such comfort. Most tents were floorless, so during rainy weather, we really were roughing it. Dad would always dig a trench around the tent's perimeter to keep us dry. Then when the rain started—which seemed to usually be in the middle of the night—he'd roll out of bed to dig it even deeper and loosen all umpteen ropes.

Sometimes the rain lasted for days, and everything got damp. Removing our moisture-laden clothes was an effort. The beds felt like cakes of ice as we pulled up the damp covers. Sometimes Mom heated rocks in the campfire, wrapped them in newspaper and put them in the cots—but it didn't help much.

One time it rained continuously during our camping trip, chilling Mom to the bone. Then she woke one morning and saw slugs crawling up the inside of the tent and telltale slimy tracks on the bedding! After that, my folks invested in a brand-new tent…with a sewn-in floor. ❦

She Discovered Stars on the Appalachian Trail

By Virginia Lytle
Saxonburg, Pennsylvania

CAMPING ISN'T what it used to be, judging from a photograph of my parents on a camping trip in 1912. Their dressy attire included floor-length skirts, hats, bow ties and dress suits!

I had a different adventure in 1937, when I hiked a 37-mile section of the Appalachian Trail, from Pennsylvania to Maryland, with a group of Girl Scouts. We killed a half dozen rattlesnakes on that week-long hike.

We slept under the stars, and on the first night, snug in our bedrolls, one of the counselors pointed out the Big Dipper, Little Dipper and other constellations shining above. What a beautiful picture—trees, stars and no streetlights.

When I woke in the middle of the night, the sky was as beautiful as before…but the stars had *moved*!

The world is coming to an end, I thought to myself. I lay there quietly, waiting for whatever was about to happen. Of course, nothing did.

In the morning, I told our counselor what I had seen. She explained, "That happens every night. It's called the apparent motion of the stars."

Two years later, I made my own telescope in a college physics class. That summer, I was a nature counselor at the Girl Scout camp. Teaching the girls about stars was a special experience.

My family has been camping for over 40 years now. The trip sharpest in my memory is driving across the U.S. with our four children and a trailer, but nothing will beat the night I discovered the stars on the Appalachian Trail. ❦

ON TOP OF THE WORLD. Virginia Lytle enjoyed the solitude atop Pole's Steeple along the Appalachian Trail in 1937.

Church Camp Eased Strain of Depression

By Eugene Fazekas, Towanda, Pennsylvania

THE HIGHLIGHT of summers in the 1930s was a camp sponsored by our Presbyterian church in Cleveland. Reverend Csutoros was the director, but he believed religion should be taught in Vacation Bible School, Sunday school and church. Camp was a place to have fun.

Reverend started Camp Kossuth in 1932, during the Depression. He had three goals: To provide three good meals a day; to take city children into the country to see the beauty of God's creation; and to develop fellowship and happiness when it was needed most.

The first year, camp cost only 75¢. Reverend and the women of the church kept the cost down by soliciting donations of food and supplies. One year, a dairy owner balked at providing milk, so Reverend had my brother Steve and another boy stop there and leave him 2 gallons. The owner thought Reverend was making fun of him.

"No," said Steve. "Reverend says *you* need the milk more than we do." (After that, he gave us 2 gallons every day.)

Each year, the men and older boys prepared the campsite by building a dam across the creek to form a swimming hole. The

DIG THOSE ARGYLES! Rev. Stephen Csutoros (top with wife and son Steve) was a dapper dresser as well as a fun guy, says Eugene Fazekas. But when it came time for dressing up, it was hard to beat the camp counselors (above) decked out for the annual School Daze skit at the Brainard Road camp in 1935.

early years were rustic. Each small white tent held eight to 10 children. The boys slept on straw ticks on the ground, and the girls used army cots. We washed up in basins outdoors or at the creek. The mess hall was a large tent, and the women from church cooked our meals in a shack on wood-burning stoves.

Every morning, Reverend inspected the tents. The three best ones received a pennant to fly from their poles. The balance of the day was spent on handcrafts, nature lessons, first-aid classes, fire-building, knot-tying, hikes, games and swimming. At the evening campfire, we enjoyed skits and songs performed by the counselors.

Like most camps, ours always had a few practical jokers who short-sheeted the beds or filled them with rocks. Reverend was one of the biggest pranksters, so he was a prime target. One morning when we went outside for exercises, his pants were flying from the flagpole!

We spent our time doing simple things that didn't cost much. There was no archery range, no tennis court, no horseback riding, no big lake. But there was a special spirit that brought us back year after year. ☙

TAILOR MADE. The camp swimming hole was made by damming the creek. The kids at left are on the sandbags.

Getting There Was Half the Fun

By Mary Elizabeth Martucci, South Bend, Indiana

WHAT I ENJOYED most about summer vacations in Williamsport, Pennsylvania was the 200-mile train ride. The Depression didn't allow for expensive vacations, but Papa worked for the Pennsylvania Railroad and had an annual travel pass.

The streetcar took us to within two blocks of the train station and we walked the rest of the way, Papa carrying our large worn-out suitcase, Mama with the lunch basket and we kids trailing behind. Papa, tired of shifting the heavy suitcase from side to side, often swung it up onto his head!

The huge ornate station house was bustling, with long wooden benches lining the center of the main floor. Papa headed straight for the shoe-shine stand while we kids went to the snack bar. What a thrill to climb the high stools and enjoy a soda—a once-a-year treat.

When the stationmaster announced our train's departure, we scrambled for the grand oak doors leading to the platform. Papa always received a special greeting when the stationmaster saw his pass.

Trains waited on the tracks, engines sputtering and steam billowing. The porter helped Papa with our bag and settled us into "choice" seats in front. With the beautiful scenery of the Allegheny Mountains outside the windows, the train seemed to float over the tracks.

Mama packed a lunch but always set aside a few pennies and nickels for treats. During the trip, the porter came through carrying a basket filled with cookies, cakes, peanuts and candy—things we never had at home.

The best thing about the trip was that when our vacation ended, we got to enjoy the train ride home again. ❧

"Tent Gang" Members Paid Own Way for Camping Trip

IN THE SPRING of 1935, six friends and I decided to go on a camping trip to Canada. We weeded and mowed lawns, washed cars and did odd jobs to make money. By the time school was out, we had $250 and we bought a 1923 Chevrolet for $15.

In mid-June, we stuffed our tent, cooking utensils and bedding into five trunks, packed our Sunday clothes in suitcases and set out for Canada.

We traveled for 3 weeks, visiting Montreal, Ottawa, Quebec and Niagara Falls. We slept on bedrolls in the tent and cooked every meal but Sunday dinner. We'd find a church to attend, then treat ourselves to dinner at a restaurant.

The next summer, six of us made another trip to Canada, revisiting friends we'd made the year before.

The members of the "tent gang" are scattered across the country now, so we can't get together often. But whenever we do, we always reminisce about those memorable trips.

—*Richard Graham
Emlenton, Pennsylvania*

HEADED NORTH. Pennsylvania "gang" went camping, twice, to Canada. Author is second from right.

Memories of 'The Shack' Are Rich

By Vivia Keegan, Venice, Florida

EVERY YEAR, we spent a week or more at a place my uncle owned near Bridgman, Michigan. We called it "the shack".

The old cabin sat atop a small dune on Lake Michigan. To reach it, we had to trudge a half mile or so along the beach, loaded down with supplies.

Inside the one-room structure, bedsprings were set on sawhorses and topped with mattresses for beds. The "kitchen" consisted of a camp stove and orange crates gathered in one corner. Water came from an outside hand pump. Our days were filled with all sorts of fun, from skinny-dipping to making baked beans in the sand. We'd dig a hole, line it with stones, build a fire and let it burn to ashes, then put a sturdy pot of beans in the hole and leave it overnight. The next day, we had delicious baked beans.

We combed the beach for driftwood for an evening campfire under a glorious full moon that made a shining path on the water. We felt its magic as we sang and toasted marshmallows.

One special memory is of Grandma reading to us. Most of the time we listened while stretched out on the beds, dropping off now and then for a lazy nap. Grandma's books were precious to her, and they became precious to us as well. ❧

STORY TIME. Vivia Keegan (with hair bow), sister Dale and cousin "Red" listen as Grandma reads. That's "the shack" in the background.

SUMMER SIPPIN'. Picnics and pop went together in the good ol' summertime. These kids, in a 1948 photo from Gail Engeldahl of Hartford, Wisconsin, are fillin' up.

Stashing Caps Was High Point of Vacation

By Dorothy Smith, Hanover, Indiana

MY BROTHER was crazy about bottle caps and had a shoe box full of them.

Unlike today's popular "Pogs" (a modern version of a Depression-era game played with cardboard milk-bottle tops), these caps were free.

Anyone could find a Coca-Cola or Pepsi cap, but unusual ones were sought after. Phil's collection came mostly from our Chicago-area bottlers, so when Dad announced plans for a vacation in far-off Minnesota in 1939, Phil saw opportunity beckon.

We set out for the long drive in our 1936 Olds. With the open windows blowing the July heat and dust into our faces, we stopped often at service stations for refreshments. Each time, Phil eyeballed the glass bottles nestled in ice in the big coolers, looking more at the caps than the contents.

Then he'd try to persuade the rest of us to try something new—Podunk grape, Big Indian strawberry, North River orange. They had caps Phil had never seen before. What a hero he'd be when we got back to Chicago!

Phil further expanded his collection by sticking his hands into the bottle-opener receptacle on each cooler, grabbing caps discarded by other motorists. The adults laughed every time his hands came up full of caps.

Phil lined up his finds on the back window ledge of the car, admiring and examining them as we rolled through Wisconsin. By the time we crossed into Minnesota, the collection covered the entire ledge. Meanwhile, Dad was steering down roads no wider than today's country lanes.

KING OF CAP COLLECTORS. Dorothy Smith (above with brother Phil) says his bottle cap collection was the envy of his friends—and, as her story tells, provided hilarity for the family.

Magic of Summer Nights Fueled Child's Fancies

I LOVED SUMMER as a little girl—especially the nights. After working all day, we often went to visit our cousin, who owned the local country store.

Neighbors would gather in the twilight to laugh and talk—a form of entertainment as lost to current generations as quilt-making. As the scent of honeysuckle drifted on the breeze, I caught lightning bugs in pint jars and gazed at their strange glowing light.

The ride home was a treat, too. I'd stretch out in the back of the truck, watching the sky. To me, it seemed a fairy's path—the moonlight shining through the leafy upper branches was like black Spanish lace, and the stars were like sequins.

On nights when we stayed home, we sat in the dark on the porch, listening to the symphony of crickets, katydids, tree frogs and the occasional owl. We seldom spoke. Our voices seemed a rude interruption of the harmony.

Even storms added to the magic of the nighttime sky, and I never feared them. I liked to sneak outside and dance in the rain until my cotton pajamas were plastered to my skin. I'd watch as the lightning flashed fluorescent designs against the dark blue velvet of the clouds. When I went to my first fireworks display, I enjoyed it—but it wasn't nearly as exciting as a good storm.

—*Sandi Keaton*
Monticello, Kentucky

We were all singing lustily when suddenly Dad spotted a roadside sign and read it aloud: "Dip ahead." Well, this was no little dip! The car went airborne and as we crashed down, so did a shower of bottle caps. They pelted Dad, Grandpa and Phil in front, as Mother, Grandma and I waited in the backseat for the torrent to end. Bottle caps were everywhere.

Dad was sure that one of the car's springs had broken, but we were all laughing too hard to care.

We stopped and retrieved most of the caps, and Mother found something to store them in, but we couldn't locate all of them. For the remaining miles to Lake Ada, caps bounced out of hiding places into our laps and onto our feet.

Our vacation was great, and when we returned home, Phil's new collection was the envy of all the other boys. He preened like a peacock whenever they looked over his stock.

As for the rest of us, we kept finding more caps in the car for months afterward. I'll bet there were a few lurking yet when Dad traded it in 2 years later! ❀

Kathi Corder/Unicorn Stock Photos

Bright Dandelions Held Promise of Summer

By Joan McConniel, Mountain Ranch, California

WHEN BRILLIANT yellow dandelions fill my yard, I wouldn't think of running for a weed killer. I enjoy every single one, smiling and reminiscing as I pick a bouquet for my kitchen window.

My love affair with dandelions goes back to my childhood. Our Midwestern winters were long and cold, and even Christmas and an occasional snowman didn't stem my impatience for spring. The dandelions' arrival immediately made things bright and cheery.

My friends and I gathered them from every parkway and lawn, using the hollow stems to make chains.

When we made one long enough, we'd hang it across the street from one giant elm to another, waiting for an infrequent car to drive through and break it. Giggling, we'd race to retrieve what was left and begin all over again.

Many carefree days were spent on these projects, and we took great pride in decorating our neighborhood. We made bright yellow necklaces for the horses that pulled the delivery wagons, too, and ran to drape them over the animals' necks while the driver made his rounds.

Dandelions also signaled summer was just ahead, when we could run barefoot on the cool lawns, skate the days

---

"We took great pride in our neighborhood decorating projects..."

---

away, gather locust shells, catch fireflies and play kick-the-can until dark.

Much later, after years of living out West, I returned to my old neighborhood for a quick visit. The street signs were still there, but everything had been leveled for blocks.

Gone were the majestic elms, the lovely two- and three-story homes, the mulberry tree that once held me safely on its limbs. Not even the dandelions survived.

The only thing I recognized was the cement stairway that once led to my grandmother's house—the only one still standing in the whole block.

Tears stained my cheeks as I realized how much I had taken for granted. Those days were a special moment in time, gone forever except for the gift of memory.

I can't skate my days away anymore, and there aren't any locust shells or fireflies to gather around here. It's been a long time since I've seen a giant elm, and our pines and oaks aren't spaced very well to show off a rope of dandelions.

But I can teach my granddaughters how to make a dandelion chain, and we'll find something to decorate. If we're lucky, the old cow across the road will stand still long enough to let us adorn her with a lovely bright necklace.

For now, I can sit on my porch swing and smile as I admire my dandelions and remember a time when children's lives were carefree and filled with simple pleasures. ❧

WONDERFUL SUMMER JOB. That's what her mother, Lydia (third from right), had working for a wealthy family in Ravenna, Ohio in 1914, says Vi Lien of Kent, Washington. Seen here with co-workers, Lydia had only come to America in 1912. During her first job, she met many new friends at picnics and parties.

ARBOREAL ANTICS. It wasn't summer until you either climbed a tree, as these kids did, built a treehouse, put up a hammock or just sat in the shade.

Trees Formed Boundaries For Outdoor Playhouse

THE FIRST DAY after school let out, we'd fly out the door into the grove of trees that protected our farmstead from the cold winter winds. During summer vacation, this was where we built our own "little house on the prairie".

We'd pick a spot where the trees were spaced just right and start tying strings from one tree to the next, forming a square "room". When the room was finished, we diligently cleaned away all the weeds and twigs and swept down the dirt until it was hard and firm.

As summer progressed, we enlarged our "houses" in case we had company. Our most frequent guest was Mother, and as luck would have it, she insisted on bringing refreshments for the day.

I'll always look back fondly on those special times when I was growing up in the 1930s.   —Delores Utecht
Wayne, Nebraska

Crawfish Catch Fed Whole Boardinghouse

MY MOTHER spent most of her summer fishing for crawfish in the ponds at the cotton gin lot outside English, Texas. Her gear consisted of a short stick and a piece of twine, with a small square of lean meat for bait.

Her widowed mother ran a board-inghouse, and the boarders often teased Mom about her fishing. One time they offered her a prize if she would catch enough crawfish for supper. Of course, they thought she never would, but she did.

It took several "hooks", and hours of running up and down the banks. She said she never forgot the surprise and delight on the boarders' faces as her mother brought in a huge platter of fish tails, rolled in cornmeal and crisply browned.   —Mary Jane Lowry
Blossom, Texas

Youngsters Held Their Own "Crawdad Cookout"

A SMALL CREEK ran through our town, and one of its many dams was close to our house. We'd walk across it whether it was dry or not. Swimming below the dam was good, too. (We were a fearless bunch!)

Catching crawdads, or crayfish, below the dam was good sport, too, and there were plenty of them. One day, someone suggested, "Let's clean 'em and cook 'em! "

A LOT OF YACHT. Sister Shirley and her dog, "Peggy", enjoyed the folks' yacht in upstate New York in the '30s, says Brenda Stevens of South Glen Falls, New York. The boat was docked on a branch of the Mohawk River.

Someone went home to fetch a skillet, and someone else got flour and lard. Meanwhile, the rest of us caught the crawdads, then cleaned them right there in the creek. The water wasn't polluted then, and most of us had already swallowed gallons of it while swimming anyway.

To my knowledge, none of us knew how to cook. But we girls had helped our moms a lot in the kitchen, and we knew the crawdads should be cleaned, floured and put in a skillet with lard. What we didn't know was how many of those little tails it would take for eight to 10 kids to get a taste!

The boys built a campfire and we had our own cookout without a grown-up in sight. I don't remember who cleaned up or put the fire out. What I do remember is that it was good clean fun—and the crawdads tasted great!
—*Joy Duvall, Thayer, Missouri*

Corner Drugstore Was Heart of His Hometown

THE VERY HEART and center of my Texas hometown was Leggett's Nyal Drugstore.

When I think of Leggett's, I see images of strawberry ice cream sodas, cherry phosphates, root beer floats, and that wonderful store-made vanilla ice cream packed in square cardboard containers with wire handles.

I can still see the racks of "funny books", the 10¢ adventure comics we read so avidly. My friends and I seldom *bought* any—we just read them and put them back in the rack.

Most of all, I remember Eddie and Sally Cleveland, who owned and operated Leggett's for many years. They were at least partially responsible for raising several generations of youngsters. We weren't just their customers, we were "their kids", and they took an active interest in us.

When I came home on leave from the Air Force in the late 1960s, the corner drugstore looked the same as always, although the 10¢ "funny books" were now a quarter, and a nickel cone cost a dime.

During that visit, I noticed my son

---

rummaging through the comic books. "If you're not going to buy one, don't handle them," I cautioned.

"Did you buy them when you were his age?" Eddie asked me. As I grinned, remembering, he said gently, "Then leave the kid alone." —*Buck Young Baytown, Texas*

FREE READ. Her dad, Doug Bennett, snapped these comic book connoisseurs at a drugstore in the '50s, says Suzanne Saltsman of Guerneville, California.

Relief from City Heat Was Welcomed

By John Bress, Lehigh, Florida

WHEN I WAS growing up, summer seemed like an endless string of Sundays.

Summers in our third-floor railroad flat in the Bronx, New York were long and hot. Air-conditioning was found only in theaters, and refrigeration only in supermarkets. To cool off, we drank pitcher after pitcher of lemonade and orangeade, bought cool ices from street vendors, visited the beaches and ran through the water spraying from opened hydrants.

In the evenings, when the worst of the heat had passed, we'd sit on the stoops until 10 or 11 p.m., adults talking, kids playing, all sharing their food, drinks and events of the day.

The ground-floor tenants would turn up their radios so we could hear our favorite programs. Everyone danced, sang and laughed together, their cares forgotten for a while.

Most of my friends attended the summer camps sponsored by churches or local organizations like the Police Athletic League. I was fortunate—I had an aunt who lived on a farm in the Cat-skills. Visiting her was like an excursion to another world.

In the cool mornings, I helped milk cows and collect eggs. Sometimes we hiked into the fields to pick berries. We came home covered with berry juice, but it was worth it—those berries would make a delicious pie.

After lunch, we kids followed a "secret path" through the bushes and trees to a pond. As we reached the clearing, we shed our clothes and plunged into the bracing water.

Afterward, we'd stretch out in the grass to let the sun dry us. On the walk back home, we'd stop at a spring for a long drink of delicious water and a short rest.

In the evening, after helping with some small chores, we'd bring the cows in for the night, take a hot bath, sit down for dinner—fresh vegetables, meat, homemade bread and pie. Stomachs full, we'd relax on the porch, listening to the radio and cranking the ice cream maker.

Next morning, we woke to roosters crowing, birds chirping and the aroma of breakfast cooking. Another refreshing summer day in the country. Nothing to do but have fun. ❦

HYDRANT HIGH JINKS. All it took to keep kids cool in the city was a friendly water utility worker and a wrench.

White Lie Put a Bug in Sister's Ear

By Lillian Brown
Schererville, Indiana

PROVIDING FOR six little ones during the long, lean years of the Depression was a king-size job. We wore hand-me-downs and repaired our shoes with rubber stick-on half soles.

Mom and Dad's summers were consumed with planting and caring for every foot of ground that could be turned into garden. This was long before home freezers, so as the various fruits and vegetables ripened, canning and preserving began, which was then carefully put away for the cold winter.

Those who've ever done any gardening know that potato plants are susceptible to a hard-shelled bug resembling a brown beetle. If not watched and kept off the plants, these little bugs can wipe out a potato patch real fast.

Now, my sister Betty was Mom's little shadow. One afternoon, Mom and Dad had declared war on the potato bugs and were going down the rows, dusting the plants with some kind of a powder, then shaking the bugs into a bucket.

As usual, Betty was tagging alongside Mom. She asked Mom what she was going to do with the bugs in the bucket. Hoping Betty would run along and play so she could finish her work without being pestered, Mom answered that she was going to bake a pie.

A week or so later, Mom baked two pies, a raisin and an apple. When she cut the raisin pie at the table, Betty sprang from her chair and started screaming, "Don't eat it! It's potato-bug pie! Don't eat it! It's potato-bug pie!"

The rest of us kids lost no time pushing our chairs back and heading out the back door, screaming, "Potato-bug pie! Potato-bug pie!"

Mom got us back to the table, but we would only eat the apple pie. Mom and Dad enjoyed the raisin.

I really do like raisin pie, and to this day, whenever I bake one, I can't help but chuckle as I think back to that summer, my dear sister Betty and the big panic over "potato-bug pie". ❦

BUGLESS. There are no bugs in this pie, but watch those little sisters!

FABULOUS FOURTH. It was time for fireworks and parades when the Fourth of July arrived. Her daughter, Gail (right), won second place with the float Dad made in 1941, says Elizabeth Parsloe of Lake Park, Florida. Gail won first place the year before with a cake float built on her Taylor Tot.

Fourth of July Festivities Filled the Whole Day

BEING A CHILD in Ridgewood, New Jersey on the Fourth of July was so exciting—a family fun time. The town celebration lasted all day, beginning with a morning parade. How I loved the fire engines' bells and sirens!

My younger brothers proudly rode their bicycles, decorated in red, white and blue crepe paper, behind the booming drums of a marching band. One year, my sister rode her white horse to represent "the spirit of liberty".

After the parade, everyone ended up in the park for food and games. Families picnicked on the grass under the lovely old maple trees. Vendors sold hot dogs, ice cream and soda. Games for all ages lasted all afternoon—three-legged races, sack races, egg-in-spoon races, balloon races and "serious" running competitions.

In the evening, we enjoyed a stirring band concert. Finally, as darkness fell, came the long-awaited magnificent fireworks. The booming explosions seemed to reach right to the bottom of my stomach! The ground displays were beautiful, too—Niagara Falls, the Statue of Liberty, a "waving" flag, and warships firing bombardments at each other. What glorious memories!

—*Joan Mayer, Adairsville, Georgia*

They Looked Forward to The Fourth All Year Long

EVERY JULY in Milwaukee, Wisconsin, the "Sane Fourth of July Association" provided entertainment all over the city in hopes of keeping us kids from the dangers of firecrackers. The festivities always included a doll buggy and coaster wagon parade.

One year, my entire family worked on pink and white crepe-paper roses to decorate my buggy, and my doll and I wore matching crepe-paper dresses. I won a silver bracelet engraved with the date, July 4, 1927. I wasn't too thrilled at the time—

I'd have much preferred a new doll. But I still have the bracelet, and a doll would have been long gone by now.

What wonderful memories—school bands playing patriotic music, flags everywhere, the scent of green grass under the hot sun, the fun of races and games, picnic lunches and suppers, the cozy feeling of lying on a blanket with my head in Mother's lap while watching the splendor of the fireworks. No wonder we looked forward all year to that glorious day! —*Jeannette Heim Concord, California*

Kids Lit Up the Night

IN THE '40s, Mom and Dad usually sat on the neighbors' porch after dinner and chatted while we kids played hide-and-seek and caught fireflies.

One night, we had a contest to see who could catch the most fireflies. We soon had jars filled with 'em. Wouldn't it be great if we could take them somewhere very dark and let them go?

I suggested my *house*, since Mom and Dad weren't there. We went into the living room, turned off all the lights and took the lids off the jars. The room was filled with hundreds of twinkling lights. We were awestruck at the beautiful sight. It was better than the Fourth of July!

Suddenly the front door opened and Mom stood there staring in disbelief. Her screams were heard all over the neighborhood. A lot more than my pride was hurting that hot summer night!

—*Barbara Hackman Monroeville, Pennsylvania*

PROPER PICNICKERS. Swimsuits covered all in 1899 for this Fourth of July gathering. Photo is from the family album of Eleanor Dougherty, Brooksville, Florida.

Front Porch Was a Summertime Oasis

By Janet Bick, Bethel, Ohio

WITH EVERY SLAM of its weathered screen door, our front porch was the center of activity. The floorboards of robin's-egg blue often resounded with the slap of a jump rope or the rhythmic thump of a bouncing ball.

We were happy simply to sit there, feet dangling over the edge, as we licked at shimmering spikes of ice chipped by the iceman and wrapped in newspaper. We laughed as they melted through the soggy paper and left chilly spots on our feet.

At the end of a hot day, the porch was a paradise of cool breezes. It was a welcome spot for congenial neighbors, who sat in the gleaming white swing or tall wicker rockers, chatting about the day.

We watched as pastel shades of pink, blue and gold melted together in the sky.

When at last darkness fell, the air filled with fireflies. Then all of us kids abandoned the porch and raced about to capture the fireflies in a jar, squealing with delight as we released them.

Come bedtime, we lay on a frayed patchwork quilt covering the warm floor. Moonlight filtered through the trees, bathing us in a pale glow.

SHADY PORCHES were welcome places for visiting in the summer, as was this one in cherished photo of relatives from Maribeth Fleischmann of Cudahy, Wisconsin.

The scent of honeysuckle at the front step blended with the mossy earth beneath the trees. The squeak of the swing, the creak of the rocker, the hushed voices around us became a lullaby, and sleep overtook us—the end of another great summer day.

WAGONLOAD of melon eaters was her kids and a nephew in 1951, says Dorothy Hickman of Cedarville, Ohio.

Spring Water Chilled "Perfect" Melons

WE LOVED the Sunday drives to my grandmother's home in the North Carolina mountains, with sweet scents drifting through the open windows of our Model A Ford.

One of our regular stops was a small country store with a hand-operated gas pump out front, picnic tables in back and spring water spilling from rocks at the base of a cliff.

Dad would park under a shade tree, and we'd scramble out, racing for a wooden watering trough. Ripe watermelons floated in the ice-cold water, which was funneled to the tank from the spring. Dad carefully selected a perfect melon and carried it to a picnic table to carve generous slices.

When I remember those visits, I recall the contentment I felt, sharing the simple pleasures of those innocent bygone days.
—*Pegge Hagler, Springfield, Virginia*

Kids "Waited Out" Juicy Treasure

BACK in the early '20s, I lived in a small Pennsylvania city called Pottsville.

Most long-distance shipping was done by rail, and with few motorized vehicles around then, local deliveries were made by horse and wagon.

In early summer, the watermelon cars came in from the south and my friends and I would go down to watch the unloading.

There were usually two men in the car. One would hoist a melon and throw it to a man at the door inside the car, who threw it to a guy outside to place in the delivery wagon.

Our purpose wasn't just to watch the men unload the car. We were waiting for them to drop one, because then we could scramble to get the pieces. We ate our treasure right there and often had enough to take some home.

We were rarely disappointed, as usually one or more melons were dropped. As an adult, I've sometimes wondered if they weren't fumbled on purpose.
—*Hilburt Umpleby Marion, Pennsylvania*

MAKING TRACKS. A train car full of watermelons was just what kids like Hilburt Umpleby waited for.

The Missing Ingredient

By Charles Niles, Janesville, Wisconsin

THERE'S NOTHING quite as good as homemade ice cream, created with rich cream, fresh fruit and a cooked custard base. That's how we made it in the '30s, when we lived on a dead-end street in Beloit, Wisconsin.

It was the Depression and everyone was in the same boat that was slowly sinking!

One thing that helped keep us barely afloat was cooperation. Dad had a 1-gallon ice cream freezer he'd bought before the Crash, but neither our family nor any other on the street had enough money to buy all of the ingredients.

That's how it became a neighborhood project. Usually, there were six

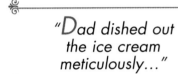

> *"Dad dished out the ice cream meticulously..."*

families involved and each contributed something. One would come up with a cup or two of sugar…another four eggs (from their own chickens, of course)… and yet another scraped up a few cents to buy 25 pounds of ice.

The cream was skimmed from the top of a bottle of milk from whichever family could afford it that week. Someone else contributed the rock salt and, perhaps, raspberries, strawberries, cherries or some other fruit in season.

Took Turns at the Crank

My dad cooked the custard, mixed all the ingredients and supplied the freezer, and every kid who was big enough took turns cranking the freezer handle.

When the crank could no longer be turned, it was time to remove the paddle from the mix. Dad would laboriously scrape *almost* every drop back into the freezer pail, but he never quite got it all. Everyone who'd helped turn the handle had a tongue out because that first taste was always the best.

Next, the freezer was wrapped in several old blankets and put in the shade until the ice cream got solid. No one had to be told when it was done—somehow our "internal clocks" just knew.

There were so many of us that we

each got only a small amount. As I recall, there were 15 kids and 11 adults. That's 26 people to share a little less than 128 ounces of ice cream—not 5 ounces per person!

Dad dished it out meticulously, ensuring equal portions, but we were always left wanting more. Maybe that's why it tasted so good.

When World War II came along, we stopped making ice cream. Dad was working 7 days a week in a war plant and no one had the time anymore. By the time the war ended, we'd gotten out of the habit.

I'd gone into the service just before the war ended, and when I got out 3 years later, it seemed that most people bought all their own ice cream at the store.

Out in my garage today there's an electric ice cream maker that's never been used. I bought it to try and recapture the flavor of the ice cream of my youth. Then I realized that wonderful flavor was more than mere taste on the tongue.

Without sacrificing something to make the ice cream; without struggling

HOMEMADE. It took a little work, but hand-cranked ice cream was the best.

to turn the handle; without fighting to see who gets to lick the paddle; and without sharing it with the whole neighborhood, most of the essential ingredients are missing. ❧

Music and Ice Cream Filled Summer Nights

IN THE 1930s, 8 miles was a long way to travel for a band concert, but that's what we did every Wednesday night.

As soon as Mama and Daddy got off work, we'd pick up my aunt and uncle and drive to the park in Naperville, Illinois. As the band played, fireflies flitted in the balmy summer sky and Uncle Walter kept time to the music, waving an imaginary baton.

After the concert, Daddy drove us to Prince Castle, an ice cream parlor that looked just like a fairy-tale castle.

Uncle Walter always carried a "good" teaspoon in his shirt pocket for these occasions. He just couldn't wait to order a "strumberry" ice cream cone—which he ate with his teaspoon. My own cone usually melted all over my hands because I was so intrigued by watching *him* eat!

—*Bette Mann*
North Fort Myers, Florida

BIG ENOUGH? This charming 1920s ice cream stand invited those with BIG appetites.

COWBOY PROJECT. When you wanted something done, you did it yourself, and if money for toys was scarce, kids rustled up entertainment from scratch, like this group building their own "home on the range". All it took was a little imagination, some spare lumber... and probably a few words of advice from Dad.

Chapter Two
Imagination Was The Best Toy Store

A little ingenuity and lots of elbow grease made
some of the best playthings money just can't buy.

The other day, my grandson asked, "Did they have Nintendo games when you were a boy?" Well, no, we didn't. Nor did we have *Toys R Us*, with aisle after aisle stacked to the ceiling with a dazzling variety of things created for the amusement of children. Gosh, we didn't even have our own private TV's in our bedrooms.

The child pondered this terrible state of affairs. "But what did you *do? What did you play* with?"

How do you explain how you had lots of fun, even though you had fewer than a dozen "store-bought" toys the whole time you were growing up. How do you explain discovering the most marvelous toy there ever was—your own imagination—and how suddenly the most ordinary things blossomed with intriguing potential.

Wooden cheese boxes, for example. Put four wheels on one and you had a trailer your toy truck could pull. Cut a few square holes in the sides and you had a fort that would shelter your toy soldiers against the next Indian attack. Stand it on end, add a few shelves and you had a cupboard for doll dishes. Nail a couple of pieces of lath across the bottom and a hand-whittled propellor on the front and you had an airplane—sort of.

Or, hey! Here's a discarded broom. With a little imagination and a few scraps from Mom's ragbag, you could create a "stick horse". Here comes the cavalry to the rescue!

The Mind's Own Magic Kingdom

My favorite "toy" was my big sandpile in the orchard just north of our home. Sometimes I turned it into a "farm" with pens for the livestock (rocks and scraps of wood). At other times, my sister, Mary, and I would shape a magnificent castle with grand walls, a moat and a drawbridge to keep the bad guys at bay. It was amazing how much fun you could create from a truckload of sand.

My childhood summers included herding cows up and down our country gravel road, where the grass in the ditches provided good grazing. Playing baby-sitter to a bunch of cows is not the most exciting job on earth, so I had plenty of idle time.

And, as they say, idle hands are the devil's plaything. Soon I was honing my pitching skills, pegging rocks at telephone poles. Here was the Cub's Phil Cavarretta at the plate, bases loaded, bottom of the ninth and two out. I check the base runners, wind up and let my feared fastball go. It's over the heart of the plate, and Cavarretta fans air. *Strike one!* Well, one thing led to another, and soon I was zinging rocks at the glass insulators. (Sorry, Northwestern Bell. I know I did a bad thing, but surely the statute of limitations has run out by now.)

Meanwhile, Mary was busy on the front porch making dolls from wooden clothespins, just the way Joan Thomas tells about later in this chapter.

I suppose it was pure necessity that enriched our powers of imagination, as the following stories recall. Money was often scarce, but we found plenty of ways to have fun without it.

—*Clancy Strock*

A REAL KID'S PLACE. The enchanting mix of children's books, Dad's homemade toys and Mom's yummy cookies made Ernestine Peircey's home a place where all the neighbor kids wanted to be.

Dad's Handmade Toys Were Hit of the Neighborhood

By Ernestine Peircey, Middlebury, Connecticut

OUR FAMILY may have been poor, but our parents made us feel rich. We didn't need a lot of store-bought playthings to have fun.

Dad built many of our toys, including a plane and zeppelin, and his handmade dollhouse made me the envy of every girl in my grammar school.

At Christmas, the dollhouse was updated and placed in front of the tree with my brother Dave's train, which got new cars every year. For little brother Donny, Dad would find a store-display Santa Claus and stand the life-size figure in a corner to surprise him.

Dad was *full* of inventive ideas. Instead of leaving teeth under the pillow for the tooth fairy, we left things in the front hall for the *pixies*, and they left us chocolates! Mom made all our Halloween costumes and was a great cook. When we moved to a new neighborhood, she invited the kids on the street inside to make cookies. When they took their treats home, their mothers called Mom to thank her. They couldn't believe it!

Our house was the place where all the kids wanted to play after school. There'll never again be a mother and father like mine. ❧

TOY HORSES like the one above were pretty tame stuff at Ernestine's house...just check out that dollhouse (at top) and the airplane (right) she and her brother are about to take off in! Ernestine says that although holidays were special, their house was fun all year-round.

tree trunk were cigar-box bookcases filled with books of Boy Scout adventures. With a series of extension cords strung from a second-story bedroom, we even had lights.

Never was such a royal palace created as that cubby in 1934!

—*Charlie Knox, St. Paul, Minnesota*

Toppled Tree Made Ideal Pirate Ship

NEAR OUR HOUSE, but far enough away to seem removed from civilization, was a large oak tree that had fallen, with a Y-shaped fork parallel to the ground. It was the perfect setting for a pirate ship.

The trunk was our main deck. We cleared out the limbs between the fork and made a ladder to climb down "below deck". An old sheet stretched across the fork served as a roof. Our "flag"—a skull and crossbones painted on a piece of canvas—was raised on a pole nailed to the trunk.

We spent many summer days "sailing the high seas" and raiding other "ships" of all their treasure.

—*James Niemann Sr., Hematite, Missouri*

WALKING TALL. Growing up in Nebraska in the early 1920s, Herbert Stevens and his brother enjoyed playing games on these homemade stilts. Herbert, now of Cincinnati, Ohio, says they fell down so often that he can't imagine how their mother managed to keep their pants clean and mended!

Two-Room "Cubby" Was Boy's Treetop Retreat

WHEN I WAS 10, having a tree house, or "cubby", was all the rage.

The iceman helped start mine, nailing the first two-by-fours to the tree with big spikes. I don't remember much about the rest of the construction, but my mother was always ready to help when my friends and I got into a tough spot.

When a rivalry developed with the next-door kids, who had a much larger cubby, Dad built an addition large enough for two small boy-sized cots. This was during the worst year of the Depression, so that brand-new lumber represented a real commitment to "keeping up with the Joneses"!

My "dining room" was cozy, with a magazine-covered table in one corner and Mom's tieback curtains hanging at the glass window in back. There were rugs on the floor, and pillows for leaning against the wall. Nailed to the

TOYS WITH LIMBS. Getting up in the world was fun when we were kids...you climbed a tree. It didn't matter if you just sat on a branch, like the girl at left, or had a nifty tree house like the one above.

Wooden Shingles Made Sleek Speedboats

By Earl VanGorder, Tonawanda, New York

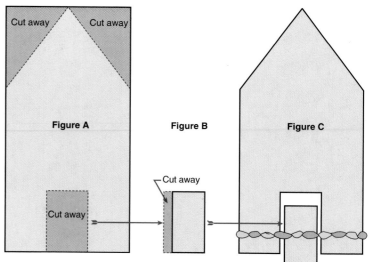

Figure A   Figure B   Figure C

DURING the Depression, when ready-made toys were a luxury, we learned to make great speedboats and had lots of fun racing them.

All we needed was Dad's saw, a rubber band and a piece of wood about 1/4 inch thick. A broken wooden shingle worked great. If there was a construction or home repair job going on in the neighborhood, there were always plenty of those. The dimensions didn't matter, as these boats could be made in just about any size.

First we cut the wood into a rectangle (see Figure A), removing the shaded portions. After cutting out the smaller rectangle, we sawed off a bit of it for the propeller (Figure B), then reinserted it. A rubber band stretched over the back kept the propeller in place (Figure C).

Then we wound the propeller backward as many turns as possible, put the "boat" in the water and watched her speed away as the "motor" unwound. The boat could be dressed up a bit with a little "cabin", but it moved faster without one.

Now, go find a shingle, get that saw going and watch your "paddle wheeler" scoot across a mud puddle or pond! ❧

Thread Spools Provided Limitless Possibilities

By Wanda Harris, Idaho Falls, Idaho

MY MOTHER sewed most of our clothes, so she went through lots of wooden thread spools—and we children found many uses for them.

Spools could be used as blocks, stacked high for towers, or glued or tied together to build a whole city.

We drew animal faces and backsides on construction or wrapping paper, glued them to the spool ends and played "zoo". The cages and fences were made of cardboard, with a paper doll for the zookeeper.

We could only afford the store-bought bubble solution as a treat once a summer. The rest of the year, we put a little dish soap and water in a bowl and dipped one end of a spool into the mixture to blow bubbles.

My girlfriends and I painted small spools with watercolors, poster paints or food coloring mixed with water, then strung them on yarn for necklaces. Paper flowers between spools made a Hawaiian lei for a pretend luau.

We even tried wrapping spools in foil to make wind chimes, but the sound was more "clunky" than musical. Aluminum pie plates cut with different-sized holes worked much better. ❧

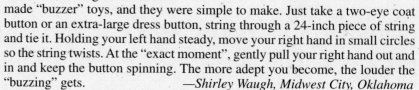
Entire Family Participated in Racing 'Spool Tractors'

By Mrs. J.M. Reifel
Seattle, Washington

WITH 11 children, our mother did lots of sewing, so we had plenty of thread spools for making toys. The most exciting was the tractor (see the photo below). All you needed was a spool, rubber band, a quarter-inch length of candle and a large kitchen match.

Little notches were cut all around both ends of the spool, then the matchstick was cut to the same length as the widest part of the spool. The rubber band was threaded through the spool, then the match was threaded through the band and glued to the end of the spool.

Next we removed the wick from the candle and threaded the rubber band through the hole in the wax. Then the head of the match, which had already been struck so it's wouldn't light, was threaded through the rubber band. Now we were ready to wind it up. The tighter it was wound, the longer it'd run.

Our dad would make three or four tractors at a time, and we'd gather game boards, books, blocks and boxes to make a race course. We spent most cold winter days speeding our tractors up, over and under anything we could arrange in a straight line.

This toy was popular at Halloween. My brother discovered the trick of winding the tractor and holding it against the window so the matchstick tapped the glass as it flipped around. It made a frightening noise and was more fun than ringing doorbells and running! ❧

FLIGHTS OF FUN. Lucky Lindy had nothing on Stella Svane and her brother. Dad made them a plane (left) for their trans-backyard flights of fancy. Actually, the kids had already been to Europe.

Kids Got More Expecting Less

By Stella Svane, Rutherford, New Jersey

THE DEPRESSION was a blessing in disguise. My twin brother and I grew up expecting less, so we were happy whenever we received a gift.

My brother, mother and I were in Germany when Charles Lindbergh made his transatlantic flight. When we got home, our father had a grand present for us in the backyard—a two-seater airplane, made from old carriage and phonograph parts and thick butcher paper. My brother and I spent many happy hours "flying" to Europe and back.

Our father also built strange-looking machines that produced whirring noises, with buttons we could push to ring bells. An old motor, some wires and a few batteries were all he needed.

Before backyard pools were in fashion, Dad dug one out, cemented it and painted it green. It was slightly larger than a bathtub, but on a hot day in New York City, it gave us hours of joy.

We all loved New York City and visited the points of interest. When the Empire State Building was completed, we were there. We visited museums and the aquarium.

Our lives were full and happy because we had parents who loved us and cared about our education. Money isn't the answer. Love is. ❧

BELLS AND WHISTLES. Some of the toys Stella's dad made (above and bottom photos) were like Rube Goldberg contraptions designed to capture a child's imagination. But there were also boxcars (below), old trunks to play in and a real in-ground backyard pool.

BONNIELU TOYS

Father's Homemade Toys Meant Business

By Bonnie Lu Vanzant, Mt. Dora, Florida

AS AN ONLY child, I never lacked for entertainment because Dad always made me things to play with. At first, he made my toys in an old pump shed, using whatever scraps he could find. Later, after he helped construct a high school, he used the leftover lumber to build a larger workshop.

The workshop soon was a busy place. Toys were hard to come by in the 1940s, and when friends and neighbors saw mine, they asked Dad to make them some, too. Dad eventually went into business making "BonnieLu Toys". I still have the stamp (see above) he used to mark them.

Every Saturday, we loaded an old ice truck with wheel barrows, play ironing boards and irons, wagons and doll furniture and sold them to city stores in central Florida. As toys became available from other sources, Dad phased out the toys and started making windows and doors. ✤

PERSONAL TOY FACTORY. Despite wartime shortages, Bonnie Lu Vanzant never lacked for toys ...her dad, Elliott Close (above right with wife Vera and Bonnie Lu in 1944) made them. Bonnie Lu (below) still has some of his handcrafted treasures.

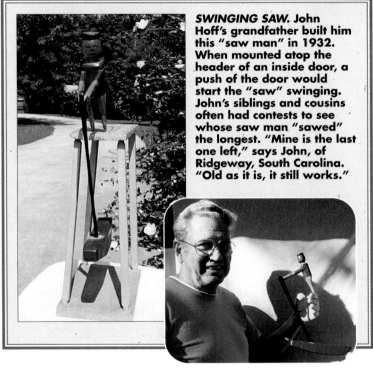

SWINGING SAW. John Hoff's grandfather built him this "saw man" in 1932. When mounted atop the header of an inside door, a push of the door would start the "saw" swinging. John's siblings and cousins often had contests to see whose saw man "sawed" the longest. "Mine is the last one left," says John, of Ridgeway, South Carolina. "Old as it is, it still works."

Dad Was Neighbor Boys' Favorite Playmate

By Lois Hyndman, Corpus Christi, Texas

A SOFT WHISTLE from outside as we finished supper signaled the neighbor boys were waiting for my father to come out and play. It was easy for me to share him with them, though, since they included me in the fun.

Dad organized many activities for the long summer evenings. One year, he spent his lunch hour making paddles for games of paddle tennis.

When he found an old beat-up putter, he laid out a miniature golf course that encircled our yard and buried empty tomato cans to make the holes. (Our lawn was nonexistent until we all grew up, but our parents were raising children, not grass.)

Another year, my uncle bought us tennis rackets, and Dad painted a line across the garage door so we could practice. He didn't seem to mind that he had to repair the door at the end of the summer. (I'm sure our games of "ante over" weren't much good for the roof, either.)

We played horseshoes, badminton and "run-sheep-run", a form of hide-and-seek. At least one night a week was spent playing "work up" at the softball park down the street, with Dad as umpire. When it got dark, Dad called a halt to the evening's activities and sent everyone home for a good night's sleep.

Our neighborhood was poor by today's standards, but every one of Dad's "playmates" grew up to be fine, productive adults and good parents—in part, I'm sure, due to his example. ✤

whistles and feather pens.

When the sap rose in the hazel trees in spring, we cut sticks 1/2 inch thick and 6 to 8 inches long. After tapping the stick repeatedly with the handle of a pocketknife, we could gently slip off the thin layer of bark.

We whittled out a notch near each end and carefully slivered out holes to blow into. We moistened the wood, put the "skin" back on and our whistles were ready to use.

For ink and pens, we started with a tennis ball-sized green oak ball, squeezed its juice into a tin can, added a little water and dropped in a handful of rusty nails. After about 3 days, the "ink" would be ready.

Then we'd gather a few big turkey feathers, slice off the big end at a slant, make a slit in the point and the pens were ready to dip into the "ink".

—*Arlene Titus*
Happy Camp, California

LET THE GOOD TIMES ROLL. As a child in Seattle, Washington, John Halvorsen and his buddies often made "roller coasters", sliding a marble down a doubled-up garden hose. He rigged up this version at his home in El Paso, Texas for his grandson (above). The boy liked it so much that John bought him a 75-foot hose and a bag of steelies for his birthday!

"Streetcars" Lit Up The Sidewalks

ON SUMMER EVENINGS, my friends and I pulled "streetcars" along the sidewalks of our block. There were no real streetcars in our little town, but we'd seen them on visits to the city.

Ours were made from shoe boxes (Daddy's bigger boxes were preferred), with three windows cut out on each side, one in back and a large one in the center of the lid. If we had colored tissue paper, we sometimes used it to make "window shades".

A string was attached to the front of the box so it could be pulled, and a candle fastened with tallow sat inside.

As we pulled our lighted "streetcars" up and down those bumpy brick sidewalks, imagining ourselves in big cities or foreign lands, our parents sat on the front porch, watching and quietly talking over the day's events. I wish children of today could have such simple pleasures.

—*Helen Allen*
Wellington, Ohio

Inner Tubes Provided Toy Pistols and Darts

BACK when car tires had inner tubes, it seemed like there was always an old one available. We'd cut it into circular strips about 1/2 inch wide to make into parts for a target pistol.

Next we assembled a piece of wood about 6 inches long by 2 inches wide and 3/4 inch thick, a nail and a wooden clothespin. By pulling on the nail and pressing on the bottom of the clothespin, the clamped inner tube was released and flew toward its target.

To make our own darts, we'd take a wooden match and cut off the head. Then we cut 1/2 inch off the sharp end of a straight pin and pressed the blunt end into the end of the matchstick.

After cutting a cross about 1/2 inch down the other end of the stick, two little pieces of paper were folded and inserted in the cross on the match. The paper made vanes like feathers on professional darts.

We thought we really got good at throwing those darts, although Mom constantly reminded us to *be careful.*

—*R.E. Alexander, Erie, Pennsylvania*

WHITTLIN' WHISTLES. An "old pro" teaches kids the valuable art of making whistles by hand.

They Crafted Their Own Whistles and Pens

MY SISTER and I were raised on our grandparents' homestead in northwestern California. Few other kids lived nearby, but we always found plenty to keep us occupied, like making our own

One day, we found an old truck tire and rolled it around the yard—until one of the boys had a better idea. I stuffed myself inside, pulled my elbows close, crossed my arms and gripped the edges of the tire.

My brothers grinned in anticipation as they pushed my head inside the rubber casing. The boys stood on either side, holding the tire upright, rocked the

Hollyhock Dolls Were Ready for the Ball

WHEN the hot days of early August arrived, we picked hollyhocks to make "dolls" in colorful ballroom dresses. We peeled back the green part around the bud, exposing tiny holes into which blossoms could be inserted. As you can see by the picture (above) of some I recently re-created, we really used our imaginations back then.—*Shirley Boak*
Port Charlotte, Florida

Stick Horse Provided Years of Riding Fun

MY COWBOY HERO was Roy Rogers, and at one point I had such an identity crisis that I wouldn't answer to anything except "Roy Ann"! So it was natural that one of the toys I played with for years was my stick horse, "Paint".

GET A HORSE! This girl has one, although it's a bit fancier than the pine-wood pony in Ann's memory above.

Paint was made out of a scrap of pine molding from one of Dad's building projects. One end of the stick was notched, with a heavy cord tied around it for a bridle. We even referred to Dad's storage shed as "the barn" because Paint "lived" there.

—*Ann Snuggs*
Pine Bluff, Arkansas

Rich Kids Went for Simple Clothespins

IN RURAL IOWA, summer vacation meant days of isolation from other children, so I made up stories, using rocks or oddly shaped weeds to represent the characters.

My best make-believe people were made of wooden clothespins. My mother often had to buy more and never understood what *became* of all of them. (I never told her that some of my make-believe people "died" and were laid to rest in a grove of trees!)

Several years later, while baby-sitting for a wealthy family, I introduced my charges to clothespin people. The busy socialite parents were amazed when their children abandoned all their fancy toys to play in the laundry room with the housekeeper's clothespins! —*Joan Thomas*
St. Louis, Missouri

Old Truck Tire Became a Thriller Ride

AS FARM KIDS living near Aberdeen, South Dakota in the 1940s, my brothers and I had only our creativity to keep us busy after chores.

SMALL FRY IN AN 8-PLY. No matter where they lived, Jacqueline Warner (swinging above in 1940) of Florence, Kentucky could count on her dad putting up some sort of swing.

tire back and forth, then started it rolling. That sensation of rolling over headfirst was unequaled until later when I took my first Ferris wheel ride.

Around the yard I rolled, my squeals mingling with the boys' shouts of laughter. My brothers ran on either side of the tire, taking turns balancing and spinning it until we reached the slope between the garage and the chicken coop. Then the race was on!

The boys rushed down the hill, trying to keep up. Usually they caught me before the tire flopped onto one side, bouncing in circles until it settled.

My brothers never had the "pleasure" of riding in the tire—they were too big. Eventually I got too big as well for the truck tire, but I had the memory of many thrilling whirls.

—*Inez Bauer, Portland, Oregon*

"Worm Hospital" Was Crawling with Patients

ONE OF OUR more imaginative activities was building a "worm hospital" out of a cardboard box. We made cardboard ambulances and used clamshells for the beds. Of course, we had to dig up our patients.

The shells were filled with dirt, and we used leaves or small pieces of cloth for blankets. We spent hours tending our "patients", since it was very time-consuming keeping them in their beds!

—*Harriet Meola, Scottsdale, Arizona*

Dogwood Popgun Worked Surprisingly Well

MY FAVORITE plaything was a dogwood popgun made from a hollow 8-inch piece of bamboo. A hickory stick was whittled down to make a plunger that fit inside the bamboo barrel.

In fall, we'd gather a handful of dogwood "balls", or seeds, then use the plunger to shove one into the barrel as far as it would go. A second ball was placed in the open end, then you pushed hard and fast with the plunger.

It was surprising how far the balls would go, and that gun really "popped"!

—*George Barbee*
Clarksville, Tennessee

"Spam Trains" Chugged Along for Years

WHEN MY SONS were small, their favorite Christmas gifts were trains made by their grandma and grandpa. The cars were painted Spam cans fitted over blocks of wood, with wooden checkers for wheels.

The steam engines were large wooden spools, with smaller spools for smokestacks. The cars were connected with metal hooks and eyes.

Rather than wrap the trains, Grandpa arranged them beneath the boys' beds with just the drawstrings peeping out. One by one, he got his grandsons to pull out their trains.

These thoughtful and loving gifts provided hours of fun for many years.

—*Bette Bedney, Peoria, Arizona*

Hoop-Rolling Wasn't Just for Boys

I WAS A TOMBOY and cared not a whit about dolls. Just like the boys at

NUTTY KIDS. Taking a break to "smoke" their acorn peace pipes were the author (right) and nieces Sharon Crossman (left) and Susan Jordan. As the girls are on the stoop, the house was obviously a non-acorn-smoking area.

What Fun Squirreling Away Acorns

THE HOUSE I grew up in was nestled in a woods, and every fall, the colorful oaks became loaded with acorns. That's when we set out with berry buckets to collect the biggest and best to use for acorn-pipe powwows and acorn-top army battles.

Acorns for the pipe bowls had to be fat and soft enough to carve. We removed the caps, and my father carefully scored and cut away a small portion of the top with his pocketknife. Then it was our turn to scoop out the acorn meat. Once hollowed, Dad made the pipe stem from a wooden matchstick.

Next, we staged Indian wars, racing around and whooping it up until we were exhausted. Then we had a peace powwow around an imaginary campfire and sat around "smoking our pipes" until we got our energy back.

Meanwhile, Dad was patiently drilling little holes into the caps of our acorn armys so we could push toothpicks about halfway through to make little "tops". We each ended up with about six or eight and colored the caps with crayons so we could tell them apart.

Our battles were waged on a flat tree stump or the picnic table in the backyard. On the count of three, we'd quickly spin our acorn tops until they were all in motion. Flying our colors, they danced across the tree stump battlefield to tumble and pitch each other off onto the ground. The person with the most tops still spinning at the end was the winner.

What happy afternoons those were! —*Barbara Jordan-Schoonover*
Hermosa Beach, California

my country school, I much preferred pushing a hoop with a stick.

My iron hoop probably came from the hub of a wagon. It was about 8 inches across and close to an inch wide. I rolled it with a 3-foot piece of lath that had a crosspiece nailed to one end. The goal was to push the hoop as far as possible without it rolling over.

On the 2-mile walk to school, we be-

came so proficient at rolling our hoops that we sometimes made it all the way there without having one fall over. That was no small thing, since the roads were seldom-graded sandy paths filled with ruts and horse tracks. It took skill to balance the hoop with one hand while carrying a lunch bucket and book in the other! —*Kathryn McGaughey*
Denver, Colorado

Mom's Bubble Recipe Beat Store-Bought

By Betty Borkenhagen
Eagle River, Wisconsin

WHEN MY CHILDREN were small, we lived in a rural area and couldn't easily "run to the store". To help me keep them entertained, my mother gave me the recipes *she'd* used during the Depression for making soap bubbles, paste and clay.

Bubbles made from Mom's solution always seemed bigger, brighter and "tougher", so we had more fun watching them ride on the wind.

Here are her recipes. (Note that they are all for playing and should not be eaten.)

BUBBLE SOLUTION
1 pint soap flakes (not detergent)
2 tablespoons glycerin
1 pint water
Heat mixture; shake and strain. Cool. Store in a covered jar.

HOMEMADE PASTE
1 cup flour
1 cup sugar
1 teaspoon powdered alum
1 quart water
3 drops oil of wintergreen or oil of cloves
Mix flour, sugar and alum; add water gradually. Cook until thickened; add oil. Cool. Store in a covered jar.

HOMEMADE CLAY
1 cup flour
1 cup salt
1 tablespoon powdered alum
1 cup cold water
Few drops oil of wintergreen or oil of cloves
Food coloring (optional)
Mix flour, salt and alum. Gradually add water, then oil. Add food coloring if desired. Knead until well mixed. Store, tightly covered, in the refrigerator.

RECIPE FOR FUN... When it came time to blow bubbles or mold clay, as these girls are doing, Mom's recipes were the best.

Archive Photos/F. Parker; inset, John E. Spangler

Pods Were Prime for Meat Market

ONE SUMMER DAY in 1936, when I was 8 years old, I couldn't think of anything to do. My mother brought several potatoes out of the house and showed me how to carefully slice them to resemble different cuts of meat. I made a meat market out of an apple crate.

Next I added "seafood" with pods from our sumac bushes. When opened, the pods looked just like *fish*, scales and all. A makeshift weight scale completed my store. Thanks to Mother, my empty hours were filled—although I'm sure she got quite tired of "going to the store" that day!
—*Jean Elliott, Claremont, California*

Goin' Pod Fishing

MILKWEED PODS made great fish. My sister, Geneva, and I would beg a pin and string from Mother, then climb a tree to break off a nice straight limb to make a fishing rod.

I'd crawl under the porch with a handful of milkweed pods, and Geneva would stand on the porch and cast her line over the banister. I'd grab the "hook", pin a pod on the string and give it a yank. With great joy, Geneva would pull up her "fish". When I ran out of fish, it was Geneva's turn under the porch. I was just as excited by each "catch" as she had been.
—*Ruth Weaver, Joshua, Texas*

Funnies Made "Home Movies"

MY GIRLFRIEND and I made our own "movies". Each day, we'd cut a comic strip out of the paper and color it. (I chose "Blondie" and she picked "Tillie the Toiler".)

The funnies were glued together into a long strip. When it reached a good length, we'd wind it around an empty toilet tissue roll. We cut a large square on one side of a shoe box for viewing our "movies". A slit cut on the back of the box let us pull the "funnies" through for winding onto another toilet tissue roll.
—*Maxine Edwards, Coronado, California*

With Corncob Dolls, Who Needed Barbie?

BARBIE DOLLS were unheard-of when I was a girl, but I had lots of corncob dolls.

I started by carefully shucking an ear of dry corn, keeping

the shucks attached at the top. After removing the kernels for the hogs, I'd wet the shucks, roll them into curls and secure them with bobby pins. When the curls dried, I'd remove the pins, arrange the "hair", and dress my doll in a scrap of material with a ribbon or string tied around the middle.

At one time, I had 26 of these dolls, each with a name starting with a different letter of the alphabet. As I recall, I had to ask Mom for names that started with X, Y and Z.

—Ann Lang, Protivin, Iowa

"Flying Ginny" Took Them for a Spin

OUR HOMEMADE "flying ginny" was great fun. Our brother cut down a tree, leaving the stump about waist-high. Then he drilled a hole in the stump and threaded a bolt through a board placed on top. One child sat on either end of the board while a third pushed it until it was going really fast. Some parents might think this too dangerous, but none of us ever got hurt, and we had a great time. —Gayle Langston
Montevallo, Alabama

MERRY GO-ROUNDERS. These high-flying funsters didn't need a fancy amusement park carousel. A tree trunk, some wire, pipe and ropes were enough.

J.C. Allen and Son

Pretty Petal Paint

DURING SUMMER, I loved putting purple morning glory blooms in a jar of water and shaking it until I had a pretty purple dye. With an old toothbrush, I'd "paint" to my heart's content—small blocks of wood, sticks, rocks, anything I could find. It didn't matter that a good rain would wash it all away. The fun of the painting was all that mattered.

—Sara Howard
North Wilkesboro, North Carolina

CALENDAR GIRL. Lois June Bittner and her log cabin playhouse were pictured on the calendar her grandfather gave to his grocery store customers in 1936. Her grandfather built the playhouse, which featured electric lights and handmade furniture. Hazel Hillegas of Friedens, Pennsylvania, who shared the photo, remembers many happy hours playing there with her friend.

Girls Treasured Newspaper Dolls

By Jane Wood, Wilson, North Carolina

AS MY SCISSORS slide across the dotted lines of a grocery coupon, I feel like a little girl again…trying desperately to keep my mother's best dressmaking shears on the line tracing the beautiful paper dolls printed in the Sunday newspaper in 1938.

Two dolls and two interchangeable outfits would occupy me for an entire week. When the next newspaper came out, a new set of paper dolls would present a challenge to pudgy 5-year-old fingers. When Mom had the time, she pasted the flimsy newsprint dolls onto cardboard to make them last longer.

The dolls were dressed by pushing their heads up through a slit. The clothes were held in place with small squares of paper that folded over the shoulders. The dresses were extremely ill-fitting, and I pretended that having hair showing through a hat was normal.

My friends and I kept our paper dolls in a shoe box, and we never went visiting without it. When we gathered at someone's house to play, all the dolls were introduced. The difference between newsprint dolls and store-bought ones was striking, but we showed no favorites.

We made make-believe homes for our paper friends from cardboard boxes, pasting on pictures of furniture clipped from the Sears catalog.

SUCH A DOLL! Funny paper clipper Gail Engeldahl of Hartford, Wisconsin props "Bumstead" family on the mantel in '49.

Our paper playmates were kind, agreeable and always smiling. It was contagious somehow. We all tried to be pleasant, too, as we dressed and redressed, positioned and repositioned the dolls on undersized furniture.

We became master ventriloquists, speaking for them out of the sides of our mouths. Their "conversations" centered around events they had attended, like grand balls, where they danced their way into the heart of Prince Charming.

Today, clipping coupons will save me only pennies. But my memories of clipping paper dolls over 50 years ago are priceless. ✿

Building Racers Filled Boys with Pride

By Chuck Maitzen
Grand Haven, Michigan

THE TOY I remember best from the 1920s and '30s was the sidewalk racer I designed and built.

All that was really needed was a discarded milk box or crate, a 4-foot length of two-by-four, an old clamp-on steel roller skate and a small can of paint. How satisfying to "do it alone"! I sanded the two-by-four plank, nailed the two halves of the skate onto either end, nailed the crate to the front, fashioned two slats into handlebars and painted the box with several coats for a long-lived gloss.

Only then did I add the finishing touch: a tin-can headlight with holes punched in the bottom to emit the powerful beam of a 1-inch candle. Then I could stand back and critically appraise my work. It was the finest pushmobile in the neighborhood!

My buddies and I were really something as we tooled down the street, wheels clicking over every crack in the pavement. As we gripped the steering handles, we kept one foot on the plank, pushing off with the other as hard and fast as our short legs could go.

After affectionately recalling those days to my son, I gathered the materials for one more pushmobile. Providing only advice and an occasional steadying hand, I watched as he built his very own version of the sidewalk racer I'd known as a lad. When he sped off on it for the first time, there was no prouder boy on earth.

Will the time ever come again when boys build their own "mopeds"? Probably not. But I hope so. 🎍

SIDEWALK RACER. Chuck Maitzen Jr. whizzed down the sidewalk on the racer he built himself—with a little advice from Dad, who had built many such pushmobiles in his youth.

MAYTAG MOTOR MOGUL. Her son John (above) and husband, Glen, built this go-cart from some lumber and the motor from a Maytag washing machine, says Celene Harper of Evansville, Wisconsin. There was always plenty of raw material around when kids (like those at right) wanted to build some transportation. Bikes were nice, but there was nothing like a "car" for careening down those backstreet hills.

CELLAR SKATERS. When he saw a neighbor toss out a pair of old roller skates in 1953, Ben Stoner of Landisville, Pennsylvania made a scooter to show his kids (above) how he and his brother used to play. He still has the scooter.

SCOOTING ALONG. Clyde Rowley shows off the apple-box scooter he made for his skeptical grandchildren. "I was amused at their amazement that Grandpa was telling the truth about these things," Clyde recalls with a chuckle.

Skating Was Her Great Escape

WHEN I WAS 9 or 10, my favorite pastime was roller skating. My skates were the kind that clamped onto your shoes and tightened with a key.

Our neighborhood had very little traffic, so I usually skated in the street. The cement street in front of our house was very noisy to skate on, but a few blocks away was a stretch of smooth, quiet blacktop where I spent many enjoyable afternoons.

I usually skated alone, but I was never bored. During that peaceful skating time, all alone, I could let my imagination soar and dream a child's dreams.

—*Georgia Greenemeier, Lakewood, Colorado*

Scooter Builder Hasn't Lost Touch

By Clyde Rowley, Everett, Washington

BUILDING A SCOOTER was a serious "basement project" for my friends and me during the Depression. In those days, 25¢ would buy a pair of used clamp-on skates, which powered two scooters when taken apart. Everything else was free.

We could pick up a two-by-four from any construction site, handlebars from woodpiles and the apple boxes from grocery stores. Our mothers provided the tin cans for headlights and taillights. Sometimes we could find an old license plate or hood ornament.

When we had all our materials in hand, we'd head for my parents' basement and start building. If one of us had managed to scrounge some leftover paint, our scooters would be "deluxe".

When we finished, we'd take our creations out onto the front sidewalk and have a parade for our cheering parents. (No wonder they were cheering—we had been busy, constructive and out of trouble, and now we were proud and happy.)

We couldn't hear much of the cheering, though. All those skate wheels on concrete made a lot of noise.

My grandchildren had never heard of these apple-box scooters, and I rather think they believed Grandpa was telling "tall tales". So I set about looking for parts. What a shock Grandpa got.

The skates were $1 at a "thrift" store, and a wooden apple box from a fruit stand cost $1.50. If I hadn't already had the two-by-four, handlebar sticks, tin cans and paint, who knows how much more I might have spent! ❧

Household Castoffs Made Award-Winning Dollhouse

IN THE 1930s, I was given a "make-it" book showing fascinating things to craft from household items. I made a dollhouse of cardboard cartons and spent hours furnishing it.

A living room table was a thread spool, matchbox and a circle of cardboard. Another piece of cardboard covered with sandpaper was marked off with bricks for a fireplace.

Round powder boxes were wrapped in fabric for chairs. Tiny perfume bottles filled with colored water became lamps with candy-cup shades.

A small shallow box with sections of corrugated cardboard painted different colors became a bookshelf. The walls were covered with wallpaper scraps, and each cutout window had curtains.

Foil gum and candy wrappers were shaped into goblets. Beads strung on thumbtacks graced the vanity, and a child's shoe box and four pencils formed a canopy bed.

When my daughter was young, I recreated the dollhouse from memory and we entered it in the New York State Fair. To my surprise, it won a red ribbon and was featured on a Syracuse TV show!

—Doris Monterey
Evans Mills, New York

Paper Dolls Gave Girls Hours of Rainy-Day Fun

ON COLD or rainy days, the girls in my neighborhood gathered to play with the paper dolls we'd cut from the Sears, Roebuck catalog.

Unlike store-bought paper dolls, ours didn't have clothes to fasten on with tabs. We solved that by cutting out several people in the same age group and just changing the whole doll when a new outfit was needed.

Each girl had a "house" laid out with strips of paper. For the price of a 3¢ stamp and a magazine coupon, we could obtain a large book of wallpaper samples for making "furniture". Some of us became proficient at folding the paper into sofas, tables, chairs, beds and dressers.

These make-believe people did much visiting and entertaining, and we also built churches and community centers so they could attend parties and dances. Our dolls provided hours of happiness. I was well into my teens before I gave them up!

—Juliette Chambliss, Emporia, Virginia

SWEET SNIPPER. Cutting paper dolls on a rainy day remains a great way to while away the hours.

ALL DOLLED UP. Mary Riggs of Trinidad, Colorado cherishes this Effanbee "Rosemary" doll she and her sister received for Christmas in 1926. "We'd almost worn out the Sears catalog, looking at and wishing for that doll," Mary recalls. Each Effanbee doll had its name embossed in the back of the neck. Mary made this new dress for the doll in 1989.

Matchstick People Filled Her Shoe-Box Dollhouse

WHENEVER I WAS bored or confined to my room, I could count on matchstick people to occupy my time.

To make them, I separated a matchbook into four pieces of paper, folding the outer pieces into arms and the others into legs. The women could be "dressed" with bits of tissue, and one spring, I made hair from my dog's fur when he started to shed!

The matchstick people's homes were shoe boxes. I cut the lids to make walls. If we'd kept the lightweight cardboard divider that used to be placed between shoes, I could mold that into furniture with a flour-and-water paste.

If I found a roll of Scotch tape to use instead, I was in heaven—but I usually got in trouble, too, because it often took a whole roll to complete a house.

I colored the walls with crayons or made them look like wallpaper. I made curtains from tissue. When we visited Grandma, I'd bring home several squares of her colored toilet tissue.

Now my hobby is building wooden dollhouses. I enjoy building and furnishing them just as much as my shoe-box houses.

—Patt Houghton
Plymouth, Indiana

❤ ❤ ❤ Loving Hands Crafted Doll Bed from Crate ❤ ❤ ❤

ONE OF THE MOST treasured Christmas gifts I ever received was a homemade doll bed from my parents during the Depression. Dad made the bed from the sides and back of an orange crate. Using leftover paint, Mother painted it and then made white flannel sheets and a pillowcase trimmed with pink satin.

What a delight to find that bed under the tree on Christmas morning, with my very own name on it! I still cherish the sight of it in my bedroom today.

—Wilda Middlebrook
Cresco, Iowa

A '50s Christmas That Took a Nosedive

By Bruce Dettman, San Francisco, California

I WOULD'VE rather helped my uncle scrub grungy car parts than watch Willie Mayes launch a grand slam over the left field bleachers at Candlestick Park. Uncle Bill could make the most humdrum occasions special simply by the pleasure of his company.

As an Illinois youth, he "rode the rails" to California, performed daredevil motorcycle stunts, and later acted as a human guinea pig for the Army testing new weaponry in World War II. And when I was about 10 years old, my Uncle Bill saved Christmas.

That was the year in the late '50s I was hoping for my first hi-fi. (Actually, *hope* wasn't the issue, since during a late-afternoon reconnaissance raid, I'd already spied the machine beneath my parents' bed.) But I was dying to hear the recordings of *Davy Crockett* sung by Fess Parker and Elvis' *All Shook Up*, which I'd also gotten a sneak peek at.

Our relatives always got together to open gifts on Christmas Eve, and I'm sure my mother dreaded the moment I unwrapped Uncle Bill's present. One year, he got me a regulation-size plastic bowling ball and pins, inflatable by water, which I set up in the living room when no one else was home. Somehow, the house survived.

On this occasion, after attacking the large wrapped box with all the restraint of Dracula browsing a blood bank, I discovered a gas-operated replica of a World War II fighter plane. Even my new record player paled in comparison. I wanted to forget everything else under the tree (especially since the remaining packages bore all the signs of sweaters and socks) and rush out into the street to send it skyward.

"In the morning," my father reasoned.

"Even the hotshot pilots don't learn at night," my uncle added with a wink.

The Big Moment Arrives

The next day was a typical California Christmas—seasonally crisp with a radiant blue sky. Not even waiting for pancakes, I coaxed my father, uncle and brother to the local playground.

The playground was quiet, save for a few kids shooting baskets with a shiny new ball and the distant sound of a tether ball chain clanging against the pole.

We kneeled over the plane as my father prepared to take it up. Everyone was giving me tips on what to expect when I took hold of the controls, but I was too excited to really listen.

My father barked for me to stand back as he guided my new powder-blue baby up into the sky. Around and around it buzzed, then my uncle put the craft through its aerial paces, and next my brother took a turn. Now the kids from the bas-

FIRST FLIGHT. Much like the author, this anxious pilot couldn't wait to launch his model plane in '56.

ketball game had joined us in addition to some new arrivals twirling Hula Hoops and fast-drawing their Mattel Fanner 50s.

"Me next!" I hollered.

Do you think you've got the hang of it, Bruce? they asked.

"Yes!" I squealed. They might as well have asked if I thought America could whomp the Russians or if Flash Gordon would eventually catch up with Ming the Merciless!

Okay. It's all yours.

I was Eddie Rickenbacker, Sky King and Captain Midnight all rolled into one. Gingerly I reached for the controls and felt the tightness of the line as the plane bent high and to the left. The model climbed and climbed.

"Bruce!" my father yelled. "Lower her nose. Don't jerk her that way!"

I heard him, but everyone was screaming at me and my plane was no longer paying attention to my commands. It continued to climb for a few terrifying seconds, paused in space, then plunged kamikaze-like to the concrete.

What Would Uncle Bill Think?

There wasn't much left—just scattered debris of powder-blue plastic. The cleanup crew following the Hindenberg disaster probably found more wreckage.

I stood there in shock, my head feeling like a thousand tons as it dropped toward the ground. All eyes were on me, even my dog's. I finally glanced up to see my father shaking his head and my brother mouth *you idiot.*

But my main concern was Uncle Bill. Would he ever forgive me? Would he ever invite me back to his garage to clean spark plugs?

On top of this, I was sure I'd ruined what was left of Christmas. There was still the entire day to get through…eggnog, homemade fudge, turkey dinner, street football, a blaze in the fireplace and listening to my uncle and father have their traditional after-dinner political squabble.

I looked up to see my uncle standing over me and braced myself, trying to keep back the tears.

"Well, nephew," he said with a bemused smile. "I guess the Navy's the place for you."

Not another word was spoken, and as if taking a cue, my father—even my *brother*—refrained from discussing "the crash" until several days later, when the pain was mostly gone.

I made certain to sit next to my uncle at breakfast that morning…and for that matter, whenever possible for the rest of his life. Uncle Bill passed away last year at the age of 73, but he left me a colorful legacy of memories, and I will always consider him the most magnanimous of men. ❦

BRING ON SPRING! With a new mitt for Christmas, a surprised Don Preiser (above) was ready for baseball season. His dad, Gordon, of Lancaster, Pennsylvania snapped the excitement back in the '50s. Those days waiting for nice weather were prime time for some "deep" reading (right) when comics went "3-D".

'Look What I Got!'

Our Gang Wanted a *Real* Football

By Gene Baggott, Houston, Texas

THE FALL I entered third grade, we were without a football in our neighborhood. Oh, we had some old ones filled with grass and leaves, but they didn't pass well and couldn't be punted with any accuracy.

Seven of us decided to do odd jobs to earn the money for a new ball. Three of us raked leaves, earning 50¢. Tommy earned a dime by washing a neighbor's dog, and Midge went to the store for his grandma, who gave him a cookie. He ate it.

At this rate, we'd be riding our *snow sleds* before we had enough money for a football. We were glumly sitting on my back porch when Dad came home.

"Golly, guys," he said, "you look like you just heard you have to go to school on Saturdays. What's the problem?"

When we explained, he offered us a deal. I was having trouble learning the multiplication tables. If they could help me learn them in the next 2 weeks, he'd buy us a football. Could we do it?

Everybody started yelling. "Yeah!" "Okay!" "You betcha!" Then we all went to work.

No gang of kids ever learned faster or better. On the way to and from school, we'd shout out our numbers. Instead of counting to 100 for hide-and-seek, we'd recite a multiplication table. We even used them to make up signals for a couple of trick football plays we planned to use.

At the end of 2 weeks, Dad had us all back on the porch. He was going to test me to see how much I'd learned. But *all* the gang wanted to be tested! Dad was amazed.

After we'd passed the test, he went into the house and came out with a beautiful full-size football. Mom was right behind him with a real thriller—she'd found some men's undershirts on sale and dyed them a brilliant orange. They were just cheap cotton shirts, and miles too big, but none of that mattered. We were a *team*! 🎵

READY, SET, SMILE! That "pigskin" William Kolbush, now of Pascagoula, Mississippi, is ready to hike in Scotia, Nebraska in '33 doesn't look very official, but the rest of the team doesn't seem to mind.

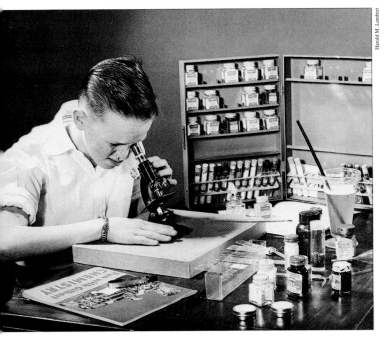
Harold M. Lambert

Microscope Kit Concocted Get-Rich-Quick Scheme

WHEN I was 7, my best friend, Georgie, wanted me to run away with him. He was 10 years old—practically an adult—but I didn't want to go—until he hit upon a scheme to make us rich.

We were playing with my microscope set, which included a little bottle of "Oregon balsam". I had no idea what it was, but Georgie reasoned that it must come from Oregon.

Georgie said we could become millionaires by going to the source of the supply, buying the stuff dirt cheap, then coming back east to sell it for a big profit.

We started out right after lunch. Each of us took an apple, and I had a nickel. We figured that it wouldn't take us more than a week to walk to Oregon from Pennsylvania. Our route took us past a popular amusement park. Since we were running away, we reasoned, why not have some fun, too?

Georgie and I couldn't afford the rides, so we spent my nickel on caramel popcorn to eat with our apples as we wandered around the park.

At about 4 in the afternoon, our stomachs began gnawing at us and we both reached the same decision: We'd run away some other day.

—*Walter Mueller*
Maple Glen, Pennsylvania

MONKEY MEMORIES. Before his family moved to a small town, Warren Christman's parents gave him this toy monkey, dressed just like the one the organ grinder who came to their neighborhood in Jersey City, New Jersey had. Warren, now of Perrine, Florida, still has the toy, with the year 1931 legible on its foot where his dad penciled it. Warren kept his love of primates alive in Florida, where he worked for the Metro-Dade County Park and Recreation Department, which operated a zoo. Warren got to take "Samantha", a real chimp, out for public and television appearances to promote an event at the zoo.

Harold M. Lambert

FUN LEARNING. Store-bought toys often taught kids things when they were too busy having fun to realize it. Her daughters, Karen and Vicki (right), whipped up a cake back in the '50s, says Rosa Claridge of Newport, Oregon. But there were also chemistry sets for boys (top), which occasionally led to explosive discoveries, and erector sets for budding engineers (far right).

Pedalers from the Past

BELOVED BIKE. George Doak of Carnegie, Pennsylvania (above) treasured this bicycle, bought when he was 10 or 11. The "Black Beauty" had white sidewalls, a rear carrying rack, a light with battery case and a tool case between the bars. The best feature, George says, was the chain-operated siren. "You could hear it for two blocks," he recalls.

BIKING SCOUTS. To earn their Boy Scout merit badges, John Kautz (second from right above), now of Fairfield Bay, Arkansas, and two friends pedaled from Chicago to Three Lakes, Wisconsin for a 750-mile round-trip in 1936. The other Scouts were Richard Bagger (left) and Melvin Frank. Donald Nass (far right) joined the trio in southern Wisconsin for the trip home. No pedaling for Louis Proper of Fairborn, Ohio (right). He motorized his bike in 1924 when he lived in California, and the summer flew by.

GAY '90S GETUPS won prizes for Esther Northrop and her sister Frances when they rode their antique tandem bicycle at gatherings in 1940. Esther is the "dandy gent" on the rear seat. In the background is their father's 1931 Franklin, which Esther recalls had an air-cooled engine.

They Looked Sweet on Bicycle Built for Two

IN THE MID-1930s, Dad bought an 1890s tandem bicycle for us to ride. The wheels had wooden rims, and there was no coaster brake—only a hand brake that worked against the front tire.

The bicycle was steered with both the front and back handlebars, so it helped if both riders agreed on their direction! My sister Frances and I spent many happy hours riding that bicycle. I often rode it alone from the backseat, too.

In the summer of 1940, Frances and I decorated the bike, got period costumes for ourselves and rode it in a parade. We won a 5-pound sack of flour as a prize (which made Mother happy). Then we rode it at a field day and won another prize—$5!

—*Esther Northrop*
Binghamton, New York

"Irish Mail" Was His Lucky Charm

MY PAL Donnie and I had a whole fleet of sleds, tricycles, pedal cars, scooters and wagons, but I was proudest of the one vehicle he didn't have—my "Irish Mail".

The Irish Mail was a pump car that had gears similar to those on a railroad handcar. It had to be steered with the feet, and mastering it was my first real achievement in life. It was a skill no one else could manage—no one else on my block, anyway.

I remember flying down the sidewalk, pumping madly, occasionally aiming at poor unsuspecting pedestrians or stray tricycle riders. Sometimes it went so fast that I could let go of the pump handle, and the darn thing would keep pumping itself!

My most outstanding accomplishment was tilting back on the rear wheels, pivoting the whole vehicle around, then pumping off in a different direction without missing a beat. I was doing "wheelies"—in 1936, yet!

My Irish Mail is over 60 years old now, and in some ways, it's still my proudest possession. I still ride it, too—but I've given up doing wheelies.

—*Jim Owens, Springfield, Ohio*

OUT FOR A SPIN. Steve Potter takes cousin Dave Wittrock for a ride in the "Jeep" his dad, Paul, built for him in 1953. Dave's sister, Judy, is awaiting her turn. "The car was first powered by a battery and starter, but soon it had to be 'gassed up'," Paul remembers. "Steve was driving it almost before he walked!" Paul, who lives in Columbus, Indiana, is currently restoring the car (below) for his new grandson.

WEST COAST RIDES. California was great motoring territory. In 1919, Stephen Petersen (above with sister) of Hillsborough, California pushed his "American Biscuit Co." car along a San Francisco street; and in 1916, Cathlyn Schmidt (left) now of Burbank, motored with brother Clyde and sister Evelyn in Hollywood.

Dump Provided Parts For Teens' Plane

I'LL NEVER FORGET the summer of 1937. That was when two friends and I built what an Ohio newspaper called "undoubtedly Cleveland's strangest airplane".

It had a 14-foot wingspan and was made of plaster lath, window shades and buggy wheels we'd painstakingly picked out of the scrap dump.

Our total capital outlay for construction was less than $2. We christened it *The Stharan*, which was a combination of our names—Stan, Harry and Andy.

The plane had a one-cylinder gasoline engine salvaged from an old Apex washing machine. The engine spasmodically turned the propeller, but that was about the most movement we ever got out of it.

We finally decided to give up on our plane. We removed the engine, towed it to an upper plateau in the park and pushed it down the steep grade toward the water pumping station, with Andy manning the cockpit. We were hoping for a glider ride. We got a nosedive instead.

—*Stan Majer*
Richmond Heights, Ohio

FLYING HIGH. This teenage trio never got their homemade plane off the ground, but their efforts got plenty of publicity in their hometown. Stan Majer (in cockpit) and friends Andy Zupancic (left) and Harry Kramer built *The Stharan* in 1937.

H. Armstrong Roberts

BOMBS AWAY! James Hesek loved playing "dive-bomber" in this pedal-powered U.S. Pursuit Plane, says wife Ann of Atco, New Jersey. Their daughter recently found a restored version of this classic toy in a catalog—for $5,000! "When Jim saw that price, he was sorry he'd done all that dive-bombing," chuckles Ann. The photo was taken May 20, 1942 in Johnstown, New York.

Plane Builder Faced Dilemma

IN THE mid-'30s when I was 9, I'd sweet-talk my grandmother out of 10¢, run down to the local hobby shop and drool over the World War I single-engine model planes. After careful deliberation, I'd plunk down my dime, run home and start building.

When finished, I had two choices. I could walk up four floors to the roof of our apartment building, wind the rubber motor and launch the plane. With any luck, it'd fly. Then I had to run *down* four floors to the street and try to catch it before it hit something, or a car hit me.

My other option was to sell the finished plane back to the hobby shop for 25¢ so I could buy and build more!

—*Bill Cohen, Sunrise, Florida*

Outhouse Plane Was a Less-Than-Soaring Success

By Bill Blake, St. Peters, Missouri

I BUILT my first kid-size airplane in our chicken coop the summer I was 8 years old. When I went back to school that fall, I really had something to tell the kids who were always calling me an "airplane nut". How many of *them* had their own plane?

I was thinking about that plane 4 years later, when my friend Charlie called to say he was coming for a visit. It would sure be neat to have another plane to play in.

My gaze fell on the outhouse. Perfect! I dashed upstairs, grabbed a school tablet and sketched the outhouse, then drew in the fuselage, tail and wings. Material was no problem—Dad and Gramps were building a new kitchen and indoor bathroom, so there were plenty of two-by-fours and lath around.

I dashed back downstairs, through the kitchen past Mom, and out the back door. Mom just stared and shook her head. (She knew something was up.)

At the outhouse, I put a brick on top of the sketch to keep it from blowing away and began pulling the bigger weeds out of the construction area. Mom couldn't believe her eyes. Trying to get me to help weed the garden was like trying to cage a wild cat.

With the weeds out of the way, I gathered a hammer, saw and nails from the tool bench in the garage, selected some one-by-twos from the woodpile and headed back to the outhouse.

I dug a hole and anchored a 5-foot two-by-four in it for a tail post. The one-by-twos were nailed to the front and back of the outhouse at ground level, then nailed to the tail post for the bottom of the fuselage.

More lumber liberated from the woodpile formed the cabin. A crosspiece, a section of cardboard and tin can lids made an instrument panel. An apple crate served as a seat, and an old hoe sawed in half became the control sticks. Four long roof shingles driven into the ground formed the rudder pedals.

That evening, when Dad and Gramps swung the Model A into the driveway and saw the outhouse, they stared in disbelief. Dad drove right into the corn patch!

"What is that?" were Gramps' first words.

"If I didn't know better," Dad replied, "I'd say it looks like an airplane fuselage."

The next morning, I was up before anyone else, ate a fast bowl of cornflakes and went out to work on the airplane's tail. Charlie was due out the next day, and I wanted to get the plane finished. When he arrived, putt-putting up the road on a motor scooter his dad had built, we immediately dashed out to spend the day flying around the world.

A couple of hours later, Mom saw us walking toward the gully. She couldn't figure this out, since Charlie

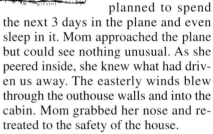

and I had planned to spend the next 3 days in the plane and even sleep in it. Mom approached the plane but could see nothing unusual. As she peered inside, she knew what had driven us away. The easterly winds blew through the outhouse walls and into the cabin. Mom grabbed her nose and retreated to the safety of the house.

The outhouse slowly disappeared as Gramps required certain pieces of wood for repairs. But I didn't mind. I seldom played in the plane, even after all the hard work I'd put into it. I just couldn't hack that powerful aroma! ✿

MODEL CHILD. His models ran the gamut from the non-flying state fair prize-winner at right to the gas-powered 7-footer below, says Hugh Smith Jr. of Solvang, California. That's Hugh below left in 1936.

Archive Photos/Lambert

JUMPING FOR JOY. All it took was a sunny day and a jump rope to keep a kid happy in the good old days. Equipment wasn't fancy back then—a leather bag of marbles, some clamp-on roller skates, an old tin can, a broom handle and a tennis ball...or maybe just the wonderful imagination of youth.

❦ Chapter Three ❦
Great Games of Our Youth

You can't put a price tag on the fun we shared playing
mumblety-peg or a brisk game of stickball.

hen I was a kid, it didn't take much money to have fun playing with my friends. Sometimes it didn't take any at all—nothing more than a fresh snowfall for a game of fox and geese, for example, and tag didn't even require snow.

The jackknife that Grampa had given you for your birthday was all you needed for a game of mumblety-peg. And it certainly wasn't hard to come up with the only item needed to play kick the can.

However, I did pay a price while learning about the evils of gambling. Playing marbles for "keeps" was strictly forbidden on the school grounds and frowned on by all upstanding parents. Ah, but the forbidden fruit is the most tempting. Naturally I yielded to temptation, and in the process lost half the treasured contents of my marble bag to some beady-eyed little crook with a deadly magic shooter! Lesson learned.

When parents got together for a sociable evening of conversation or pinochle, the visitors often brought along their kids—who could afford a baby-sitter in those days?

Home Court Advantage

If the weather was decent, we usually ended up outside for a game of hide-and-seek. The first thing you learned was the value of "home court advantage". If the game was in your own yard, you naturally knew of all sorts of neat places to hide—under the porch, up in a tree or deep in the shadows of a big lilac bush. But if you were in *their* yard, your chances of success were slim.

One thing I'd like to bring back for kids is baseball as it used to be played. It was just for kids and *not* for overexcited parents who felt the family honor was at stake every time you were on the field. Everyone who showed up got to play; you simply chose up sides. So inept as I was at the game, I still got picked...eventually.

A few lucky players had a baseball glove, but even a glove wasn't much help in handling the lumpy, misshapen balls held together with black electricians' tape. We played in parks, on the school grounds and sometimes in empty fields, where bemused cows (who had unknowingly provided the necessary bases) kept their distance.

In big cities, the street-version of the game was called stickball. It involved nothing more than a broom handle and an old tennis or handball. The neighborhood hero was the "three manhole guy" because that's how far he could hit the ball—all the way to the third manhole cover down the street. Some of those standouts eventually made it to the major leagues.

On the next pages, you'll discover a lot of other for-free games kids invented, including some you may never have heard of. They'll make you wish you were a kid again. —*Clancy Strock*

City Stickball Seems Like a Dream

By Joseph Turner, Leesburg, Florida

MY WIFE and I were in a toy store shopping for our grandson's birthday present, when I noticed the aisles were filled with weird-looking stuffed toys and gadgets. I headed for the sporting goods section, sure that "normality" would at least prevail there.

As I weighed the pros and cons of various balls, I spotted an assortment of multicolored sticks in a corner. "Can you believe this?" I asked my wife. "Stickball bats manufactured by companies whose employees probably never even *heard* of a stickball game!"

The guys I grew up with in Queens, New York *lived* for stickball, and every one of us owned several bats fashioned from our moms' brooms.

I picked up a bright red bat, its low-er half neatly wrapped with black tape. Suddenly, people I hadn't heard from or thought of for years flooded my mind's screen. *I was a kid again, playing stickball on 63rd Road...*

Memories in Replay

I could see old man Casey, a retired fire fighter, exiting his house with folding chair under arm to watch the game. He usually appeared the minute we began choosing sides and settled any disputes. All of us accepted his decisions as binding.

Next, Mrs. Hurley suddenly came into view, calling down the wrath of the banshees upon us, and especially poor Jackie Brady as he trampled her daffodils in a futile attempt to catch a foul.

Matty Molloy, a three-sewer hitter, stepped up to the plate and hit a long drive to the left. Joe Torney, in a valiant attempt to catch the speeding orange ball, crashed into a brand-new Hudson. Neither boy nor machine was seriously damaged.

The pitcher was Weario Huggins, our opponents' favorite hurler. (It was rumored, but never proved, that he pitched with his eyes closed.)

Now George Smith appeared in the batter's box, swinging three bats over his head. He had the largest bat collection of any of us and spent hours sanding, painting and taping his beauties. (Nobody can remember Smitty ever getting a hit, though. Andy Reilly claimed that Weario occasionally *hit him* with a pitch so Smitty could at least say he got on base.)

A Sudden Time-Out

When Fritz, the delicatessen owner, suddenly appeared in his sparkling white apron at the end of the block, we knew intermission wasn't far off.

Within minutes, officers from the 112th Precinct arrived to break up the game. As soon as we spotted them, we quickly hid our bats behind the hedges lining the tiny lawns bordering our playing field.

Once the cops left, players and spectators trudged to Fritz's, where the "informer" happily sold us ice-cold soda pop. We grumbled about him calling the police, but we were secretly happy for the respite and returned to the field refreshed. *The game went on until our moms started sending younger siblings to fetch us home for dinner...*

The pictures faded from my mind as I heard my wife warn me the store was closing in 10 minutes. I grabbed several bats in different colors and a few rubber balls and made my way to the checkout counter.

On the drive home, I thought a silent "so long" to Matty, Weario and the rest of the gang, thanking them for the memories. ❧

J.C. Allen and Son

BATTER UP! Whether it was stickball in the city or softball in the small towns, as the boys here are playing, kids and balls and bats were made for each other. Those curbside bleachers could get a little hard, though.

COLORADO CLUBBERS. The Newcastle nine had just drubbed the neighboring Rifle team in June 1915, says Claude Hall of Canon City, Colorado. His dad, third baseman Claude, is at front right, and his Uncle Clarence, the manager, is second from left in the back row. Nine players...no subs, Claude notes.

As Few as Three Could Play "Step Baseball"

CONCRETE STEPS and a rubber or tennis ball were the only equipment needed for "step baseball".

The game required at least three players, preferably five. The batter stood a foot or two from the bottom step. The first baseman stood 8 to 10 feet behind him, followed by the second and third basemen and outfielder. The distance between batter and outfielder was determined by the width of the street.

The batter threw the ball against the step with all his might. A ball that sailed past the outfielder was a home run. If a fly ball was caught, the fielder switched places with the batter.

A "ground ball" fielded by the first baseman counted as a strike. When the batter struck out, he moved to the outfield and all the fielders moved up.

A ground ball fielded by the second baseman was a one-base hit; by the third baseman, a double; and by the outfielder, a triple. The imaginary "men" on base moved up accordingly.
—Charles Bridinger
Costa Mesa, California

We All Wanted To Be the Teacher

WE PLAYED "rock school" on our front steps, lining up on the bottom step to start "first grade". The "teacher" stood in front of us, asking us to guess which of her closed hands held a small rock.

A correct guess meant a "promotion" to the next step. The first student who reached the top step got to be the next teacher, and "school" started again with everyone on the bottom step.
—Bertie Carnes, Gainesville, Georgia

Singsong Rhymes Livened Up Games

MANY OF OUR games in New York City were accompanied by songs. Tag called for: "Old Mother Witch, couldn't sew a stitch, she picked up a penny and thought she was rich."

When we played ball, we recited: "Down the market stinkin' fish, if you want some bring a dish, two for a penny, three for a dime, Johnny has a haircut just like mine."

For jumping rope, we sang: "Oh, say, kid, whaddya think I did? I upset the cradle and out fell the kid. The kid began to holler, I caught him by the collar, the collar broke loose and I got the deuce, deuce, deuce!"

To get a turn on the park swings, you approached someone who'd been swinging a long time and sang out: "Cry, baby, cry, stick your finger in your eye, tell your mother it wasn't I, so die, baby, die." At that point, the swinger was not allowed to pump his legs and had to let the swing slow down until it was still.

When autumn weather approached, the street games got a little wilder, especially after school let out on October 31.

Then every child turned their coats and sweaters inside out, because you were sure to be "chalked up" by some Halloween prankster sneaking up behind to draw something on your back.

The boys were a little rougher than girls with their tricks. They filled up stockings with flour and whacked you with them, leaving big white blotches on your clothes.

In the evening, there was always bobbing for apples or trying to bite the apple stuck with pennies, hung by a string from the ceiling. *—Hilda Kraus*
Westport, Connecticut

The Whole Skinny on How to Play "Shinny"

WE PLAYED a game called "shinny", which was similar to hockey. It was played on the street, with goals about 40 feet apart.

The puck was made from a Carnation milk can that had been filled with sand and crushed down. A carefully selected tree branch sawed with a crook left in the end made the perfect shinny stick.

There was only one rule: Stay on your side of the puck. Exciting? You bet. Once in a while, you'd hear, "Shinny on your own side!"

In winter, we skated on the Des Plaines River, and shinny became hockey, with the same excitement. Most of us owned racing skates with 16-inch blades; they weren't very good for hockey, but our philosophy was, "Do with what you have".

—George Biringer
Bella Vista, Arkansas

PAVED GRIDIRON. A Philadelphia street in 1943 was as good as a field for a pickup game. Hugh Smith Jr. of Solvang, California shared the photo.

Makeshift Checkers Were Just Too Sweet to Resist

By Margaret Underwood, Wilbur, Washington

MY BROTHER was 12 when his friend Eldie introduced him to the game of checkers.

Fascinated by this new game, yet knowing our family could not afford to buy it, Francis carefully counted the number of squares on the board, memorized the rules and ran home. He couldn't have been more excited if someone had handed him a $10 bill.

With a piece of brown wrapping paper and a ruler, he drew his own checkerboard and asked Mom for some of the red and white cinnamon candies left from Christmas to use for the checkers.

Then he taught his three younger sisters the game so we'd have something fun to do when it was too cold to play outdoors.

KING ME, GRAMPS. There was a time when a real checkerboard, like one being enjoyed above, cost a lot of money...50¢. But the fun was priceless.

Unfortunately, it never occurred to Francis (who had a conscience the size of the United States) that we might nibble away at the candy when he wasn't looking! We eventually substituted dry red and white beans for the "checkers".

We played all winter with no lessening of interest in the game. Every night after the supper dishes were washed and the homework done, those living room tournaments raged on.

One day, Dad surprised us with a real checkerboard set. Fifty cents was a lot to spend on a game in those lean years, but Dad was convinced we were serious about it.

We lived in an 18-room building that had been a hotel. Sometimes we rented rooms to out-of-town visitors, but we had no modern gadgets like a radio to entertain them. Instead, they played checkers with us.

Many years later, tourists passing through town would stop for a short visit to remind us they'd been our guests during the Depression. They always concluded their reminiscing by asking, "Do you still play checkers?" 🍃

First Game of Marbles Was a Rite of Spring

By Margaret Underwood, Wilbur, Washington

KNUCKS DOWN. If it's "for keeps", marbles can be a tense game and all the rules must be followed. The leather bag of mibs, as this boy is clutching, was a kid's treasured supply. If you lost your shooter, it was a sad day.

A FEW YEARS AGO, I was at a flea market when a container of old marbles caught my eye. They were in a metal box that once held attachments for a treadle-type Singer sewing machine, and the price tag on the box read $1.

I asked hopefully, "Is the box included with the marbles?"

"No, it isn't," she said. "And the price for the marbles is $1 *each*."

Back at home, I hunted up my old red plastic purse filled with marbles from my childhood. I was rich! There were emmies, aggies, grannies, glassies, shooters and even a couple of dough babies.

In the 1920s, we played marbles as soon as the last snow melted and the ground dried. At morning recess, we cleared an area about 6 feet by 10 feet, then stepped off the distance for the "lag line" and dragged a shoe in the dirt to make a groove. The child who tossed a marble closest to the line would shoot first.

Next, we drew an almond-shaped ring at least 1-1/2 feet wide and 6 inches deep. From an agreed-upon line, players used their shooters to try to knock opponents' marbles out of the ring. The game continued until all the marbles were shot out, or the bell rang.

My older sister had a large collection of marbles, but I lost so often that Mom made me stop playing "for keeps". When I won the county spelling competition, my teacher bought me a bag of 100 marbles for 10¢. I couldn't have been happier if they were diamonds! 🍃

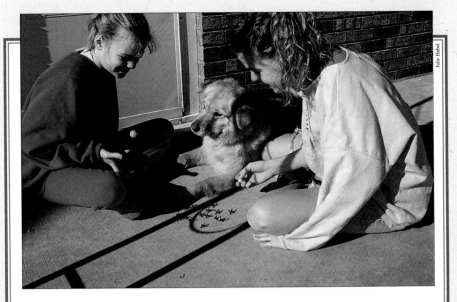

Jacks Could Be Played Anywhere—Even in the Car!

By Annie-Laurie Robinson, Williamston, Michigan

OUR FAVORITE GAME was jacks. It could be played inside or out, in any season. We played in our grandmother's huge bathroom, on hardwood floors and on sidewalks. We even played on the floor in the backseat of our '37 Buick. (We always seemed to have skinned and bleeding knuckles.)

Jacks were sold with little rubber balls, but we abandoned them for those that came from the center of golf balls. We'd cut off the white cover and unwind the yards of a rubber band-type material inside, which sometimes seemed to snap off by itself. In the center was a wonderful hard ball with a super bounce.

We played with up to 10 jacks at a time, throwing them out onto a flat surface to start. There were many variations of the game, but the simplest involved picking up the jacks one at a time, bouncing the ball in between "pickups". Then you'd pick up two at a time, then three and so on until all the jacks were picked up.

If you failed to pick up the required number or moved a jack you weren't picking up, that was a "miss" and you lost your turn. Sometimes it was hard to tell if a jack had moved, and many arguments ensued.

I wish I had my old jacks. Today's aren't as heavy as the ones of my youth. I plan to teach my granddaughters how to play—and my husband might even find some of his golf balls missing! ☙

Children Flipped Over Mumblety-Peg

KIDS LOVED to play mumblety-peg, which involved flipping a pocketknife in various ways to make the small blade stick into the ground.

A player had to perform each "event" three times to continue. In the first event, he held the end of the blade and flipped the knife for a "stickup". In the second, he balanced the knife between his forefinger and middle finger and slapped it with the other hand, then repeated the sequence with the opposite hand.

Next, the player flipped the knife off both wrists, elbows and shoulders. In the final event, "Over the Mountain", he flipped the knife over his head. If the knife didn't stick, the player could say "risk it" and get one more chance. If successful, he continued. If he failed, he had to start all over.

The winner—the first player to complete every event—whittled a peg the length of a knife blade and drove it into the ground. The player who was the furthest behind had to "eat the peg" by pulling it out of the ground with his teeth! —*Jack and Evelyn Corzine New Port Richey, Florida*

Shortage Was No Barrier To Fun and Games

IN THE '30s, when I lived in Sand Springs, Oklahoma, my grandpa helped my brothers and me make a bag swing —a gunnysack filled with rags and tied to a rope or cable. We'd throw the swing out, hop on it when it came back and sway out over a sandpile where we could jump off.

On the school playground, we played "gang pile". Whoever had the ball would be chased and tackled, and all the kids would pile on top of each other.

We also played "horse and rider" where smaller kids would ride on the stouter ones' backs, trying to dismount their opponents. The school grounds were hard red clay, so we were always scratched and bruised.

"Root the Peg", also called mumblety-peg, was played with a pocketknife with both blades open. Points were awarded for the different positions (shown at right) in which the knife fell.

You got 25 points for position 1, 50 points for 2, 75 for 3 and 100 points for position 4. A game was usually 500 points.

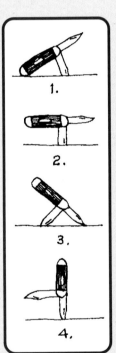

"Territory" was played with a pocket knife or ice pick. A large circle was drawn in the dirt with a line through the center. These were the territories the players started with.

Then they took turns flipping the knife (or pick) in the opponent's territory. The angle that the knife struck was used for drawing a line to cut up the territory.

The old boundary line was wiped out with a bare foot. When one piece of territory was down to a size smaller than the owner's foot, he lost the game.

We probably got dirtier and more roughed up than kids do today with video games, but we had fun just the same.

—*Robert Gilmore, Anchorage, Alaska*

SCHOOLYARD FUN. There was no need for expensive playground equipment years ago. Just the teacher, a hoop and some kids.

Clanging Maypole Chains Signaled Start of Spring

SPRING wasn't official until our principal gave word and the Maypole chains were lugged up the stairs from the boiler room and installed by our faithful maintenance man.

Like magic, swings started pumping, the slide received its first waxed paper rub, and the sandbox was full of happy children.

The Maypole chains hung from a 10-foot galvanized pole. Each chain ended in a triple-bar grip, like a miniature ladder with three smooth rungs. The grips clanged against the pole, sounding lovely, deep tones that seemed to beckon us to play.

When each child had a grip, someone signaled "Go!" and we'd all run around the pole a few times, then start lifting our feet off the ground. After a few circles, I could remain in orbit for 10 passes around the pole. (It was best when the opposite kid outweighed you, because then you'd be the high man that time around.)

The workers at the Kirby Vacuum Co. across the street would hang out the second-floor windows and fan themselves during breaks, following us with envious eyes as we flew around the pole.

Diehards like myself stuck stubbornly to a first-and-third overhand grip, skipping the rung in between. Many a summer night we suffered as the family popcorn bowl passed us over while we sat soaking our blistered palms in a dishpan of warm water.

The Maypole reigned for many summers. Then one spring, "safety" reigned and our beloved Maypole stood naked and shamed without its chains. Mothers who'd tended our loosened teeth and skinned knees rejoiced, but we kids were gloomy. We gathered on each other's porches, recalling the thrill that caught in our throats when our feet left the ground and we felt ourselves being tugged upward.

Eventually, the pole was removed, the playground shrank and a new building sprouted on the site where we had once taken wing. But sometimes I can still hear the clanging call of the Maypole and remember the pride of being "high man in the air". —*Claudia Perez*
North Ridgeville, Ohio

'Tag...You're It!'

By Anita Champeau, Norman, Oklahoma

MY DAD worked in the oil fields when I was a child, and we moved to a new town nearly every year. At each school, there was a different version of the game of tag.

In "Japanese tag", the person tagged had to hold whatever part of his body had been touched while he tried to tag someone else.

In "lock tag", the first person tagged joined hands with "It" and chased the others. The next person tagged joined hands with the first two and so on, until only one player was left to chase.

"Skunk tag" had no home base where players were safe from being tagged. Instead, players had to stand still, holding their nose with one hand and their left foot with the other. As long as the player could maintain this position, he couldn't be tagged.

"One-legged tag", played only by boys who could take such roughhousing, required two teams. One boy from each side would try to knock down the other while hopping on one foot. If a player let go of his foot or fell, he was "out" and another member of his team took his place.

Another boys-only game was "tractor tag". Two players got on their hands and knees, facing in opposite directions. Two others straddled their backs, then reached behind and tried to tag the other rider. When one rider was tagged, he became the "tractor".

Another thing I remember from my school days is all of the creative games the teachers thought up.

In "Teapot", one student would leave the room while the others thought of a word with two or more meanings, such as "train". When the student returned, we'd substitute the word "teapot" for "train" in sentences.

For example, someone might say, "I like to ride on a teapot." Or: "Charles is going to teapot for the wrestling team." Once the word was guessed, the player who offered the last sentence became the next "guesser".

Another game was called "Spinning a Yarn". The teacher would start telling a funny story while holding a skein of yarn. At some point, she'd toss the yarn to a student, who had to pick up the "thread" of the story, then throw the yarn to someone else. ❧

Jump Rope Had a Language All Its Own

JUMPING ROPE was one of our favorite pastimes. You could jump alone if your friends weren't around, but the best way was to have two girls throw the rope while a third (and sometimes fourth) jumped in.

When we really wanted to show off, we'd yell *Hot pepper!* and the throwers would turn the rope as fast as they could. Jumping rope was always accompanied by chants, calls or songs. These were our favorites:

Cinderella, dressed in yellow
Went upstairs to kiss her fellow.
How many kisses did she get?
1, 2, 3, 4, 5 (until you missed)...

Down by the ocean,
Down by the sea,
Johnny broke a bottle
And blamed it on me.

By June Williams
Mount Pleasant, Texas

I told Ma, Ma told Pa,
Johnny got a whipping
So ha, ha, ha!
How many whippings did he get?
1, 2, 3, 4, 5...

I'm a little Dutch girl
Dressed in blue.
Here are the things I like to do.
Salute to the captain,
Bow to the queen,
Make a funny face at
The naughty, naughty king.
I can do a tap dance
And never, never miss.
I can do the hokeypokey
Just like this.
1, 2, 3, 4, 5...

Down in the meadow
Where the green grass grows,
There sat (girl's name)
As sweet as a rose.
She sang, she sang,
She sang so sweet,
Along came (boy's name)
And kissed her on the cheek.
How many kisses did she get?
1, 2, 3, 4, 5...

Ice cream soda,
Delaware punch,
Tell me the initial
Of your honey bunch.
A, B, C, D, E...

Engine, engine, number 9,
Running on Chicago Line,
Please tell me the exact time.
1 o'clock, 2 o'clock,
3 o'clock, 4...

Mother, Mother, I am sick!
Call the doctor
Quick, quick, quick!
Call for the doctor,
Call for the nurse,
Call for the lady
With the alligator purse.
In came the doctor,
In came the nurse,
In came the lady
With the alligator purse.
How many pills
Did she have to take?
1, 2, 3, 4, 5...

Julie Habel

"Tippity Over" Was a Schoolyard Favorite

DURING RECESS, all the students at my country school played a game called "tippity over". We split into two teams and went to opposite sides of the schoolhouse. One team would throw the ball over the roof, and the other team had to catch it before it hit the ground.

Once the team threw the ball, they never knew what to expect. If the other team caught it, they charged around the building to "capture" a member of the opposing team. If they didn't catch it, they threw the ball back over the roof for the other team to catch.

The object of the game was to capture the entire opposing team, which never seemed to happen before the bell rang. But there was always the next recess! —Bobbie Stewart, Chambersburg, Pennsylvania

Harold M. Lambert

JOIN THE CROWD. You had to work to push this schoolyard merry-go-round, but there were plenty of kids to do it.

Backyard Coronation Was Nothing to Sneeze at

By Elizabeth Poehlman, Seattle, Washington

MY friend Liz and I had great imaginations. With no TV to interfere, we created our own world of make-believe.

We'd already visited Europe, crossed the Plains in a covered wagon and performed in the circus—all without leaving our backyards. So it wasn't difficult to turn the most pageant-filled historical event of our lives into a home-

grown production. In June 1953, we staged our own coronation of Queen Elizabeth II.

Liz, a year older and more regal, was queen, and I was the Archbishop of Canterbury. Liz's little sister, Carolynn, played the dean of Westminster—and every other character needed to put on a coronation of backyard proportions.

We found out about the coronation from newspaper stories and an official program we somehow obtained, then edited the ceremony to our purposes. After researching the crowns and objects that would be used, we fashioned our own with cardboard, gold foil paper, fabric, glitter, papier-mache and a dowel.

The garden swing, hanging from a pipe between two cottonwood trees, was draped and canopied with bedspreads. A sturdy wooden garden chair was covered with a gold blanket for the throne.

Liz's gown was a pale pink lace evening dress dug out of the back of a closet. Her coronation robe was a maroon kimono we edged with white sheeting since we didn't have any ermine.

My archbishop's vestments were made from white sheets and remnants of old richly patterned chintz drapes. We didn't have a clue what Carolynn

should wear in her multiple roles, so we outfitted her in my uncle's military school parade hat, an old cutaway coat and trousers.

On the day Queen Elizabeth assumed the throne in London, a gallery of "royal guests"—our friends and their mothers—assembled in the backyard for the Ohio coronation. My Girl Scout leader, who was a professional photographer, volunteered to take pictures. Mother used my Brownie camera to take candid shots, and my sister manned our 8mm movie camera.

The cameras captured a serious, quite flawless kid-sized ceremony. Liz *was* queenly—until the very end when she got an itchy nose (see photo above). As she regally walked from the "cathedral" with orb in one hand, scepter in the other, the cameras caught her wriggling her nose as she tried to ward off an *unqueenly* sneeze. ❧

MAJESTIC MEMORIES. With her friend Liz getting the royal treatment (above), Elizabeth Poehlman did the crowning, while Liz's sister, Carolynn, handled the standby tasks.

The "Aunt Jane Game" Finally Unveiled

THERE WAS a huge window in our living room overlooking the front porch. My mother had hung a lace curtain from the top of this window—but had no idea that it also served as a prop for a game my sister and I made up called "Aunt Jane."

Aunt Jane was a career woman—a legal secretary in New York City—directly across the Hudson from our home. She visited us about twice a month and always dressed in the latest fashions.

One sign of a well-dressed woman in those days was a delicate veil attached to her hat. Upon Aunt Jane's arrival, she always greeted my sister and me with a kiss through that veil. No other visitor ever greeted us this way, and being very young, we thought it was so amusing.

We played the "Aunt Jane" game again and again. I'd put the lace curtain over my face and kiss my sister, then we'd reverse roles.

My aunt was a fine lady—who never knew she provided us with the idea for one of our favorite childhood games.

—*Ruth Overwyk, Polk City, Florida*

With Dad's Props, Girls Became "Angels of Mercy"

MY BEST FRIEND and I spent hours playing pretend. Sometimes we were high-society ladies, sneaking into our mothers' vanities to apply makeup, jewelry and generous supplies of toilet water.

If we were lucky and our moms were away for a few hours, we could try on their dresses and high heels, then parade around serving tea and cookies to our dolls.

One day, Dad came home to find us prancing around the house in our borrowed finery. Being a doctor and an "overaged kid" himself, he suggested we become nurses and save people's lives. Dad encouraged us by offering an assortment of linen wrappings, candy "pills" and his old stethoscope.

We went full steam ahead, with grand ideas for healing everyone in the neighborhood. Unfortunately, we couldn't find willing patients. None of our brothers would volunteer. We finally attached an assortment of splints and wraps to our dogs, cats and rabbits, who didn't seem to mind too much.

When my mom came home and saw the family pets hobbling around, she didn't know what to do. Dad saved us by telling her, with a straight face, that he was just giving us a lesson in training for careers as nurses!
—*Edythe Robinson Starke, Florida*

NURSES IN TRAINING. Edythe Robinson and her best friend, Nancy Brockman, looked the part when they pretended to be nurses. Despite grand plans for "healing everyone in the neighborhood", their only patients were family pets.

STYLISH SHOW. There was no end to the things to do for Lois Tesch of St. Paul, Minnesota (on right in photo at left) and her friends. On this day in the 1930s, they borrowed clothes from the neighbor ladies and held a "Gay '90s" bustles-and-bows fashion show.

Battered Truck Drove Youthful Imaginations

MY FOLKS lived in a suburb of Detroit during the Depression. Dad worked in the auto plants, and we lived with his parents, since short workweeks and checks were not uncommon.

A book I believe was called *Five Acres and Security* became next to the Bible in their plans to find the perfect place, and in 1940, we moved to what is now Farmington Hills. We went from city folks to truck farmers overnight.

Down the hill behind our house, in a grove of trees near the barn, sat an old Model T pickup. The seats and floorboards were long gone, the tires were flat, the headlights and windshield were broken, and a sapling was growing where the truck bed should've been. But to two preteen boys, it had all kinds of possibilities.

We did what we could to replace the floor and laid rugs over the bare seat springs. We also cut out the sapling and made a rear seat of boxes for our younger siblings.

After a morning of hoeing corn, picking berries or pulling weeds, Mom would go to the kitchen to make lunch, and my brother and I hotfooted it for the old "T". We "drove" all over the countryside until it was time to eat. The big steering wheel and all those levers, knobs and pedals gave us plenty to pretend with.

After the war, Dad sold the "T" to some young fellows who were going to get it runnin'. We always wondered if they ever did.
—*Bob Patchin Villa Park, California*

SUITS TO A "T". This Model T runs, but that wasn't a requirement for two boys with active imaginations (see memory above).

A Few of Our Favorite Things

OUR FAMILY enjoyed all sorts of simple games. We especially liked "I one it, I two it", where the leader describes something like a scrumptious cake, then someone barks, "I one it".

We'd continue in a circle until someone said, "I eight it". (If the leader had described something unappetizing, poor "I eight it" reluctantly accepted that position and confessed as we all groaned and laughed.)

Daddy even taught my sisters and me how to type rows of soldiers using the "W", "8" and slash marks, and we had contests on Sunday afternoons using an old Underwood with a purple ribbon. This is how it looked:

```
///////////////////////
88888888888888888888888
WWWWWWWWWWWWWWWWWWWWWWW
```

Another favorite activity was cutting slits in orange peels so the white part made "false teeth". This was actually Mother's idea, and we never laughed harder.
—*Esther (Ferree) Russell
Asheville, North Carolina*

"Grocery Store" Popular Memory Game at Parties

A GREAT GAME for parties was "grocery store". With everyone sitting in a circle, the first player would say, "I went to the grocery store and bought an apple"—or some other item that began with the letter "A".

The next person had to repeat that and add another item beginning with the letter "B" and so on through the alphabet. When we got to "Z", we started over. Any player who missed one of the items was out of the game. The last person remaining was the winner.
—*Jean Bell, Bellvue, Colorado*

Dad Left His Mark with Game of "Pinchy-Winchy"

WHENEVER we were at a large gathering, Dad would suggest a game of "pinchy-winchy". To play, there had to be at least one person who'd never played before, and that person stood next to Dad. Anyone who laughed or giggled during the game had to drop out.

Standing in a large circle, each person pinched the ear of the player next to them, saying, "Pinchy-winchy ear". Then we went around the circle again, pinching cheeks, chins, foreheads,

necks and noses. By the time we got to the noses, many people had dropped out for laughing or snickering. (I was usually one of the first to go.)

Now here's what started the snickers: Before the game, Dad blackened his fingers with burned cork, so each time he pinched the *new* player, he left a sooty smear. That player couldn't understand why the rest of us were laughing—until we got to the end of the game and he could see the black mark on his own nose!

Nowadays, people are too sophisticated to indulge in such entertainment.
—*Shirley Wheaton, Lombard, Illinois*

Kiss Was Winners' Reward

WHEN I WAS growing up in rural Alabama, the highlight of all parties for young people was the popular game of "candy-breaking".

The hosts would buy at least 100 sticks of hard candy, making sure there were six to eight different colors or designs. Each stick was broken in half and placed in a large container, usually a dishpan from the pantry.

The candy was then stirred thoroughly to ensure that all the different colors were mixed up. A towel was placed over the pan to keep the players from seeing inside it.

Girls lined up on one side of the pan and boys on the other. The first girl in line reached under the cloth and pulled out a piece of candy. Then the first boy in line pulled out a piece. If their pieces didn't match, it was the next "couple's" turn to draw.

When at last a twosome drew matching pieces, we yelled for the boy to kiss the girl. However, if the boy didn't like the girl, it took some urging to get him to kiss her! But since the penalty for refusing amounted to dropping out of the game, he usually gave her a quick kiss, to everyone's delight.

Few of today's youngsters have even heard of this game, much less participated in it. My, my...what great fun they're missing!
—*Albert McGraw
Anderson, Alabama*

Mom's Button Box Provided Hours of Fun

By Margaret Gary, Mattawamkeag, Maine

ONE GAME our mother taught us was "button, button, who's got the button". We could play this game all day, and it always left us laughing.

We'd find a button in Mom's button box, then choose one person to hold it between their palms. The others would sit in a circle, holding their hands out.

The person with the button "visited" each of the other players and pretended to drop the button into their hands. He or she *did* drop the button into *someone's* hands, but you could never be sure which person it was.

Each player then tried to guess who had the button. The first one to guess correctly switched places with the person who originally had the button. ✂

Orange   Lemon   Island Punch   Grape

Our Wild Afternoon in a Studio Back Lot

Photos: Archive Photos/American Stock

MOVIE MAGIC was created on the back lots of studios like these...and they made the perfect setting to create a magical afternoon for two kids with big imaginations.

By Ray Schott, Huntington Beach, California

WE WERE riding our bikes one afternoon in 1937 when my buddy Bill asked, "Hey, Ray…ya ever been to Warner Brothers' back lot?"

Sure…I'd passed it many times, but all of the "No Trespassing" signs had discouraged further investigation. Bill, being more adventuresome, was not as easily intimidated.

We rode to the lot, ditched our bikes in high weeds and found a place to crawl under the fence. We came out at the livery stables! This semi-permanent set was used in so many of the Westerns of that era that it was never taken down. The street scene facade included a jail, sheriff's office, Belle's tavern, rooming house, bank and the Majestic Hotel.

Bill took one side of the street and I the other, our imaginary pistols drawn. I ran in a crouch, dodging rain barrels and hitching posts while watching for suspicious characters. When I thought I saw someone aiming at me from a balcony, I pointed my fingers at him and fired. *Got 'em!*

I was sneaking past the jail when a figure came through the swinging doors across the street. I aimed and yelled *Bang, bang!* Bill clutched his chest, contorted his face and collapsed in a heap. We laughed as he got up, brushing the dust from his jeans.

We sauntered over to the next set, a city scene with vintage cars parked on the street. We were *sure* the one outside the Midlander Bank was a getaway car and burst into the bank wielding simulated machine-guns. *Okay, youse guys! This is a stickup, and we know how to use these guns! Take us to the safe!* We took our haul to the waiting car, peeled rubber at the curb and took it on the lam.

Next we passed rows of vehicles—everything from Greek chariots and horse-drawn carriages to race cars and touring cars. It was like being at an antique auto show.

On the other side of the street sat World War I planes. With Bill in a German Fokker and me in an English Spitfire, we did loops and barrel rolls in an imaginary dogfight over the European countryside. Up another aisle, we spotted a model of the Taj Mahal, carefully packaged and stored, and what appeared to be a French Foreign Legion post.

Stopping short at the end of the aisle, we saw two watchmen making their rounds and decided to make tracks back to our secret entrance near the livery stables. These guys were for real, and our 12-year-old imaginations had already gotten quite a workout for a single afternoon. ✤

TWO SEATS BEATS WALKING. That's what Neeta Musgrove of Austin, Texas was doing —strolling home from classes at the University of Oklahoma in October 1947, when a friend suggested they rent a bicycle built for two. As Neeta's snapshot shows, they put saddle-shoe-to-the-pedal and enjoyed a beautiful autumn afternoon.

*Sprinkled among the "posed" portraits of a family
album are those zany snapshots that recall fun
times…and still bring us laughs today.*

When you turn the pages of your photo album, you usually discover all of them fall in-to three broad categories: places we've been, family events (babies, weddings, birth-days, anniversaries) and the happy times our families enjoyed.

As you get older, you discover the most priceless ones are those that bring back the happy times—those precious moments when your family was having fun together. Some bring back a smile, some a chuckle or even a happy tear.

Suddenly *you are there again!* You remember what a perfect day it was. You can hear the happy giggles and shrieks of the little ones. You can almost taste the homemade ice cream that everyone helped churn. You can smell the fresh green grass or the bratwurst sizzling on the grill.

There's Grampa, the merciless croquet player, getting ready to whack an opponent's ball off into the bushes. There's Gramma, happily snuggling the newest addition to the family in her arms. There's Uncle John, snoozing on the porch glider as cousin Jerry sneaks up to tickle his nose with a feather.

A Clown in Every Crowd

And, of course, there's always the family clown, who manages to cross his eyes and paste a goofy grin on his face just as the picture is snapped. You remember it happened during a fam-ily get-together on the sweltering July day when Dad was pushed into the kids' wading pool and didn't mind a bit.

I have a special collection of photos labeled "Clownin' Around". Most of them are of my wife, Peg, and she claims to hate them. But her parents say she was the family clown from an early age—the one who always livened up the family gatherings. Aim a camera at her and she can't resist doing something goofy, even today.

As a rule, though, girls take posing in pictures rather seriously. (Maybe they're practicing to be a future model or beauty queen.) Boys don't much want to be in snapshots in the first place, so they squinch up their faces and contort their bodies and generally make saps of themselves as a form of protest. (They don't regret it until someone shows the family photo album to their own children many years later.)

On the next several pages, you'll have a chance to savor several dozen priceless photos of families having fun together, provided by readers of *Reminisce*. They're sure to bring back many of your own best memories of family fun. Enjoy!

—*Clancy Strock*

1. Family Fun Feast

2. Tyke on Trike

3. Tea for Three Was Doggone Good

1. *FAMILY REUNION* in 1922 in Coeur d'Alene, Idaho meant good fixin's (note pork and bean cans under table) when the Broxsons, Warrens and Pitzers got together. Bernadine Pitzer Creagh of Tacoma, Washington is little yawner in rear, left row.

2. *ANCHORS AWEIGH* was the cry for this little bike rider. According to Dorothy Smith of Summerville, South Carolina, Joseph Art was 3 in 1930, when this photo was taken outside his parents' apartment building in Lakewood, Ohio.

3. *LAPPING UP* the luxury of dining alfresco and being waited on was certainly no dog's life for "Fritz", laughs Doris Beccio of Mariposa, California. She was celebrating her seventh birthday as the doll patiently waited for her cup of "tea".

4. Dig These Duds

5. The Wright Stuff?

4. *MODEL MOTHER-IN-LAW.* "Ruth Lane (left) was the smartest woman I ever met," says Paula Lane of Tyler, Texas. "She made her own clothes, was a great cook and saved everything. Outfit she's wearing was found in a trunk after she passed away at 87."

5. *PILOT TO COPILOT,* who's who? Twins John (left) and Joe Meissner had this propeller-driven photo taken in 1920, says their niece Corinne Wilson of St. Cloud, Minnesota.

6. *RUB-A-DUB-DUB,* there are six folks in this tub, or barrel, including her mom (wearing hair ribbons), says Theresa Walters of La Habra, California. A traveling photographer captured this barrel of fun in 1909 near Christie, Oklahoma.

6. Don't Roll Out This Barrel!

1. *ALL DRESSED* up and ready to ride was her Uncle Wesley in 1904, says Betty Uhl of Luna Pier, Michigan. This precious postcard shot was taken by her grandfather, who owned The Sunshine Studio in Monroe.

2. *"WATCH THE BIRDIE,* kitty," says Mary Ann Gentry of Carrollton, Kentucky (right) and her best friend, Corinne. Back in the '30s, the two friends, each of whom had a cat, rode their balloon-tire bikes everywhere—even a mile out of town to Corinne's grandparents' farm.

3. *COVER ALL* coveralls are being held out the window by her grandmother, Dora Steinfadt (left), says Barb Powell of LeMars, Iowa. Back in 1943, she helped make these giant jeans to use as an ad gimmick by Kohout's, an overall manufacturing company in LeMars.

2. Balancing Act

1. Bow-Tied Biker

3. Deep Pockets

4. No More Nasty Nails

4. **BUSHELS O' NAILS** from a razed store were gathered by St. Phillips, Montana catechism class in the '30s, says Aggie Twist of Glendale, Arizona. Some are holding up prizes won from this contest.

5. **MAYBE MOM'S** motorcycle mania is why he's owned 10 of them, says John Schroeder of Waukesha, Wisconsin. Sporty-looking mom, Violet Bousman, now lives in Columbia Falls, Montana.

6. **TEMPERATURE-TAKER DAUGHTER** Joyce didn't go on to become a nurse, notes Ralph Carroll of Mabank, Texas. But back in the '50s, at least her doll got good treatment.

5. Motorcyle Mom

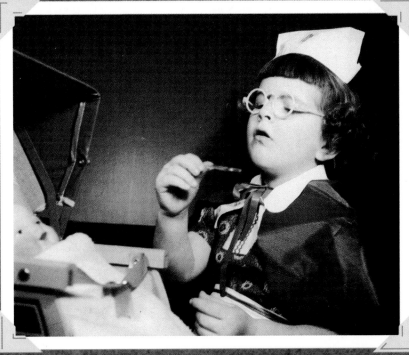

6. I Don't Like the Looks of This

1. Real Cool Hot Rod

2. Little Hoppy

1. HER HUSBAND, Edward "Koko" Baumgartner, posed in 1942 with his pride and joy, the "Kokomobile", writes Marie Baumgartner of Stoughton, Wisconsin. Edward was 18 at the time, and he and his friends had great times cruising in that 1926 Model T, which, as the door depicts, "Shakes, Rattles and Rolls". Riders couldn't say they weren't warned!

2. HOP ALONG little Hopalong. Yes, even girls dressed up like their favorite cowboys, says Mary Alice Byrne of Irvine, California. She and her sisters' favorite Western star was Hopalong Cassidy, so that's who they dressed up as. Judging from the cuffs on those jeans, Mary Alice would undoubtedly be getting a lot of wear in before she outgrew them.

3. OH, BABY, what a buggy! This was her husband's first car in 1958, jokes Michelle Alvey of Hollywood, Maryland, and she'd love to find one like it to give to him today. (Think he'd still fit?) Michelle, who might be a bit prejudiced, thinks little hubby was an adorable baby (we do, too!) and claims he still gets that same "contrary" expression on his face today.

4. A RELATIVELY high pile of relatives was created when the Meissner clan got together in 1928, says Corinne Wilson of St. Cloud, Minnesota. Corinne's mom, Elaine, is third from left on the ground, while Mom's twin sisters, Hulda and Anne, are on the ground at right. Cousin Ruth is at far left, and her sister, Gertie, is standing on Anne's knee. Got all that?

3. My First Car

4. Hey, Watch Your Step!

5. Central? Give Me the Nursery

5. A BONNIE MISS. Bonnie Dee Highfield was only 3 when she picked up the phone in 1929, says friend Virginia Oman of Polson, Montana. Bonnie recently gave Virginia a 65-year-old unfinished tatted lace dress like the one in the photo. Virginia had it completed and gave it to her granddaughter.

6. FIDDLING away the afternoon in Worcester, Massachusetts was her great-aunt, Mamie Carey, in 1918, says Sally Duttweiler of Vernon, Connecticut. Sally wonders if Mamie, who was called Mary, was playing *That International Rag* by Irving Berlin. The sheet music for the hot tune can be seen on the piano.

7. FUN PHOTO of Mom, Edna Vandre (left), was sent to her future husband after being introduced by friends on a streetcar in Springfield, Illinois, says Marcella Meyer of San Francisco, California. Once he received the photo, her dad traveled the 18 miles from the farm a little more often. They married in 1917 and raised 12 children.

7. Have Breakfast Ready

6. The Dog Seems to Like It

1. What Are You Two Doing?

2. Hound's Sweet Home

1. *CAMERA-SHY COUPLE?* No, it was good old Uncle Albert, who could always be counted on for a fun photo, says niece Gertrude Merkel, who is in the photo with him. This "parting shot" was shared by Pat Lathrop of Milwaukee, Wisconsin.

2. *FINISHING TOUCH* on homemade doghouse was putting on the shingles. Larry (right) and Bill Vance were in the backyard of their Delavan, Wisconsin home in 1943 with sister Sandi, who can just be seen behind Larry. Bill, who still lives in Delavan, shared photo.

3. *WHOA, NELLIE*, or, rather, "Moxie". Norman Girard (center, on saddle) says his dad was friends with the Moxie man, so he and his family got to ride on this "horsepowered" car back in Detroit in 1931. Norman, now of Rotunda, Florida, recalls it was a real traffic-stopper.

3. Now That's Horsepower!

4. SNEAKY SENIORS Myrna Riley Croan (left) and Janice Brummer painted their year—1955—on the school steps just before graduation during the "Senior Sneak", admits Myrna, now of Wellsville, Kansas.

5. STUFFED OSTRICH doesn't seem to mind rider Janet Watson, who was on a trip from Canada to California when this wacky shot was taken in 1911. Daughter-in-law Ruth Kennedy of Boyertown, Pennsylvania shared the photo.

6. SANDY FUN was provided by their friendly Chicago landlord. He also gave the kids a garden plot, and tubs of water to cool off in during the summer, says Roberta Gilbert of Hingham, Massachusetts.

7. FEET FIRST was the wily way these women asked for the vote, says Gordon Van Vliet of Bradenton, Florida. That's his mother, Minnie, third from right. The photo was taken around 1912 in Patterson, New Jersey.

4. Wet Paint

5. Struttin' Their Stuff

6. Bucket o' Fun

7. Foot Soldiers for Suffrage

1. Love Is Forever

1. **LOVING GRANDPARENTS** Charles and Mary Holt of Port Washington, Wisconsin weren't kidding when this photo was taken in the '20s, reports Ethel Backus of Manitowoc, Wisconsin. They showed their love for each other all their lives, she says.

2. **HORSING AROUND** about 1948 was Gail Engeldahl and sister Jayne Steffens in their backyard in Wilmette, Illinois. Gail, now of Hartford, Wisconsin, says she and Jayne still love real horses as much as the wooden one Dad made.

3. **BASEBALL BLUES.** Bob Adamek, then 9, was ready to play ball, but the weather that day in 1940 didn't cooperate, explains sister-in-law Doris of Rochester, New York. Rudolph Zirngibl is credited with snapping soggy shot. At least Bob was inside and dry!

4. **HO, HUM,** these girls look like they're ready for bed, but it's still light out. Actually, they were hamming it up during a pajama party at Silver Lake, New York in 1928, says Linda Burke of Williamsville, New York. Her mom was among these silly "snoozers".

2. Old Paint Needs Paint

3. Rain Delay

4. Sleepy-Time Gals

5. Higher Education?

5. **THIS PILE** of seniors from Shamrock, Oklahoma was obviously happy to be graduating in 1935. The "thinker" out in front is Myurldean Whiteside of Independence, Kansas, who shared this photo—and is probably still thinking over fun times with "the gang".

6. **SKATING AWAY** an afternoon in New York City's Central Park in the early '30s were Mary LaRussa of York, Pennsylvania and her "steady". Wednesdays and Saturdays were the approved "date days" back then, and a stroll or roll through the park was no-expense fun.

7. **WILD BUNCH.** Well, at least the daisies in their hair were wild, says R.S. "Bobby" Hedin (second from right) of Minneapolis. The photo was snapped one summer day in 1926 when the kids were in Kentucky. The others are Margy, Sonny and Buddy.

6. Roller Blade

7. Flower Children in the '20s

1. Good Old "T" Formation

2. Let's Take a Drive

3. Lifesaver

1. *HELMETS* were not standard equipment when the Arlex Club of West Chicago hit the line. Robert Klee of Green Bay, Wisconsin says the team played others in the area between 1890 and 1915 and recalls they even had a clubhouse for dances.

2. *SUNDAY WAS* visiting day, says Agnes Duncan of Fonthill, Ontario, who is one of the twins on the right. The gang is leaning on Dad's '37 Chevrolet, including Cornelius (left) who, according to Agnes, had his pants on backward.

3. *MADE IN* the shade is how Burke Waldron of Carson City, Nevada had it in Maysville, Kentucky in the summer of '47 when he was a lifeguard. Burke said his elevated position was an "easy perch" and all shaded, too!

4. No Tricks, Now

5. Listen to Sister

7. Passel of Patriots

6. Little Hoser

4. *TRICK-OR-TREATING* was not done when she suited up for Halloween in 1921, says Joan Tuley of Wheat Ridge, Colorado (right). But there was always a party where kids could show off Mom's homemade crepe-paper costumes.

5. "*BIG SISTER* Beth was my guardian angel," says Christina Larson of Shalimar, Florida. "She'd let me lick the cream off the milk bottle lid, and when I fell on my glass baby bottle and needed stitches, she pleaded with Mom that she 'didn't want her baby sewed'."

6. *NO BIGGER* than a squirt was her father, Edwin Leech. Seen here at age 3 in 1913, little Ed got his picture taken while playing fireman, says Judy Farmer of Mansfield, Ohio. With a coat that long and boots that high, young Edwin didn't need suspenders!

7. *FLAG WAVING* was still popular on the Fourth of July when this picture was taken in 1918. The world was still in "The War to End All Wars" and folks were very patriotic. The photo was shared by Renee Kerns of Tucson, Arizona. Looks like the folks had a fine day.

1. Tea Toddlers

1. *TIME FOR TEA* for Ruth Merritt and her buddy Burt Elstad. Accompanied by a family of baby dolls, the two were breaking bread in Bowbells, North Dakota in '33. All grown up, Ruth now resides in Yakima, Washington.

2. *DOG DAYS* of summer were a good time to go boating for Gertrude Merkel (left) and her friend Alice Mertz. This photo was taken to send to their boyfriends serving overseas in World War I, says Gertrude's daughter, Rosemary Greinke of Milwaukee, Wisconsin.

3. *ROUGHIN' IT* didn't look all that rough when these spiffy folks hit the tents near Trinity Springs, Indiana in 1912. Just like her dad (boy sitting near washbowl), Mrs. Herbert Gilligan of Encinitas, California still loves to camp and recommends it as a great family recreation.

2. Boating Beauties

3. The Family That Camps Together...

4. Portable Phone

5. Cheepers by the Dozen

4. **HELLO, MOM?** Dorothy Higgs says Mom made the clothes she's wearing here, back when she was just 2 years old. But how about those high-buttoned shoes? Dorothy, who now lives in Holiday, Florida, says she still has the buttonhook she used to fasten those shoes—but she didn't mention if her call ever got through.

5. **CHICKENS DELIGHT** Gretchen Walker (in high chair) and her sister, as they get a lesson in incubation from Mom in 1907. A "traveling picture man" took this photo at their Lebanon, Indiana home, says Gretchen, now of Edgewater, Florida. The incubator obviously worked pretty well.

6. **PROUD LITTLE MOMMIES.** Although her friends (two sisters on left) had brand-new baby dolls, Joan Potter was just as proud of her favorite baby and buggy. The three went for a stroll in December 1938 in East Smethport, Pennsylvania—just a "half whistle" from Smethport, says Joan, now of Buffalo, New York.

6. Triple Wicker Baby Buggies

J.C. Allen and Son

MELODIC MEMORIES were easy to make in the good old days, when music was an important part of a family's life. Whether it was gathering 'round the piano or organ like the family above, or enjoying a band concert in the park, music was there to be enjoyed by those making it and those listening.

Chapter Five
Music Put a Song In Our Hearts

For those who grew up in a golden age of music in this century,
all it takes is that one tune to bring back good memories.

If you were lucky enough to be born in the early part of this century, you grew up in a golden age of music…no question about it. Wonderful, wonderful music is what I remember most about those years.

Whatever your taste, there was lots to enjoy. Our unique American contribution to music—jazz—came up the Mississippi from New Orleans and spread everywhere. It was the music of the Roaring Twenties and has influenced our popular music ever since. George Gershwin even used the language of jazz to create an authentic American opera, *Porgy and Bess*.

And there were the magnificent military concert bands of Sousa and Goldman that stirred our patriotism and put our feet to tapping. Every small-town band saved *Stars and Stripes Forever* for that special moment when it marched past the reviewing stand during the Fourth of July parade.

Then came the Big Band era of the Dorsey brothers, Glenn Miller, Harry James, Sammy Kaye and others. Places like the Glen Island Casino in the east, the Aragon and Trianon ballrooms in Chicago and the Chase Park Plaza in St. Louis were filled with dancers reveling in the exciting music. Who could have predicted that *a dance band* would play a concert in Carnegie Hall? But Benny Goodman's orchestra did, and fortunately it was recorded so we can still enjoy it a half century later.

Music Was Life

Those also were the days when *we made our own music*…and enjoyed doing it!

In the town where I grew up, the elementary schools organized bands. This was during the Depression, so there was no thought of sending away for pricey uniforms. Instead, a "band mothers" group held bake sales to raise money. Then they sewed blue capes with a gold satin lining, along with matching berets. The rest of the uniform was provided by each family—white duck pants, a white shirt and a black bow tie. Not very fancy, I admit. But we felt like the Royal Palace Guard as we tootled away on the stage of the school gymnasium.

There was music in homes, too—with Mom thumping away at the piano as the family gathered around to sing. If a tune made the top 10 on *Your Hit Parade*, there was sure to be a run on the sheet music at the music store the next day. Our family sing-alongs always ended with some of Mom and Dad's favorites from their World War I courting days, like *There's a Long, Long Trail a-Winding* and *Roses of Piccardy*.

Our town was blessed with a splendid municipal band that played every Wednesday night in Central Park and gave frequent winter concerts in the town's new Armory for large and appreciative audiences. Every concert featured a vocalist or two, usually soloists in local church choirs.

Danceable music. Marching music. Music with sophisticated Cole Porter lyrics. Music to fall in love by, to whistle to, and music to inspire. You'll read personal memories of those wonderful times in the pages that follow. They're sure to put a song in your heart.   —*Clancy Strock*

Family Tied Together By the Heartstrings

By Marilyn Strickland, Williamson, New York

AS THE OLDEST of six children, I was the first to start piano lessons, but the others followed as soon as they were old enough. At 5 every morning, I was on the piano stool, practicing my scales and playing Bach.

By the time the younger ones were up, I was ready to move to the next room to practice my saxophone. Meanwhile, another child was practicing a different instrument in the den. We all played two or three instruments, so I'm sure the sounds in the mornings weren't always pleasant!

My earliest childhood memories are of Sunday afternoons when we all played together, using simple music with two-part instrumentation. As we got better, our music teacher and her friend started coming to play with us. Sometimes they brought equipment so we could cut records.

Our church had about five families with musical children, so a church orchestra was organized. My future husband, George, played in the orchestra and occasionally joined in our Sunday concerts.

On other Sundays, I was invited to the concerts at his house. I played saxophone, his Uncle Mort violin or trumpet, his mother piano and George trombone. That was some of the most fun I ever had. We really *did* play 'til the cows came home!

Our family didn't take many summer vacations, but when we did, our instruments went with us. We'd camp in upstate New York and play music in the evenings for the neighboring campers.

My sisters and I also sang at talent and variety shows and churches. One Sunday, we drove 50 miles to Mom's hometown and stood on the back of a tractor-trailer, singing for her church's homecoming.

A few years back, some of our senior church members tried to resurrect the "Mason Sisters Singers" for an old-fashioned ice cream social. It'd been years since we'd sung together publicly, except in our church choir, but three of us had daughters who were willing to join us, and we had fun putting a performance together.

Just recently, about 60 family members and friends sang a cantata, with my brother-in-law as our director. He made us wish it would never end. And maybe it won't…we have some grandchildren who like to sing, too! ♪

BAND SUITS THEM. When a church orchestra was formed, Marilyn's family was a big part of it. Above left, Marilyn (far left) and her brothers and sisters posed outside the family home in Williamson, New York. Above right, Marilyn (second from left) and her sisters were in costume for a high school "Gay '90s" gig.

Fiddling Wasn't Music To This Child's Ears

WHEN I WAS about 10, I spent many summer afternoons lying on the carpet in Grandma's parlor, listening to records on her windup Victrola. I especially loved any melody played by a violin.

Grandma said her brothers both played violin, and when they finally came for a visit, I was thrilled. That afternoon, Uncle Ed gave us a concert. He chose some of the favorites that he and his band played for Saturday night dances.

To my surprise, Uncle Ed's music sounded nothing like the mellow, sweet tones I'd heard on the records. This music was lively and harsh! I ran out of the room in a huff.

"Uncle Ed doesn't play a violin," I shouted at my astonished grandmother. "He told me he plays a *fiddle*, and I hate it!"

Today, I hear that same music when I watch square dancers on television, and I realize how young and unforgiving I was. Now I know there is music to please everyone. —*Dorothy Barna, Houston, Texas*

COUNTRY FIDDLER. Dorothy Barna felt cheated when she learned her Great-Uncle Fred was a fiddler, not a violinist! Pictured from left are Fred; his brother, Ed; Dorothy's grandmother, holding hands with a young cousin; and Ed's wife, Min.

Mountain Kin Kept Close with Music

WE WERE a close mountain family and made every occasion a special party. (We described ourselves as "the other Renfro Valley".)

My mother's youngest brother played guitar in a country band, and after they played square dances in the park, the band would come to our house afterward and "jam" almost every weekend. Then I was allowed to get out of bed and get dressed, put on my tap shoes and entertain.

Uncle Don also played at our gatherings, and when he was away in the Navy during World War II, he cut records of himself playing and added messages for us. It made us both happy and sad to hear him playing *My Rose of San Antone* and some of the other favorites he'd played from so far away. —*Reita Sellman, Alexandria, Virginia*

Lumberjacks' Music Brought Pair Together

By Dora Weber
Spring Lake Park, Minnesota

WHEN PAPA was young, he and his brother worked in the logging camps together. After a hard day of cutting and hauling timber through deep snow, they'd play the fiddle and harmonica to entertain the other lumberjacks, who kept time by clapping their hands and stomping their feet.

Before long, word of their talents spread, and they were asked to play for barn dances. That was where Mama first saw Papa, and she immediately wanted to meet him.

When she heard the logging camp where this good-looking fiddler worked needed a cook, she packed her bags and took the job.

After my parents married, Uncle Hans visited us often, always carrying his harmonica in his pocket. I don't think there was a country-western song written that he couldn't play. We especially loved it when he played *Down in the Valley*, *Red River Valley* and *On Top of Old Smoky*.

For my favorite, *Wabash Cannon Ball*, he'd cup his hand over one end of

---

"That's where Mama first saw Papa..."

---

the harmonica to produce the sound of the train engine and whistle. The sounds were so realistic that if I closed my eyes, I really believed I could see the train coming around the bend.

My brothers later took up the harmonica, and their music entertained us on cold winter evenings. Both were blessed with good voices, too. We all liked to sing the songs our parents taught us, like the Norwegian melodies of Mama's youth.

Church songs also were a big part of our lives. My sister and I once had an elaborate funeral for our broken dolls, complete with our favorite hymns. As we stood over the pint-sized "graves" Papa had dug down by the willow trees, we lowered our heads and sang, "Rock of ages, cleft for me..."

Nature blessed us with other lovely sounds—the wind in the willows, singing birds, chirping crickets and frogs, and the stream cascading over the rocks. We were surrounded by beautiful music. ♫

'30s String Band Specialized in Street Serenades

By Donald Starkey, Seabrook, Texas

"SONNY, you can pick that banjo just like the boys down South," the man said as he tossed a dollar bill at my brother's feet.

Our little string band, The Starkey Entertainers, was seated on the front steps of Fred O'Brien's Refrigerator and Appliance Store in Sistersville, West Virginia. Mr. O'Brien had asked us to play a few tunes, saying the crowd was good for business.

In the late 1920s, it wasn't unusual to see a band on a street corner or in front of a business. Invitations like Mr. O'Brien's meant earning a few precious dollars during the Depression. If we got lucky, somebody in the crowd even passed the hat.

Our band was organized by my father, a schoolteacher and self-taught guitarist. I was 13 and played fiddle. My brother, Arnold, 11, played banjo; our younger sisters, Von Dean and Louise, played mandolin.

Dad had coached each of us on some sort of string instrument before we were 5, so we'd been playing together for years. We'd strummed and sung around the stove in the living room for hours on long winter evenings after our schoolwork was done. Summer evenings often found us on the porch, serenading the night creatures.

Once we started performing in public, we appeared at company picnics, family reunions, business banquets, church socials and lodge and school functions, all within 40 miles of our Pine Grove home.

We got our "big break" in 1931, when a group of businessmen sponsored our appearance on radio station WMMN in Fairmont. For an hour, we played songs like *Peg Leg Jack*, *The Little Shirt My Mother Made for Me* and *She'll Be Comin' 'Round the Mountain*. The rest were violin instrumentals—*Over the Waves*, *Stars and Stripes Forever*, *Turkey in the Straw* and *My Blue Ridge Mountain Home*.

During the next 18 months, we also performed on station

FAMILY BAND. The Starkey Entertainers consisted of father Glenn (in rear) and children Arnold, Von Dean, Louise and Donald. The quintet made public appearances and performed on radio stations in West Virginia from the late 1920s to 1936.

WWVA in Wheeling and became acquainted with other local country performers like Big Slim, the Lone Cowboy and Doc Williams Chickie.

Our little band made music through 1936, when my brother and I graduated from high school. By then, Big Bands were becoming popular, and our interests were changing. Our family had grown, too, and our parents had younger children to tend to.

But those were happy times. Our performances kept us in pocket change and even enabled us to buy a used player piano. Dad, a wise teacher, always said the best way to keep young people out of trouble was to get them interested in something challenging that they liked. I believe he was right. ❧

DOUBLE ATTRACTION. Yet another '30s family hit was Lawsie Nash and his sons, Darris and Douglas (left). Darris' wife, Annette, of McKenzie, Tennessee shared the photo.

Father Poured His Soul Into Mandolin Music

EVERY Saturday night, Dad and I played duets. He'd sit on a soft chair in the living room, playing his mandolin, while I made an attempt to accompany him on the piano.

Years before, as a young emigrant from Italy, he'd traveled with friends who played guitar and banjo, entertaining at parties. He had no money, family, education or job prospects, but the music filled a void in his life as nothing else could.

The mandolin let Dad express all the emotions he couldn't speak—his grief at leaving his homeland and the joy of finding a good woman in his adopted land. The mandolin reverberated with all the passion in his soul.

As he taught me the songs of his youth, I was inspired to play with the same grandeur and feeling.

Now my son plays the guitar, and we play some of those same songs every Saturday night. Whenever Dad listens to us, I wonder if he recalls, as I do, those tender years when we shared the precious bond of music. —*Nora Airey Winchester, Massachusetts*

Morning-After Coin Hunt Added to Concert's Appeal

WITH SIX CHILDREN to raise, my widowed mother had little time to relax. Our only chance to spend "prime time" together was during evening band concerts, which provided me with a double pleasure when I was 7.

We'd walk to the commons in Lowell, Massachusetts, spread a blanket on the ground and listen to the great music. Mother loved to sing along, and I marveled at her beautiful voice.

The next morning, I'd get up early and run to the commons to find coins others had dropped and give them to Mom to help buy groceries. The beaming smile she gave me was my greatest pleasure. My biggest find was $1.35—big money back then—and Mom put every dime to good use.

—*Dorothy Stella*
Titusville, Florida

Remember Tune About Gum Left on Bedpost?

I CAN RECALL saving chewing gum on the bedpost—otherwise we wouldn't have had any the next day! Does anyone else remember the song *Spearmint on the Bedpost*? It went like this:

> *Does the spearmint on the*
>   *bedpost*
> *Keep its flavor overnight?*
> *If you chew it in the morning*
> *Will it be too hard to bite?*
> *Can't you see I'm going crazy?*
> *Won't somebody set me right?*
> *Does the spearmint on the*
>   *bedpost*
> *Keep its flavor overnight?*

—*Lucille Eilenfeld*
Palmyra, Wisconsin

Dad's Blue Suede Shoes

By Patti Ann Griffin, Bloomington, Minnesota

OH, HOW GRACEFUL Mom and Dad looked as I peeked down the basement stairs, watching them dance with their friends. They didn't even seem to touch the ground when they were in each other's arms, Mom tossing her hair and laughing as Dad whispered in her ear.

I saw that scene often on Saturday nights in the years just after World War II. Once or twice a month, my parents and their friends took turns hosting parties with charades, card games and dancing.

The hosts' only expense was dessert. Everyone else brought food for a smorgasbord at the end of the evening. Imagine all that entertainment at almost no expense. The laughter and camaraderie were priceless.

For these parties, Dad wore special dancing shoes made of light blue suede with a navy blue strip of shiny leather. With the addition of a double-breasted navy suit, white shirt with French cuffs and spiffy red patterned tie, he looked like a movie star.

Mother was no slouch, either. She wore a full-skirted navy dress with a jewel neckline and princess waist, accented with the rhinestone earrings, necklace and bracelet Dad had given her when he came home from the Army.

Most couples brought their children to the parties. When I was very little, Dad would put my feet on his, hold my hands and twirl me through the crowd. It was heavenly—I was dancing, with Dad, on his special dancing shoes! When I got older, Dad was my first dance instructor.

Mom and Dad have since passed away, but the memories of those days when people dressed up, brought a hot

DANCE DARLINGS. **Patti Ann Griffin's parents (above when he came home from the Army) were young and in love when they hosted many dance parties at their home back in the late 1940s. In her story, Patti Ann (at left with her dad) tells of the special memories these lively parties made and how her handsome daddy taught her to dance.**

dish and had a great time still linger. I taught my children what my parents taught me—that it doesn't take a lot of money to have a great time, just good friends. 🍂

She Still Cherishes Dad's Treadle Organ

AS FAR BACK as I can remember, our family of five regularly gathered around the old pump organ, singing hymns to our hearts' content.

Dad never had music lessons, but he knew some chords and taught them to me. He eventually decided I should learn to read music.

I fondly recall walking a good 3 miles across the hills to my music teacher for twice-weekly lessons. She taught me on her piano, but when I got home, I practiced on the old organ.

Years later, my own daughter took piano lessons at school and also practiced on the treadle organ. We finally bought a piano, but the organ still sits in my living room, one of my prized possessions.

Not long before my father's death, we all flew to Arizona to visit my daughter and my sister. We gathered again around the organ—my daughter's new one. My father, 78 years young, sat down and played, and the rest of us sang those same hymns that never grow old.

—Ovaleen Hooper, McEwen, Tennessee

PRIZED POSSESSION. Ovaleen Hooper still uses this ornately carved treadle organ, which has been played and enjoyed by three generations of her family.

Musical Misstep Was Wake-Up Call for "Air Boy"

THE ORGANIST at our Baptist church in Maine was a perfectionist who *always* remained in control, no matter what challenged her dignity.

She depended heavily on an assistant who stood to her right behind a curtain, gazing out a peephole. On her signal, the "air boy" moved a long handle up and down, forcing air into the organ's bellows. The quality of the organ's tone rested in his hands.

One Sunday morning, a new recruit was manning the pump. The organist played the offertory brilliantly, and Rev. Wheeler seemed positively inspired. When the choir joined in, the organist smiled and nodded her approval, then began singing along with all her heart and soul.

Suddenly a sour note from the organ—then another and another—resounded all the way to the back pews. The choir, trying to find its way through the toneless accompaniment, went haywire. It was a musical disaster, but the congregation couldn't keep from laughing. Even Rev. Wheel-

Dance Band Nearly Kept Couple Apart

By Joan McMillan
Walterboro, South Carolina

WITH THE DEPRESSION on in the early '30s, Daddy considered himself lucky to have a job in a drugstore, doing a little of everything.

One day, while making the store's ice cream, he looked out the window and noticed the most beautiful girl he'd ever seen walking past.

Daddy dropped what he was doing, ran outside and tried to introduce himself. But Mama, being a proper Southern Baptist girl, ignored him and kept on walking. Daddy wasn't put off for long, however. He found a mutual acquaintance to introduce them, and before long they were talking marriage.

The only thing Mama found wrong with Daddy was that he loved to dance and he played clarinet in a dance band at a place where liquor was served. (Liquor and dancing mixed with a Southern Baptist like oil and water!)

Mama did some thinking and some praying and decided they'd have to part. They did, for a while—but Daddy never gave up. He kept reminding her that he was still around and thinking of her every day.

Mama did some more thinking and praying and at last decided she simply had to marry Daddy and trust the Lord to show him the error of his ways. But music remained a big part of Daddy's life, and he continued to play with the band.

Then one weekend, a drunk threw the first punch at a dance where Daddy was playing. The fight grew bigger and bigger, until the brawlers were knocking over members of the band. To save himself, Daddy broke his beloved clarinet over someone's head!

The Depression was still on, and with a young family, Daddy couldn't justify buying another clarinet. His music career was over. But he instilled in me his love of music. He even taught me to Charleston when Mama wasn't looking. ♪

er fought to keep a straight face. The organist leaped from her bench, threw the curtain aside, and revealed a sleepy-eyed lad—*me*! She pointed at me with a murderous expression, then regained her composure and returned to her post.

Fully awakened to my responsibilities, I grabbed the handle and pumped as though the devil himself had me by the tail. The choir blended into perfect harmony.

Rev. Wheeler was still grinning as he stood at the door, bidding farewell to his parishioners. Many were wiping tears of laughter from their eyes, keenly aware that the Lord works in mysterious ways.
—*Kenneth Nye*
Dover, New Hampshire

$60 Irish Harp Launched Lifelong Music Career

AFTER my father died, a kind lady found a box of our old family photos at a garage sale and tracked me down. One particular picture (right) brought back many memories.

In it, our family, plus an uncle and our priest, were gathered around the piano while Mother played. My brothers were playing cornet and clarinet, and I was playing the Irish harp.

The harp had cost about $60, which was a lot of money then. To keep it, I had to learn to play it within a month. We found someone to give me lessons, and I gave a recital one month later on St. Patrick's Day.

Mom saw to it that I played every Christmas Eve at the hospital where Dad was a doctor. While I performed, two little girls dressed as angels gave gifts of fruit and candy to each patient.

The nuns at the hospital talked Dad into buying me a small pedal harp and asked a professional harpist to give me lessons. During that time, a hand injury kept me in a splint for a year, but I managed to keep playing and went on to win a multi-state music contest.

In college, I wanted to make the harp my major. "You can't make a living in music," my folks argued, but shortly after graduating, I began touring. For 7 years, I proved that I *could* make a living in music.

Over the years, I've played with symphonies, the ballet, and performed at supper clubs, weddings, receptions and funerals. I still play every Sunday for brunch at a local hotel. Every time I load that 75-pound harp into my station wagon for a performance, I thank the dear Lord for making it possible for me to do work that I love.
—*Genevieve Winkenbach*
Bethany, Oklahoma

Texas Clan Had an "Ear" For Down-Home Music

IN THE 1920s and '30s, many families had no entertainment, so they went to each other's homes on Saturday nights to make music. Twenty to 30 people would gather to play guitars, fiddle and piano.

My father-in-law, Wayne Barkley, played fiddle, guitar and harmonica, so it's no wonder his three sons learned to play, too. (That's Wayne and son Joe in the photo above right.) None of them read music—all four played "by ear".

After work, the boys would gather on the porch to play music with their dad. They were also glad to play for family and friends whenever asked.

When Joe was 12, he was asked to travel 30 miles to play

MUSICAL MEMORIES. Genevieve Winkenbach, seated at left, plays the Irish harp that started her musical career. Also pictured are, from left, Father Martin Reed, assistant pastor of their church; Genevieve's parents; her Uncle John Kelly; and brothers Bob on cornet and Tom on clarinet.

BORN MUSICIANS. Wayne Barkley (right) and son Joe made music on their front porch in the early '40s. Joe, in his early teens when this photo was taken, had already played steel guitar on the radio. He later had his own band and kept playing until his death in 1989.

steel guitar on the radio in Pampa, Texas. The family wasn't able to go with him, but they were glued to the radio to listen. Joe could play anything, but his first love was the Western swing style of Bob Wills.

That same year, Joe and my future husband, Earl, then just 10 years old, decided to take their fiddles to a local dance hall and play. Needless to say, the sheriff took them home and told them to wait a few years.
—*Betty Barkley*
Borger, Texas

Gramp's Gramophone Made Sundays Special

IF I COULD be a kid again, I'd go back to the Sunday afternoons when Grandfather brought out the old Edison gramophone with its large horn and wax-cylinder records.

These sessions always took place in the parlor, which was used only on special occasions. It *was* a special occasion as we kids watched Grandfather crank the gramophone and slide on a record.

Sometimes he'd let us choose which one to play, as each of us had a favorite. My brothers would listen to *Casey Jones* or *The Preacher and the Bear*, then scamper off to more adventurous activities.

But my sister and I would stay as long as Grandpa put records on that wondrous music-maker. Some of our favorites were *When You Wore a Tulip*, *It's a Long Way to Tipperary*, *In the Blue Ridge Mountains of Virginia* and *Red Wing*.

Although Grandfather has been gone for many years, we can enjoy his music anytime. I'm the proud owner of his gramophone and records, which are still in excellent condition.

Now I can crank them up with my own grandchildren and hear the voice of Addison Rinker say, "Let 'er go, boys!" as we listen to Finnegan's Jamboree.
—*Annetta Lusiak, Bristol, Wisconsin*

Father, Daughter Shared Love of the "Opry"

ONE OF MY fondest childhood memories is listening to the *Grand Ole Opry* with Dad. We'd sit as close to the radio as we could, because one minute it'd be okay, and the next, the static would be so bad we couldn't hear.

We loved Roy Acuff's *Wabash Cannonball* and *The Great Speckled Bird*; Hank Snow's *I'm Moving On*; Ernest Tubb's *I'm Walking the Floor Over You*; and Hank Williams Sr.'s *Lovesick Blues*. We were listening the night Hank received five encores for that great song.

Country music has always been part of my life, but the happiest times were listening to the "old stars" with my dad. I still listen to the *Opry* occasionally, fighting tears when Roy Acuff begins, "From the great Atlantic Ocean to the wide Pacific shore..."
—*Faye Pepper, Mantee, Mississippi*

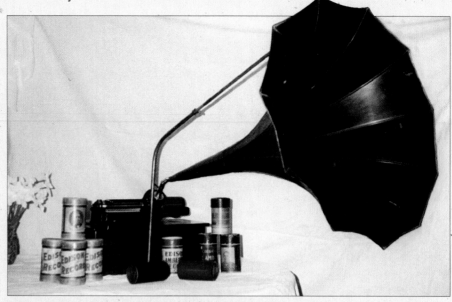

CRANK UP A TUNE. Annetta Lusiak doesn't just listen to the old songs, she uses her grandfather's original Edison gramophone. Now her grandchildren can join in the fun, and they can also do the cranking!

Rod Furgason/Unicorn Stock Photos

Word of Mouth Drew Crowds to Country Dances

MY FAMILY hosted country dances in the large detached garage on our southern-Illinois farm. Daddy didn't dance, but he played banjo in the band and enjoyed the music and camaraderie. Mama loved to dance, and she liked providing the opportunity for others to have a wonderful time.

The only publicity was word of mouth. People came from miles around, bringing chicken salad sandwiches, cakes and brownies to go with a big pot of Mama's coffee. The band played just for the pure enjoyment of it, but usually someone passed the hat late in the evening anyway, collecting about $40.

We did square dances, some wonderful but nearly forgotten dances like the schottische, and waltzes, two-steps and polkas. My favorite was the Grandpa Dance—every man had a lady on each arm, and when the music got fast, he'd swing each lady alternately. I was so small it was easy to swing me right off my feet!

Anyone who wanted to dance did, including the little ones, and everybody had a good time. It was perfectly acceptable for girls and women to dance with each other for all but the slow songs. Occasionally a couple of fun-loving men would even dance together!
—*Clara Locher, Honolulu, Hawaii*

Picture Discs Added Visual Appeal to Record-Buying

By Wayne Daniel, Chamblee, Georgia

PHONOGRAPH RECORDS were never known for their visual appeal. Some manufacturers tried to beautify them with colorful center labels, but they were basically just black discs with holes in the middle—until 1946.

That's when Vogue, a new record manufacturer, put picture discs on the market. Each side of the record had a full-color illustration covering the entire disc, plus a small picture of the artist.

The records were an instant hit with the record-buying public. In the days before television, it was always exciting to see pictures of our favorite radio entertainers. The $1.05 price tag was twice as much that of traditional records. I was a senior in high school, depending on an after-school job for spending money, so buying even one Vogue record required fiscal sacrifice.

My first was by Phil Spitalny and His All-Girl Orchestra. I'd heard them often on the *Hour of Charm* radio program, and was hoping for a picture of the entire orchestra on the disc. I had to be content with twin pianos on one side and a violinist on the other.

I also bought Lulu Belle and Scotty's *Have I Told You Lately That I Love You*, with *I Get a Kick Out of Corn* on the flip side. They performed what was

> *"I had to be content with twin pianos on one side and a violinist on the other..."*

then called "hillbilly music", so I was surprised that their picture showed Scotty in suit and tie, and Lulu Belle in what looked like an evening gown. I'd expected overalls and gingham!

Some of the other popular artists recording for Vogue were bandleaders Art Mooney, Clyde McCoy and Frankie Masters, vocalists Marion Mann and Joan Edwards, and country artist Patsy Montana.

The illustrations usually revealed something about the song's content. For

PRETTY SOUNDS. The late '40s saw a change from the old black 78-rpm records. That's when Vogue started to press these "Picture Records" that showed the musical stars featured in the songs. Phil Spitalny and His All-Girl Orchestra (left and above left) was Wayne Daniel's first purchase. The old *Sugar Blues* man, Clyde McCoy (above), was also popular with Wayne.

example, the picture on bandleader Shep Fields' *I Can't Begin to Tell You* showed a young man sitting at a desk, pencil in hand, with a pile of crumpled paper in front of him—clearly struggling to write a love letter.

Besides being pretty, Vogue records were advertised as unbreakable, warp-proof, wear-resistant and subject to less surface noise than ordinary records. But

by 1950, the company was out of business and the picture records quickly became highly prized collector's items.

Today, a Vogue picture disc can bring anywhere from $40 to several hundred dollars, depending on its rarity and condition. Those that have been well cared for are just as attractive and sound just as good as they did when they were first pressed. ❧

Herbert L. Stormont/Unicorn Stock Photos

'Maple Leaf Rag' Meant Time to Roll Back the Rug

By Helen Ueberbacher, Stamford, Connecticut

THE CONDITION of my mother's sheet music is proof of its years of constant use. These taped, yellowed, plastic-encased relics remind me of years and years of pleasure.

Mother was a skilled pianist who supplied sound effects for the silent movies as a teenager around 1912. She sat beneath the flickering screen with a dim light shining on the music for chase scenes (fast and furious), love scenes (soft but throbbing) and mad scenes (thundering bits of Beethoven).

Later, after my sisters and I were born, scant extra money went toward the purchase of the latest sheet music. Mother played each new song until everyone knew the words to every verse and the chorus. Mother loved to play, anytime, for anyone who would sing. Friends often gathered around our piano, joining in loud—and often pretty good—harmony.

Alexander's Ragtime Band was usually Mother's opening number to get the singers going. Scott Joplin's *Maple Leaf Rag* roused the men to roll back the rug in the dining room so the fox-trotters could dance to *The Teddy Bears' Picnic.*

Irish neighbors shed a few tears mid-evening for *My Wild Irish Rose, Mother Macree* and *I'll Take You Home Again, Kathleen.* Dad always requested a song from his home state—*That's Why I Wish Again That I Was in Michigan.*

Judging by the tattered appearance of the music, some of the most popular pieces were *Smiles, By the Light of the Silvery Moon* and *Moonlight Bay. Over There* is nothing more than a lacy scrap! *How You Gonna Keep 'Em Down on the Farm* was so fragile it was pasted onto sturdier paper.

As my sisters and I learned to play, Mother's collection grew to reflect our tastes. Some of our favorites were *The Music Goes Round and Round, Cheek to Cheek, Heart and Soul, Take Me Back to My Boots and Saddle* and *Once In a While.*

It's difficult to imagine now, but we often had five women vying for time on that old piano in the front room! ❧

Musical Moments Lifted Spirits During Wartime

By Joan McMillan, Walterboro, South Carolina

MUSIC filled my life from an early age. I still remember squirming on a high stool at age 5, as Mama rolled my hair so it could be combed into ringlets for Sunday school the next morning. But at least it was Saturday night, which meant the *Grand Ole Opry* was playing on the radio just behind me.

Joy filled me as Ernest Tubb sang *Walking the Floor Over You*. Soon "the Duke of Paducah" would say, "I'm heading for the barn, 'cause these shoes are killing me!" If I was very lucky, maybe someone would sing *Red Roses for a Blue Lady*.

A year or two later, World War II was raging. Daddy was the only man in our extended family left stateside, so he kept an eye not only on Mama, Grandmother and me, but on various aunts and nieces.

Everyone was lonesome with all the men away, so we got together for meals, short Sunday afternoon jaunts or just to sit and discuss the latest V-mail.

Some of our favorite times were when Daddy took "his ladies" to Aunt Jessie's house. After supper, Aunt Jessie's daughter would play the piano and we'd all gather around it and sing songs like *Sentimental Journey*, *White Cliffs of Dover*, *Don't Sit Under the Apple Tree*, *Always* and *America the Beautiful*. When we ended with *Till We Meet Again*, every family member was there, at least in our hearts.

During that period, I fell in love for the first time—with the voice of Al Jolson. He was one of the first entertainers to perform for the troops overseas, and when he released a new album of his older songs, my aunt bought it. I was hooked.

It mattered not that Al Jolson was as old as my grandfather. When he sang about the bluebird of happiness, I *saw* that bird. When he sang *Toot, Toot, Tootsie, Good-bye*, I *felt* his train leaving. When he sang *Bye Bye Blackbird*, the music filled me from the top of my head to the tips of my toes. ♪

MOONLIGHT SERENADER. Glenn Miller was just one of the great dance bands people "swung to" in the '40s.

Archive Photos

Aragon Among Great Ballrooms of 1940s

CHICAGO had some fine ballrooms in the '40s, but I thought the Aragon on the north side was the greatest.

We danced to Big Band greats like Ted Weems, Eddy Howard, Benny Goodman and the Dorsey brothers, and Elmo Tanner's whistling could carry you above the clouds.

The Aragon often had two bands playing at once, one at each end of the dance floor. You could start dancing to the band at one end, work your way around the floor and dance to the band at the other end.

The smooth oak dance floor had a water fountain right in the middle, and the music never overpowered the mesmerizing sound of falling water. When dancers wanted a break, they could retreat to carpeted alcoves furnished with overstuffed chairs and couches. There were small cocktail tables, too, but only soft drinks were served.

The atmosphere was romantic even when the bands weren't playing. A huge tapestry painted with clouds moved above the dance floor, with a moon and bright stars above that. It was like being under the stars on a moonlit night.

—Ronald Oberst
Bloomfield, Michigan

Hotels Hosted Top Big Band Musicians

WHEN I WAS in high school, we loved listening to the Big Band broadcasts from hotels. Our favorite site was Frank Dailey's Meadowbrook in Cedar Grove, New Jersey. We couldn't afford to go

there, so we'd drive over with our dates, park in the *lot* and listen to Glenn Miller, Tommy Dorsey or whoever was playing. At least we were *there!*

Alvino Rey was one of my favorites. When he played *Hold That Tiger*, the guitar actually growled! And when Glenn Miller played his theme song, *Moonlight Serenade*, nobody spoke a word.

—Robert Went, Longwood, Florida

USO Dance Led Her to The Man of Her Dreams

DURING World War II, the Knights of Columbus USO in Washington, D.C. was the place to be on Saturday nights.

After getting through a long workweek, my friends and I would converge there in high spirits. If we were lucky, we might even find a date for *next* Saturday night.

One night in May 1944, I was standing at the foot of the spiral staircase, trying to look like I didn't care if no one asked me to dance. As the band began to play *Stardust*, a handsome sailor ap-

LIFETIME PARTNER. Peggy Sharpe (with Johnny) married the starry-eyed sailor she danced with (story at left).

proached, took my hand and led me to the dance floor. He didn't let go for 40 years, and *Stardust* was always our favorite song.

—Peggy Sharpe
Spotsylvania, Virginia

DANCING DAILY for 144 days! That's what 3,456 hours came to for Betty and "Popeye". Glen Grewell of Enon, Ohio, who shared this photo, says Betty was his wife's cousin. Marathon dancing was big back then.

Dance Music Was Just What the Doctor Ordered

By Marian Erdman
Charlotte, North Carolina

IN THE 1940s, I was a hospital recreation worker at an Army hospital in Georgia. Many of our patients were hospitalized for months or even years, so the recreation program provided a welcome respite from their treatments and suffering.

We often took the patients on trips outside the hospital, and the community was generous in donating tickets to events they might enjoy, including Big Band dances.

When Stan Kenton and his orchestra came to town, I was thrilled to be among those assigned to take 100 patients to the performance. The 12 "bed patients" were transported in an enormous ambulance, and their stretchers were placed right in front of the bandstand. The rest of us were seated on the edge of the dance floor.

R&R IN SWING TIME. GIs enjoyed a slow dance at a USO club in France when Don Condon of Janesville, Wisconsin snapped this photo in 1944.

When the music started, every foot was tapping, and many of the ambulatory patients found willing dance partners. Those who didn't dance enjoyed just listening to the music.

Suddenly a young soldier came running over to me. "Come quick!" he cried. "One of the bed patients is jitterbugging!"

One of the bed patients *jitterbugging*? I was horrified.

I rushed across the dance floor toward the stretchers. A crowd was watching a young woman dance with a patient who was in a body cast from his ears to his hips!

The man moved only his feet and arms, but he skillfully guided his partner out and back again, keeping perfect time to the music. They were having a wonderful time and I didn't want to spoil his fun, but I was frantic. "What should we do?" I asked a nurse.

"It's all right," she assured me. "He's supposed to have the cast removed in a day or two anyway."

The patient finished his dance, got a round of applause and hobbled back to his stretcher. He was smiling and appeared none the worse for his venture onto the dance floor. In fact, *he* probably recovered from the episode sooner than I did! ♫

Doris Day's Performance A Sentimental Favorite

WE USED to travel 50 miles to a pavilion on Pleasant Lake near Jackson, Michigan, where we danced to the music of Big Bands. On warm evenings, the huge windows were lifted up and hooked to the ceiling, providing a clear view of the lake. A mirrored ball hung from the ceiling, making rainbow-like designs on the waxed hardwood floor.

One evening during World War II, we drove over to hear Les Brown's orchestra. He introduced a budding female vocalist, who performed a new song called *Sentimental Journey*, and the vocalist was Doris Day!

Little did we know that song would become one of the greatest hits of the war years. —*Annie-Laurie Robinson*
Williamston, Michigan

A Graduation They'd Never Forget

IT WAS 1942 and World War II had just begun. My friends and I were working in an aircraft factory and knew we'd be going off to war soon.

Our girlfriends were still in high school, so we decided to make their graduation something they'd never forget. We took them to the Cocoanut Grove at Hollywood's Ambassador Hotel.

At this time, the famous ballroom was known all over the world as the Ballroom of the Stars, and it was the permanent home for Freddie Martin and his orchestra.

As soon as we were seated on the dance floor, Mr. Martin asked if we wanted to hear any special songs and whether anyone was celebrating a birthday. His music and kindness made the night extra-special. We felt like stars in our own little world. (Also, my date from that night later became my wife for 43 wonderful years.)

Another thing I'll always remember about that night is when the waiter asked us what we wanted to drink, 12 voices answered in unison, "Milk". He walked away shaking his head!
—*Robert Pure, Port St. Lucie, Florida*

Music Parties Brought Neighbors Together

IN THE late 1930s, almost everyone in our sparsely populated Illinois neighborhood played music. On Saturday nights, we'd meet at someone's home for a "pound party". Each family brought cookies and sandwiches, the adults played instruments and everyone sang.

When I was 12, I got a used tenor guitar for Christmas and it became my constant companion. My uncle spent hours teaching me to play. My heart's desire was to play with the adults at those Saturday night parties, and after about a year, I did.

One of my favorite radio performers was Patsy Montana, and I often tried to sing and yodel the way she did. Years later, I saw her in person. Patsy was such a tiny little thing with a big guitar, and although in her 80s, she still sounded and looked like a girl to me.

I was overcome with emotion, crying tears of joy as she sang *I Want to Be a Cowboy's Sweetheart*. That song rolled away 57 years, and I was 13 again.
—*Lucile Good, Tucson, Arizona*

Record Shop Was Perfect Place to Spin Away Time

By Anne Tierney, Temple City, California

ONE OF MY favorite after-school pastimes was moseying into the local record shop. I rarely had the money to buy a record, but I pretended to be a serious-minded customer.

The 78-rpm records were filed alphabetically behind the counter in little cubicles similar to the mail slots at a hotel. At our little shop, all the clerks were men who had affected the dignified bearing of a butler.

I'd ask if the store had a recording of a particular song, and the clerk would reply, "By which artist would you wish?" He'd turn to the row of records, remove one, place it in a faded green sleeve and hand it to me. Then I'd go to a glass-enclosed sound booth to listen, gab with a friend and while away an hour or so.

Most of my requests reflected what I'd recently heard on the radio or seen at the movies. Our family was devoted to *Lux Presents Hollywood*, a brief re-enactment of a current movie, and *The Railroad Hour*, based on operettas and Broadway musicals. On Monday nights, we'd eat a quiet dinner as we listened raptly to that week's new program.

TRY IT BEFORE YOU BUY IT. There were times when you didn't have to buy a phonographic "pig in a poke".

The movies introduced me to Bing Crosby and Dennis Morgan, and I developed crushes on both. After seeing *My Wild Irish Rose*, I just *had* to save enough money—about $1.40—to buy the record. I played it over and over, and I still have it.

I also remember spending precious baby-sitting money on Nelson Eddy's *Stout-Hearted Men*, with *Lover, Come Back to Me* on the flip side.

When I heard about the new 33-1/3-rpm records I was shocked. Imagine a whole album on one measly record! I took great pride in collecting my 78s in rigid-bound albums with title backs like books. They looked so nice lined up on a shelf. *Now* they'd have just a sliver of cardboard jacket. Horrible!

Worst of all, you could no longer touch the record or hear the music before you bought it. No more dignified clerks to serve you…no more listening booths to congregate in. It may have been progress, but I was disappointed. ❧

Coin-Toss Contests Kept Jukeboxes Going All Night

I OPERATED a jukebox route from the time they became popular in the '30s until 1941, when I joined the Navy. I drove about 1,100 miles a week, mostly on dirt and gravel roads through the Ozarks. Sometimes, just getting to some of my stops was an adventure.

In those days, the only jukeboxes were 12-record machines without all the flash and lights that came along later. The records were the old 78s that had to be handled with care. Common jukebox brands were Wurlitzer, Seeburg, Rock-ola and Mills (that one was built on the order of a Ferris wheel, which would turn until coming to the selected number).

Jukeboxes changed every year, and the Wurlitzer 24-record machine with bubbling lights has become a classic of the jukebox industry. A real boost to the business was the wall or booth boxes that became popular.

It cost 5¢ to play a record, but the kids got real professional at carving nickel-shaped slugs out of wooden spoons while sitting at the fountain or in booths at the drugstore.

The best incomes came from the honky-tonks. The employees marked their jukebox coins with fingernail polish and flipped with customers to see who'd play the next record. When the operator checked the machine, the marked coins were returned to the employees.

Since the customers were well aware of this practice, this kept the jukeboxes playing well into the night. They often asked employees to flip for a record, knowing they had a 50-50 chance of hearing a song for free.

—*John Sessions, Harrison, Arkansas*

JUKE JOY. A glowing, bubbling Wurlitzer was a teen dream.

OH, FRANKIE! It was *swoon* time when young "blue eyes" arrived.

The biggest thrill was when stars like Tommy and Jimmy Dorsey and Glenn Miller came to town for bond drives and stopped at the store to sign their records.

When Frank Sinatra visited, as you might expect, throngs of teenagers were out in force.

He had just signed my record and handed it to me when it was knocked out of my hand and broken! I was crushed, as I couldn't afford to buy another one.

Suddenly someone grabbed my arm and ushered me through the crowd back to Sinatra. He had witnessed the whole thing and gave me another record—signed, of course. I'll *never* forget that day. —*Audrey Ball, Toledo, Ohio*

Sinatra Saved the Day

AT THE OLD five-and-dime stores, the clerks in the music departments used to play the latest songs on the piano, or just play the records. We rarely had the money to buy them, but it was great fun to listen.

Four in a Booth Enjoyed Cocktails for Two

IN 1945, I was 15 and going steady with a clarinet player in the Seattle Youth Symphony Orchestra. My beau and I were screening a record in a glassed-in booth at the music store and both wondered what the three sailors in the next booth were laughing and gesturing about. We couldn't imagine what was so funny!

Then my boyfriend had to go upstairs for a few minutes to check with his teacher on a lesson time—so imagine his consternation when he came back to find all three sailors in the booth with me, playing Spike Jones' *Cocktails for Two*. We were all especially tickled by the "yickety-yickety" part where the talking hand signals came in.

We wound up buying the record, which became a longtime favorite. My boyfriend and I eventually broke up and married others, but whenever I hear that silly song, I remember way back when we were more concerned with "yickety-yickety" than politics and the economy. —*Roeena Cohn, Chico, California*

Music Soothed These Savage Teens

By Sonya Jason, Woodland Hills, California

DURING WORLD WAR II, my "first love" was on active duty when I started working for Bell Telephone in Pittsburgh, and I longed for him to come home. Oh, the memories of those rare furloughs, when we moved across a crowded dance floor in a close embrace!

I was one of about 50 teenage girls working on an assembly line on the top floor. It was tedious work, and at quitting time, we all made a mad dash for the lone elevator. The pushing and shoving occasionally led to near-riot conditions, and the hostilities began to carry over to work the next day.

Management pleaded for more ladylike behavior, but our stampedes actually worsened. Something drastic had to be done.

One day, during our usual 4:48 p.m. race for the elevator, the piped-in Muzak suddenly stopped, and out of that ugly brown box on the hideous green wall we heard the most beautiful voice in the world singing, "All of me, why not take all of me..."

MUSIC HATH CHARM. Sonya Jason recalls how Frank Sinatra stopped her and co-workers from dangerous "stampedes".

I think my feet paused in midair, and so did those of all the other girls. At 5 p.m., the elevator operator stopped at our floor and braced herself for the usual pandemonium, but when she opened the door, no one was there!

She peeked into our work area and saw girls leaning back in chairs, on benches and against walls. Some had their eyes closed; others gazed off into space. We were listening to Frank Sinatra, remembering the magical times we'd danced to his music with our sweethearts.

That voice was all it took to civilize us, and not one of us moved until the final note.

As the speakers switched back to the traditional Muzak "instrumentals", 50 girls floated dreamily to the elevator, patiently waiting to be brought back to earth...and the ground floor.

From that day on, at exactly 4:48 p.m., silence prevailed. The other floors continued to get Muzak, but we got Frank. Then we marched in an orderly manner to the elevator and out of the building with Frank's music echoing in our ears and our hearts. ❧

Teens Too Busy Dancing To Make Mischief

THE CLASS of '37 at Glendale (California) High School was a magical class living in a magical era. Despite the Depression, my friends and I had "home parties", dancing to radio tunes like *Oh, You Nasty Man, Stay as Sweet as You Are* and *Three Little Fishes*.

There was a uniform board made up of our peers and a monitor in each homeroom that kept us in line. We had no designer clothes. We wore skirts down to our ankles and blouses, and nobody thought a thing of it if you wore the same outfit every day. The boys wore "dirty

BEACH BLANKET BUDDIES. "This is 'the gang' at Balboa in southern California during Easter vacation our senior year," says Flora MacKay (top). **"This was *the place* back then, and 20 of us kids threw in $5 each to rent a room. We're all still friends and many of the couples have been married for over 50 years."**

cords" (if they could stand up by themselves, they were ripe for school). You had to keep them hidden so that Mom wouldn't throw them into the wash.

Our class "dated". Most of the boys couldn't afford to go steady, and we girls didn't feel the need of a commitment as the girls did later in the war years.

Gasoline was 10¢ a gallon, and a few boys had their own cars…the ones with the rumble seats were the greatest. The boys were good at one-arm driving and we girls learned to shift gears.

After a date or a football game, there was The Rite Spot or the Night Owl,

and after a prom, it was Lucas on Vermont Street, where for 75¢ you could have soup, salad, pasta, an entree, a drink and dessert and, for 5¢ more, a little box of miniature petit fours.

We ate hamburgers made by Bob Wian (who made the Big Boy famous) and shared 10¢ malts at the Danish Maid. There you would see straw wrappers hanging from the ceiling that had been blown up by the boys showing off their lung power.

For a nice date, we'd go dancing at the beautiful Crystal Ballroom. For 25¢; we could go to the Pasadena Civic and dance to a big-name band.

One night, while the orchestra was playing *Pennies from Heaven*, everyone threw pennies into the air. We danced to all the greats. Someone once remarked that we danced so much we were too tired to get into trouble.

—*Flora MacKay*
West Covina, California

Surprise Guests Added Glamour to Teen Dance

WHEN I WAS a high school senior in 1939, we all took turns hosting dances. For my turn, the dance would be in the empty restaurant next to my dad's hotel. We'd rent a jukebox, wax the floor and have a ball.

My family lived at the hotel, and I loved sitting on the long porch, talking with the tourists. One night I got acquainted with some Hollywood performers who were doing a show at a big nightclub in town. They were very kind and listened graciously as I talked excitedly about the dance I was hosting the next night.

A good number of teenagers came to the dance, and the place looked great. We were about to take a break at 9:30 p.m. when a bus pulled up out front. It was the entertainers from the hotel!

In came the women in glittering gowns and the men in tuxedoes, carrying their instruments with them.

We just stood there, awestruck. My friends glanced at me and gulped in amazement.

When the performers were ready, the emcee announced with a smile, "We've come here from

Hollywood to help Harry entertain his guests. We hope you enjoy it."

The show was fantastic, with singing and dancing, magic, comedy, even a sharp-shooting act.

Afterward, as the group hurried to the bus for its act at the nightclub, I ran up to thank them. The manager said, "Son, we did this because we like you, and we hope the best for you."

I believe the performers enjoyed the show as much as we did. They just wanted to do something good—and they did. And my reputation at school improved quite a bit after that, too!

—*Harry Gross, Jeffersonville, Indiana*

Dancers Moved Under Canopy of "Stars"

THIS cherished photo shows me with my prom date, Dave Bergman, in 1959. I worked on our senior prom's decorating committee that year, when the theme was "Sparkling Stars".

We cut out star shapes, dipped them in wax and glitter, then attached them to different lengths of string and hung them from the ceiling to give the feeling of a starry night. It didn't look like much by daylight, but when all those stars were lit by a revolving ball, the gym looked like a starlit ballroom.

Hoop dresses were popular for proms then. It's fortunate the cars were roomy, or we never could've gotten in and out! Strapless dresses weren't allowed at my school, so many dresses had jackets, and rhinestone tiaras provided glitter.

—*Fran Hendren, Sylvania, Ohio*

Fans of 'Champagne Music' Bubbled Over Meeting Their Idols

By JoAnn Cooke, Reseda, California

IN THE EARLY '50s before Lawrence Welk had a national TV show, his band had a local program in Los Angeles, California that my friends and I never missed. Roberta Linn was the Champagne Lady then, and we loved watching Lawrence waltz or polka with her. As a dancer, he was everything our romantic hearts desired.

But the main attraction really wasn't Lawrence Welk himself. It was the music—and *the band members*. Each of us had a crush on a different musician.

As soon as the show was over, we telephoned each other. "Did you see…?" "Wasn't he great?" "He's so cute!" For that next week, until the show was on again, we relived each moment, each musical number and each smile or special look of our particular favorite.

My sister, Charlene, loved Myron Floren, who played accordion and sometimes directed the band. Some of the other girls liked trumpet player Rocky Rockwell and deep-voiced Larry Hooper.

My favorites were trombone player Barney Liddell and singer-saxophonist Garth Andrews. Barney's family image was part of his appeal to me, since I wanted to be a wife and mother. Once I sent his little girl a stuffed dog and received a wonderful thank-you note from him. How I treasured it!

Garth was the handsome, romantic band member, and I wasn't the only girl with a crush on him. We thought he was married (but ignored that) and were thrilled to learn he drove a yellow Hudson.

We were even more thrilled when we learned we could watch our idols *in person*. The band re-

BOYS IN THE BAND. Lawrence Welk band members (from left) Larry Hooper, Bob Pilot, Garth Andrews, Clarence Willard, Dick Dale and Rocky Rockwell posed in 1952.

hearsed on Thursdays at the Aragon Ballroom at Venice Beach, so whenever we could borrow the car, we drove to watch them in summer, or if we had a Thursday off from school. Lawrence usually wasn't there, but it wasn't him we wanted to see anyway!

During one break, we actually got to meet the band members, and they were even willing to go outside so we could take snapshots. They were so nice and friendly, we thought we were in Heaven! (Looking back, I've wondered that since their dance audiences were mostly middle-aged, they might have been somewhat flattered by the attention of several adoring teenage girls.)

Some years ago, when one of the "girls" was approaching 40, her mother sent friends and family members squares of fabric to personalize for a memory quilt. I knew immediately what to do with mine. I embroidered a champagne glass, bubbles and Garth's name. She loved it!

My sister recently gave me an autographed copy of Lawrence Welk's autobiography, *Wunnerful, Wunnerful!*, that she'd found at a garage sale. A note inside indicated it had been a gift for someone named "Millie". Maybe Millie isn't still a fan of Lawrence Welk and his Champagne Music Makers, but I always will be. ♣

WHAT A THRILL! JoAnn Cooke and her friends got to meet their heartthrobs, Barney Liddell, Myron Floren and Garth Andrews (left to right below). Thrilled beyond words, JoAnn stands with Barney at right. And since her sister, Charlene, had a crush on Myron, she posed with his Hudson (below right). It was all too "wunnerful, wunnerful".

READING BY RADIO. There was a time when reading was the only way to get the news, or be entertained at home. Then radio came along, went national, and the world was literally at our fingertips. We still had the movies, though, and there was nothing like them...or so we thought until something called television surfaced.

Chapter Six
Broadcast to Silver Screen
...That Was Entertainment

*There were marvelous matinees, maudlin radio soaps
and Milton Berle when television was young.*

W e'll never again see an entertainment bargain to match what a dime or quarter bought at the movies before World War II.

It wasn't just that you got up to 4 hours of the best (and worst) that Hollywood had to offer, either. You were also transported into a grand world of red carpets and uniformed ushers, gilded statues and plush seats, and perhaps even a monstrous Wurlitzer theater organ that rose out of the basement. And, praise be, a cool darkened shelter from the blazing sun and 100-plus temperatures of the Dust Bowl years. (If the banner on the theater marquee boasted "20 Degrees Cooler Inside", that alone was reason to buy a ticket.)

The Fox Movietone News featured sports heroes in action, current fashions, floods, fires, earthquakes, celebrities at play and world events…not much different from the fare we get nowadays on the network evening news.

The animated cartoons and Pete Smith short features provided some welcome laughter…*and then* came the double feature. But on Friday nights (Saturday afternoons for the kids) there was still more—the much-anticipated drawing for a set of dishes, a $2 gift certificate at the dry cleaners or a brand-new bicycle.

Meanwhile, national network radio had dawned. It brought us everything from H.V. Kaltenborn with the news to soap operas, ringside descriptions of Joe Louis' bouts and *The Lux Radio Theater* and *Maxwell Coffee Hour*.

Radio Gave Something to *Tsk* About

My grandmother and Aunt Edith were essentially housebound. Even worse, there wasn't much scandal going on in the neighborhood. But no matter—the soap operas provided all the gossip and lurid goings-on they could handle. Every week when our family stopped in to visit, the first hour was devoted to *tsk-tsking* with Mom over the shocking developments involving Mary Noble and husband Larry, Ma Perkins and a host of soap opera characters.

Radio brought an incredible range of entertainment into our homes, but after World War II, we soon abandoned our radio favorites for something new called television.

In the early days, TV didn't have much to offer other than wrestling and Milton Berle, and John Cameron Swayze became America's Newsman. Most of the day, what you got when you turned on your Philco, Muntz or Admiral 12-inch black-and-white set was the test pattern.

Nevertheless, the first family on the block to own a set also became the most popular. If you were among the privileged to be invited for an evening of TV viewing—and hoped to be invited back—you made sure to arrive with fresh popcorn or chips and dip.

Gradually things got better, thanks to Dave Garroway, *What's My Line?, The Fred Waring Show* and *The U.S. Steel Hour.* Some of our favorite radio stars tried to bring their shows to television. A few succeeded (Jack Benny and Bob Hope) and some flopped (Fred Allen).

Think about it…weren't we lucky? No country in history has ever been so magnificently entertained by so many talented people. It was, indeed, the Golden Age of Entertainment.

—*Clancy Strock*

Brother's Lost Clothes Were a Real Show-Stopper

By Jacqueline Zelo, Nesconset, New York

I HAD MIXED feelings about going to the movies when I was young. I was enthralled when Mario Lanza sang *The Drinking Song* from *The Student Prince*, and I've dreamed of owning a Basenji ever since seeing *Good-Bye, My Lady*. I still even remember the words Michael Rennie used to open the saucer in *They Came from Outer Space*.

But sometimes I wonder if the Saturday matinee was invented by hardworking parents who needed a break. Every parent in our apartment building cheerfully talked it up all morning until after lunch, when a crowd of about 20 kids left, quarters in hand. We'd be out of their hair until dinnertime!

At the theater, white-uniformed matrons with flashlights maintained something resembling order—nobody under 12 in the balcony, no throwing popcorn

---

"The houselights came on as all of us searched..."

---

from the balcony, no unnecessary talking or leaving seats (sure!), no arguing or fighting. They turned into Olympic sprinters whenever an exit door opened trying to sneak in a non-paying customer.

I enjoyed the matinees but resented having to take along three younger siblings—especially my brother. He talked continually, never sat still and lost a scarf, hat or mitten each week! Because of him, the matrons knew us by name, humiliating me to no end.

My mom never quite believed I'd dressed him properly or tried to keep track of his things. How could his scarf "just disappear" if he was sitting in a seat all afternoon?

One Saturday, Mom attacked the problem with safety pins. She attached my brother's jacket to the suspenders on his ski pants, pinned his mittens to his sleeves, pinned his scarf to his hat and then attached both to his jacket.

I can't remember what movie it was ...only that it was in 3-D and there were frightening special effects like a falling cable car. It took a lot of effort to watch a 3-D movie. If you didn't hold your head at a certain angle or if you moved it one iota, the glasses fell off, and just looking through them meant

having a slight headache all afternoon.

When the movie ended, *all* of my brother's outerwear was gone! The matrons could find nothing with their flashlights. The exits opened to let the other kids out, and adults began moving in from the lobby for the evening show.

To the manager's astonishment, my mother showed up and *insisted* we keep looking. The movie was in progress, and the manager said a thorough search couldn't be conducted until morning.

"Out of the question," Mom said. The manager didn't know my brother

had only one jacket. He didn't know my mother, either!

The houselights came on and the projector went off while the manager, the matrons, Mom and we four kids searched. We finally found it all under Row 2—kicked 20 rows from where we'd been sitting.

I was quite sure the entire population of Woodside, Queens was watching as my mother held the grimy clump of clothing high in the air. When they applauded, I wanted to die of embarrassment. When I think about it now, I nearly die laughing. ✦

MATINEE MAYHEM! At least the old Saturday matinees provided a service...they got the kids out of the house for a few hours.

Daring Boys Found Ways To Sneak Past Ushers

MY CHILDREN marvel at my knowledge of films and stars of yesteryear, but it's easy when you grow up spending so much time at the movies.

The theaters then were like palaces. Often three balconies high, most featured heavy dark green, red or blue velvet draperies with gold tassels, polished glass, brass and marble, decorated walls with gold or silver trim, winding stairways, large oil paintings of stars, tapestries, plush Oriental print carpeting and uniformed ushers.

Even intermission was just more of a good time. Theater personnel would gather 20 or more children on stage, have them remove their shoes and mix them up in the center of the stage. The first three kids to find their shoes got a prize like candy or popcorn.

Or sometimes a huge Lowry organ would rise from under the stage and we'd have a sing-along, following the words that appeared on the screen with the famous bouncing ball.

A favorite pastime for 12- and 13-year-old boys then was sneaking into the movies. One or two boys would pay to get in while the rest went outside to the exits. At a prearranged time, the boys inside would push the doors open and 15 or more kids poured in. There were usually four ushers, so four kids got caught. The rest scattered quickly and sat down. Not bad odds, I guess.

During one film, we heard a huge crash and quite a commotion from behind the screen. We later learned one of the boys had climbed in through the skylight. As he clung to the drapes, trying to climb down, the curtains gave way. He broke his leg trying to save 12¢. But in those days, not every boy had 12¢.

I had an embarrassing moment myself in 1939 when I was 8 or 9. On my way to the movies, I ran into a classmate and invited her to come along. After paying for my ticket, I turned and saw her just standing there.

"Come on," I said, "we'll be late." She said she didn't have any money. I was so embarrassed! I ran all the way home to ask Dad for more money—which wasn't easy to explain— then ran back to pay her way. Now that I think about it, that may have been my first date.

—William Kenyon
Glendale, Arizona

"GRAB SOME SKY, PARDNER." When he was 5, Doug Davis walked, talked and dressed like his hero, Roy Rogers, says his mom, Mrs. J.W. Davis of Higginsville, Missouri. Doug wore this getup every day and knew the words to all of Roy's songs.

Seeing Movie Twice Was Worth the Punishment

WHEN I WAS ABOUT 11, I was absolutely enraptured by Nelson Eddy and Jeanette MacDonald. After seeing one of their movies on a Sunday afternoon, I *was* Jeanette for the rest of the week.

I'd sing her songs at home, up in the apple tree in our yard and at the creek, where people would stop to listen. Even when I sang in the church choir, I was Jeanette.

One Sunday, after seeing Nelson and Jeanette's poignant movie *Maytime*, I told my sister and a friend to go on home. I was going to stay and see it once more—something that was strictly forbidden.

I reveled in it again but *still* could not tear myself away, so I stayed for a third viewing. Just after the movie began, I heard my name called softly. There stood my dad with an usher.

All the way home, Dad lectured me about how worried he and Mom had been, how I knew better and perhaps there wouldn't be any movies for a while. I meekly kept silent—I was suffering, just like my heroine, but soon I'd be free to sing all the new songs I'd learned that afternoon…"Sweetheart, sweetheart, sweetheart. will you remember love-time, springtime, May…"

And if I couldn't get to the movies again soon, I could buy several old movie magazines for a nickel and cut out the pictures of Nelson and Jeanette for my scrapbook. It was worth the pain.

—*Irene Hill, Cudahy, Wisconsin*

Aiding War Effort Got Her into Movies Free

IN 1941, London was having a terrible time of it in the war, so the Beaver Theater in Toronto added a special 10 a.m. show each Saturday. Anyone who brought a piece of aluminum for the war effort was admitted free.

After a month of these shows, I was desperate for another piece of aluminum. The theater was going to show the final episode of the Fu Manchu serial, and I *had* to see it. (He was so ugly and frightening—yet compelling to look at for a 7-year-old.)

I went all through the house, the garbage, asked all our neighbors—no more aluminum! Then it came to me—Father's pills! Father had a nervous disorder, and his medicine was packed in small aluminum trays. Since one tray wouldn't be nearly enough for admission, I took all six of them.

I got in to see my movie (Fu Manchu was killed, and we all cheered), and Father wasn't the least bit upset with me. He said the pills still worked, even if they were in a jumble in the box… and he'd inadvertently helped the war effort.

—*Leslie Simms
North Hollywood, California*

Teen Wasn't Piggish About Claiming Prize

THE MOVIE HOUSE in our small town gave out a number with each ticket on Saturday nights, then had a drawing for a prize like a puppy or rabbit.

One night when I was 17, I was there with a date, and my number was drawn. The prize was a squealing *pig*. I was so embarrassed I didn't even claim it. I told my girlfriend I'd lost my ticket!

—*Ray Kelley, St. Cloud, Minnesota*

"AIR-CONDITIONED for your comfort" was a surefire way to rustle patrons in to see a Western in the days before homes had central air.

First Movie Made Indelible Impression

I REMEMBER my first movie as if it were yesterday. We lived on a farm, with no theaters nearby, so Mother watched the ads in the paper for a suitable offering in the big city.

When the day arrived, we dressed in our Sunday best and traveled 25 miles to Kansas City to see Mary Pickford in *Daddy Long Legs*.

My brother and I were mesmerized by the big screen and the irresistible star, with her bouncy blond curls and angelic face. We talked about the experience for weeks afterward to anyone who had the patience to listen.

After the movie, Dad took us to a cafeteria and told us we could select anything we wanted from an endless array of meats, salads and desserts. Sometimes Mother had to intervene, smiling as she cautioned that "our eyes were bigger than our tummies".

On the ride home, I fell fast asleep with Dad's strong arm around me, my head on his shoulder.

Looking back, I'm so grateful for the simple pleasures and all-enveloping love of my family.

—*Viola Zumault*
Kansas City, Missouri

Second Showing Left Her in the Dark

ONE NIGHT when I was 7, I went to the early show at the movie house and decided to stay for the second show, too. When my parents saw the other kids returning from the second show, I wasn't among them.

My older sister was dispatched to find me and raced down the block, arriving just as the projectionist was locking up. He'd seen me but hadn't noticed me leave, so they checked the building. When he turned on the lights, there I was, fast asleep on the third-row bench!

(I shudder to think how I would have felt waking up in that dark, silent movie house.) Needless to say, I was forbidden to ever stay for the second show again.

There were no concession stands, so we bought our popcorn from Mr. Kirkland's "popcorn mobile" on the corner. It was built on the body of a Model T Ford, with glass all around and the popcorn machine in full view.

Mr. Kirkland sold popcorn and peanuts to shoppers all day and to movie fans until the theater closed at night. Then he would simply crank up the Model T and drive it home!

—*Novelene Freeman*
Huntsville, Alabama

PRETTY MARY PICKFORD. Is it any wonder that this lovely actress managed to mesmerize a young Viola Zumault? Read her memory above right.

Moviegoers Sent Home When Theater Lost Film

MOVIES WERE a big part of my life when I was growing up in the 1920s, and we all eagerly awaited the Saturday night shows at the local theater.

To keep up with the latest happenings in the lives of my idols, I rushed to the local drugstore every month for the latest copy of *Photoplay* and then to the print shop for construction paper to make picture albums of my favorite stars like Pearl White, Gloria Swanson, William Hart, the Gish sisters and Marion Davies.

One Saturday as my mother, sister and I waited for the lights to dim, we were told there would be no show. The films had been lost!

We were given our money back, then sadly walked the one block home and reluctantly prepared for bed. Just as we got settled in, a megaphone-amplified voice drifted through the night air.

"The lost films are found," the voice announced. "We will now have the high-class show *The Affairs of Anatole*."

Of course, we were so excited and lost no time getting back into our clothes and back to the theater to see this "high-class" Cecil B. DeMille epic.

—*Ruth Kemmerling*
Schoolcraft, Michigan

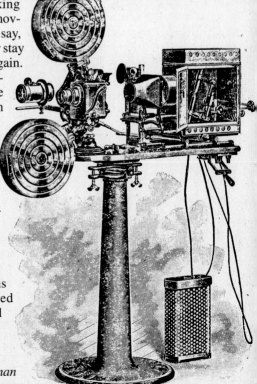

Hugh F. Smith

SUCH GRAND TIMES! This 1950 scene of Times Square shows the New York landmark bustling with life. As Harry English recalls, it made a memorable place to play hooky the day he saw "the show" and heard singer Frank Sinatra (left).

Archive Photos

"Our Great Escape to Times Square"

OUR WALK to high school took us past a subway station. I don't know why, but one morning my brother, two friends and I couldn't get past that spot. Before we knew it, we'd dropped nickels into the slot and were on our way to Times Square.

The square had many famous movie houses then—Loew's State, the Strand, the Roxy, Music Hall. But the best by far was the New York Paramount. On any given day, you could see Jimmy Dorsey with Ray Eberle and Helen O'Connell, Glenn Miller playing *In the Mood*, Benny Goodman playing *Cherokee*, or Kay Kayser and his Kollege of Musical Knowledge.

On the day we skipped school, it was Tommy Dorsey and his new lead singer, Frank Sinatra. Admission was a quarter. The emcee warmed us up with his famous greeting: "Good morning, hooky players!" We could easily identify with that! Tommy Dorsey played *I'll Never Smile Again*, which was No. 1 on the hit parade.

Then Sinatra sang *That Old Black Magic*, and the shouting raised the rafters. When he sang *Night and Day*, the girls fainted in their seats and swooned in the aisles. There was pandemonium for 10 or 15 minutes. We couldn't have asked for more.

We also saw the movie *Brother Rat*, with Ronald Reagan, Jane Wyman, Wayne Morris and Priscilla Lane. After-

ward, we went around the corner for a frankfurter and root beer, then took the subway home.

The day cost us 40¢ each—a dime in subway fare, a nickel for lunch and a quarter for the show. We still had a dime left over to see a movie on Sunday!
—*Harry English, Brooklyn, New York*

Roy Rogers and Dale Evans Were Matinee Favorites

SATURDAY MATINEES were a great treat for me when I was growing up. I'd get 10¢ for my ticket and 5¢ to spend. To get the most out of my nickel, I'd stop at the market and get a really big dill pickle, which lasted longer than a candy bar. Then it was on to "happy trails" with my favorite performers, Roy Rogers and Dale Evans.

Since retiring to the high country, I've been fortunate to see Mr. and Mrs. Rogers at local charity functions. I even met them in person once, and it was the most exciting event of my life. What wonderful, gracious, pleasant people they are. I hope God blesses them with many more happy trails together.
—*Barbara Tuhey, Victorville, California*

Rudy Vallee Fans Saw Their Idol Every Week

By Margaret Chaiet
West Hills, California

ALL WEEK LONG, my friend Esther and I anticipated our weekly trip to the Brooklyn Paramount to see our idol, Rudy Vallee, and his orchestra, The Connecticut Yankees.

I was in my early teens, and there was no one more star-struck. We got there at 10 a.m. to get front-row seats.

Waiting for the stage show was almost unbearable. There were "coming attractions", a newsreel and a short comedy or cartoon.

I especially liked *Out of the Inkwell*, in which an artist drew a pointy-headed figure that jumped off the drawing paper and got into all sorts of trouble. Then the artist had to capture him and get him back into the inkwell until the next week.

Next came the movie, and then the Mighty Wurlitzer rose majestically from its pit, playing popular songs. We sang along, following the bouncing ball as it leaped over the lyrics projected on the screen.

Finally, the curtains parted to Rudy Vallee's theme song. The "vagabond lover" held a megaphone to his lips and crooned *My Time Is Your Time*. We swooned.

After the show, many of us who were members of the Vallee Boosters ran to the stage door to get a glimpse of our idol. He'd sign autographs, tell us for our newsletter where he'd be appearing, and ask what we'd like him to sing on his radio show.

"When I say 'heigh-ho, everybody' on the radio, I'm saying it to my fan club," he told us.

On the way home, Esther and I would stop at Kresge's for a chow mein sandwich and a root beer, and to buy lipstick or hair curlers or rouge.

It was a perfect day, well worth the long train ride into the city on the Culver Line El. And there was always next week! ❧

Trip to Drive-In Called For Pajamas and Pillows

BACK in the '40s, Mom would always wait until just before suppertime to announce that we were going to the drive-in.

My brother and I would be so excited we could hardly eat. It never made any difference to us what movie was playing—we were just glad to go.

After supper, as we played outside, we'd watch the evening sun drop slowly to the treetops.

Finally, Mom would call us in to take baths and don our pajamas. She *never* had to call us twice! Soon we were parading to our green 1954 Ford sedan, our arms full of pillows.

Dad would buy our tickets at the booth, then select our spot. After pulling the car onto a small gravel mound, he'd remove the speaker from its stand and hook it onto his window, letting the soft music waft into the car as my brother and I squabbled over how much of the backseat each one was allowed.

At last, the lights above the screen faded and we saw advertisements for the concession stand and coming attractions, followed by a cartoon and then the main feature. My favorite was *Old Yeller*. It was the first movie that made me cry.

BIG OLD CARS like this were great for stretching out to see a drive-in movie. There was plenty of room to bring pillows, blankets and your favorite doll.

About halfway through the film, Dad would make his pilgrimage to the concession stand for our traditional order—popcorn for him to share with Mom, Junior Mints for my brother, Milk Duds for me and soft drinks all around.

My brother and I leaned back contentedly against our pillows as we slowly savored our treats in the darkness.

When the movie ended and we began the drive home, I'd curl up under my blanket, close my eyes and smile while my body rocked as the car made its familiar turns. I was happy—we'd been to the drive-in.   —Doris Stroud
Paducah, Kentucky

Charles Farrell

Janet Gaynor

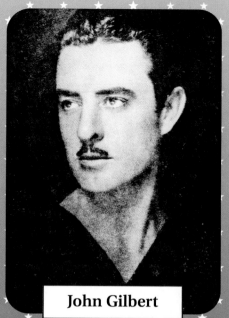

John Gilbert

Laura La Plante

'20s Movie Stars Had Her Moonstruck

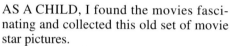

AS A CHILD, I found the movies fascinating and collected this old set of movie star pictures.

One of the first movies I ever saw was *Seventh Heaven* with Charles Farrell and Janet Gaynor, which was released in 1927. One of the songs from the film was *If I Had a Talking Picture of You*.

We were shopping one day and bought a recording of the song for our hand-cranked Victrola. Sadly, the first time we played the record, our poor canary fell dead off his roost!—*Grace Rainey, Whiting, New Jersey*

Ronald Colman

Gary Cooper

Gloria Swanson

Mary Nolan

Silver Screen Inspired 'Silver City'

By Robert Hill
Fort Mill, South Carolina

I WAS standing in line at a movie theater some years ago when a voice behind me said, "Hey, Bobby, let's go to Silver City." It was my old friend Randolph Spillers, and as boyhood pals, we'd gone to Silver City almost every day.

Silver City was our pretend Western town, complete with jail, saloon and corral. My friends and I built it in a gully behind our houses. The "buildings" were burlap sacks strung over poles, the jail had bars made of skinned tree branches, and the saloon's plank bar was held together with rusty nails. But to us, Silver City was very real.

Our inspiration came from the Saturday matinees. Our heroes were *real* cowboys like Buck Jones, Ken Maynard and Hoot Gibson—cowboys who would *never* be caught playing a guitar or kissing a girl. It just wasn't done.

Each of us assumed the identity of our favorite cowboy. There was never any doubt about who I'd be. I was hooked on Buck Jones. (Once I wrote him a letter and received an autographed photo, with a letter addressing me as "Dear Friend". Me, a friend of Buck Jones!)

Nearly every day after school, we'd ride our faithful stick horses into town and tie them at the rail in front of the saloon. Wallace Rogers was the saloon keeper—a fact I'm sure he kept from his Baptist minister father.

Wallace was our only real entrepreneur, selling soft drinks in toothpick holders for 50¢ each. We used milk bottle stoppers for 50¢ pieces, and soft drink caps for quarters. Wallace's papier-mache cash box was full of both, and he emptied it periodically so he could announce his new net worth.

We never walked through town. We mounted our stick horses wherever we went, urging them on with spurs fashioned from coat hangers and Coca-Cola caps. Most of us carried stamped tin pistols from the five-and-dime, but George Rogers whittled his own six-shooter, complete with smoothed bark to simulate handle grips. Needless to say, it was much admired in Silver City.

I was the sheriff, but I didn't have to campaign for the job—just build the jail. The sheriffing business was slow sometimes, as the citizens didn't always allow me to incarcerate them.

We solved that by allowing some younger kids, including Randolph, into Silver City. They were so eager to join our elite ranks that they didn't mind playing jailbirds…

Someone was calling my name. It was Randolph, now leaving the theater. "How'd you like the movie?" he asked.

"Huh?" I said. "To tell you the truth, I didn't really see that movie. I was in Silver City the whole time." ❧

DOWN THE HATCH. The fellows in this old movie still shot down their swill as Hoot Gibson (left) looks on. As Robert Hill recalls, Hoot was one of the Western stars emulated in his boyhood memories of "Silver City".

Marshall Prescott/Unicorn Stock Photos

OLD-TIMER TUNER. Sometimes, you had to work for your entertainment. There was an art to honing in on the few radio stations available in the old days...but the satisfaction of finally tuning in to a faraway station was all part of the fun.

Grandfather Turned Radio Listening Into a Knee-Slapping Adventure

By James Adams
Durham, North Carolina

MY GRANDFATHER was a wonderful guy I called "Papa". He was a man of few words, with a dry sense of humor, and as a boy of 8, I thought one of his special gifts was subtly building an insignificant event into a humming adventure.

When we sat on the porch that ran the length of his unpainted, tin-roofed house in central Mississippi, I'd ask if we could listen to the radio.

Papa's homemade hickory rocker, with its stretched black-and-white cowhide seat, would continue its slow rhythm. "Maybe," he'd say, not looking at me. "What day is it, anyway?" (He *knew* it was Saturday.)

He might muse a bit about the pretty sunset...or whether I should try to teach his dog to talk. Then he'd suddenly say, "If we're going to keep the skeeters off, best you be gettin' some cow patties lit, don't you think?"

Homemade Bug Repellent

I was off the porch fast as the flash of lightning bugs. I grabbed the bucket from under the porch, ran to the cow lot for five or six dried patties and raced back to light them. The smoke crept up around the porch in the still night air,

banishing any mosquitoes to the front yard.

Meanwhile, Papa removed the 6-volt battery from his Chevrolet coupe and put it near a screened window on the porch. The wires from the radio in the front room protruded through a small, neat hole in the screen.

Then he would pull his watch from his bib overalls, squint at it and silently

---

"He's shucking down the corn on this one, ain't he?"

---

put it back in his pocket. I could hardly stand the suspense.

"How much longer, Papa?"

"Oh, 'bout as long as a piece of rope with a knot in it, or 10 minutes or so ...I'm not sure."

I didn't know anything about rope with knots, or even how long 10 minutes might be. So I'd silently count to 100, then 200. Somewhere between 300

and 400, I would get bored and quit.

It didn't matter anyway. I knew that Papa would turn on that radio at precisely 7:30. It would be tuned to WSM, the 100,000-watt station from Nashville, Tennessee, and we would listen to the *Grand Ole Opry* for exactly 1 hour.

Hour of Fun

We'd listen, laugh and compare the talents of performers like Roy Acuff, Minnie Pearl, the Stanley Brothers and Doc Watson.

During a lively number, Papa would slap his leg and say things like, "He's shucking down the corn on this one, ain't he?" Papa was a self-taught fiddler, and he always told me ahead of time when one of the musicians was about to mimic a steam-engine whistle or the sound of yelping hounds.

This happy hour of sharing and learning ended at 8:30, during the fourth commercial break. Papa would get up in the middle of a Martha White flour commercial, turn off the radio, unhook the battery and carry it back to the car, saying, "Don't want to run the battery down all the way, now do we?"

What memories, being there on the porch with Papa and his radio. ❧

Early Radio Buffs Built Their Own

RADIO WAS big entertainment in the 1920s, but in the early days when equipment for households was just being developed, most people bought components and built their own.

My brother-in-law put together a conglomerate of batteries, wires and tubes popularly called a superheterodyne. Surprisingly, it worked. In Chicago, Monday was "silent night", with no local broadcasts, so enthusiasts could try for "distance". Tuesday was devoted to bragging about getting stations from California or New York.

My effort was to build a crystal set, made by wrapping coils of copper wire around a Quaker Oats box and connecting the wire to a sensitive crystal controlled by a "cat's whisker". All of this was attached to my bedspring, which served as an antenna. Tuning was accomplished by a slider on the coil.

The best program came on at 10 p.m.—Wayne King broadcasting from the Aragon Ballroom. I went to bed with the earphones in place and usually woke up around 2 a.m. with the earpiece in my eye or around my neck.

By 1930, radio was growing up and so was I. With a loan from my sister, I bought a beautiful 1929 Pontiac convertible. Car radios were practically unheard-of, but I wanted one. I obtained a small radio, wound copper wire inside the top for an antenna and connected more wire to the battery. It worked—I could tune in stations up to 75 miles away.

—*George Biringer*
Bella Vista, Arkansas

Neighbors Heard the Latest News Together

ONE OF OUR neighbors had the first radio in Greensboro, North Carolina.

He was a thoughtful man, and whenever something was on that would interest his neighbors, he'd bring the radio to the front porch and turn up the volume. Everyone gathered on his porch, or on those of his closest neighbors, to listen.

I remember sitting in the yard one night as we all sat in perfect quiet as we listened to a championship boxing match. Nobody called it that, though—we called it a prizefight.

When the local station broadcast election returns, we all gathered again to see how the candidates were doing. In those days, it took a long time for the ballots to be counted and carried in from the polling places to election headquarters.

Returns often came in all night, so about 11 p.m., the kind neighbor would apologetically turn the radio off, as all the men had to get up early for work the next day. We'd read the rest of the election results in the morning paper.

—*Eunice Pitchford*
Hendersonville, North Carolina

FOLKS WERE SOLD ON RADIO. Leona Weber of Markesan, Wisconsin shared this 1930s advertisement from her keepsakes. For $285, this radio-phonograph combination offered a "rich brown walnut cabinet with satin finish, super-heterodyne circuit and nine tubes...*tone* control and new, improved electrical phonograph reproduction, including home recordings."

Radio Got Brief Workout During Joe Louis Fight

IN THE 1930s, my brothers and I used to stretch out on the floor on our stomachs, watching the radio and listening to old favorites like *Inner Sanctum*, *The Whistler* and *I Love a Mystery* (with Jack, Doc and Reggie).

One evening when Mother and Dad had gone to the movie on bank night, Dad came rushing in to tell us he'd won $175. In those days, that was like winning the lottery. The first thing we bought was a new radio with an electric eye that moved in an arc. The closer the lines came together, the clearer the station.

Not long after that, Dad invited all the neighbors over to listen to the Joe Louis fight. He moved the radio out onto the lawn with lots of extension cords.

Everyone came over, and Dad went inside to get a basin of popcorn Mother had made. By the time he got back, the fight was over. Joe Louis had thrown one punch and knocked out his opponent!

—*Kenneth Givens*
Las Vegas, Nevada

Gail Denham

"Sum Fun" Added Up to Some Fun Times with Mom

IN THE LATE 1930s, a radio station in Des Moines, Iowa produced a show called *Sum Fun.*

Listeners were instructed to note every number they heard in a brief story that was read during the show, then send in the sum of the numbers to the station. The first listeners to send in the correct sums won prizes.

I liked that program, because my usually harried mother always stopped working to enjoy the game with us.

—*E.H. Jones*
Bellingham, Washington

Birthday Girl Waited To Hear Name On the Radio

MY FAMILY lived on a small farm in Kentucky, and on my fifth birthday in 1927, I was allowed to use the earphones to our crystal set and listen to the radio for the first time.

My father usually listened to the news then, but on this day, "Big Ford and Little Glen" at WHAS in Louisville were going to read the names of those who had birthdays and had sent in a card.

I listened with great anticipation, but my name was never called. I cried and accused my mother of forgetting to mail the card.

Meanwhile, my father took the earphones back to listen to the rest of the program. Afterward, he said Big Ford and Little Glen promised to send autographed postcards to those whose names weren't read. I figured he was just saying that so I'd stop crying.

A few days later, though, I did receive an autographed postcard from them. I was one happy little girl. And I laughed and laughed when I saw what the hosts looked like—Big Ford was little, and Little Glen was big! I treasured that postcard and I still have it.

—*Wanza Staley, Jupiter, Florida*

REMEMBER "BREAKFAST IN HOLLYWOOD"? Sarajane Cebula (left) of Fort Bragg, California was on the set of this morning radio show February 2, 1949. "One thing they did was to interview the oldest person in the audience," recalls Sara. "My parents, Henry and Jane (center) are pictured here with my 85-year-old grandmother, Ernestine Rissi. She was visiting us in southern California and had the honor of being picked for the interview with the master of ceremonies. She even sang a song with a voice that was still quite strong! She lived to be 98."

THE EASY LIFE was looking at pictures to the accompaniment of a '40s Philco superheterodyne radio.

They Couldn't "Name That Tune", But They Enjoyed Prizes

IN 1950, my family was called for *Name That Tune*, the popular radio program hosted by Jack Bailey. They called a half hour before the show went on the air, so I ran and got all the neighbors to help us identify the song. The operator talked to my dad about everything under the sun until the show started.

Then Jack Bailey came on the line and asked Dad's name and where we were from. We were then informed of the prizes we could win. If we named the tune, we'd win a chrome dinette set. If we didn't, we'd get a Dormeyer electric mixer, a french fryer, a toaster and a treasure chest of Old Gold cigarettes.

When the big moment came, everyone was speechless. No one knew that tune! It turned out to be *The Turkish March*, and I haven't heard it since that night. But we did have fun with our new appliances, and milk shakes and french fries became our favorites. —*Deanna Provines, Auburn, Illinois*

Behind-the-Scenes View Ruined the Make-Believe

MY FAVORITE Saturday radio show was called *Let's Pretend*, "brought to you by Cream of Wheat". (By the way, I can still sing the jingle.)

My Aunt Helen knew I loved the show, so she decided to give me a big surprise. With great secrecy, she took me to New York City one Saturday morning, a trip of about 30 miles. We stood in line with a bunch of kids and their parents, then went into a big room with a slightly raised stage. It was the studio of the *Let's Pretend* show.

I tried to keep up a good front for my well-meaning aunt, but my illusions were destroyed when I saw all those radio actors in street clothes standing in front of microphones, reading scripts, while two other people did the sound effects. The show was never quite the same for me again! —*Philip May, Parksley, Virginia*

"Hey, Mister, Can You Tell Me Why..."

REMEMBER Fibber McGee's long drawn-out answers to little Molly's questions? I was just a kid when we listened to that show, but I still recall two of his explanations.

"Hey, mister," Molly asked, "why is a fire engine painted red?"

"Well, kid, a fire engine is a truck, and it's in the trucking business. Trucking is a dance where you use your feet. Twelve inches is a foot, and a foot is a ruler. The present ruler is King George, and he married Queen Mary.

"The *Queen Mary* is a ship that sails on the ocean. There are fish in the ocean, and fish have fins. The Fins were defeated by the Reds. The Reds are Russians. A fire engine is always rushin', so it's painted red."

And how about this one: "Hey, mister, what's a double petunia?"

"Well, kid, a petunia is a flower, like a begonia. Begonia is meat, like sausage. Sausage and battery is a crime. Monkeys crime trees, and tree's a crowd. The rooster crowd at dawn and made a noise.

"Your noise is on your face, sometimes called the nase. A horse neighs and has a colt. You get a colt and go to bed and wake up in the morning with double petunia." —*Helen Foreman Hamilton, Ontario*

Boys Acted Out Parts From High Seas Drama

ONE RADIO PROGRAM I never missed in 1935 was *Cap'n Cracker and His Crumby Crew* spondered by the American Biscuit Company.

Cap'n Cracker sailed the seas and had marvelous adventures with Petey the cabin boy and crewmen Wong and Orange. Petey was my age, and I really identified with him.

In one episode, the characters were on a desert island and found a sea chest hidden in a cave. With great care, Cap'n started to open the lid, then he yelled, "No, it can't be. Petey, help me!"

The show abruptly went to a commercial. We'd have to wait until the next day to find out what happened.

WARM REMINDER. Burke Waldron of Carson City, Nevada received this cozy family photo while serving in the Navy during the '40s. That's his picture on the radio.

We were used to making our own entertainment, so we went to the hayloft and acted out all the parts. Of course, I played Petey. When we got to the climax, I looked into the chest. "Snakes!" I cried. "Wong, Orange, help me save the Cap'n!"

We had great fun wrestling in the hay, fighting off imaginary snakes.

The next day, we were glued to the radio to see if our guess had been correct. We were disappointed to learn that all that was in the chest was just treasure—gold coins, jewels and stuff like that.

I'm surprised today that I can't find anyone who remembers my favorite program! —*Ralph Blois Woodburn, Oregon*

Singing Commercials Sold This Listener

MY FIRST full-time job working in Philadelphia permitted the acquisition of a "big-ticket" item—a radio. Listening to sports, news, weather, plays, serials and the like was fun, but the most fascinating to me were the singing commercials.

One in particular had such a catchy tune and was sung in such pleasant,

close harmony that I still remember it 55 years later. The song went: "We feed our doggy Thrive-O, he's very much alive-o, full of pep and vim. If you want a peppy pup, you better hurry up, buy Thrive-O for him." —*Wes Faurot, Los Altos, California*

Her Favorites Were Real Fist-Clenchers

I WAS rather a tomboy at heart, so my favorite radio shows were *The Green Hornet, Sergeant Preston of the Yukon* and *The Lone Ranger.* The adventures they had eliminating the bad guys had me sitting on the floor in front of our tall Philco radio with my hands clenched, spurring them on.

My father didn't approve of these kinds of programs for his daughter, so I kept the volume so low I had to keep my ear an inch from the speaker.

Since I had a very early bedtime, I enjoyed Fibber McGee and Charlie McCarthy from my bedroom, which was directly over the den where the radio was. There was a heating vent in the floor, and I'd sneak out of bed and lay on the floor with my ear pressed to the grate to listen.

It was fun to outwit my parents. I guess they never realized what treasures these programs would become in later years. —*Mrs. Arthur Koller Rockport, Massachusetts*

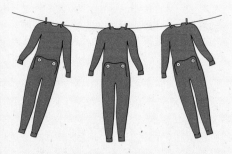

"Dancing Long Johns" Made Spooky Show Even Scarier

EVERY Friday night, Mom would turn on the radio so my brother, sister and I could listen to *Inner Sanctum*. A door would slowly open with an eerie, screechy, spooky sound, then a scary story would be acted out. To make it even more scary, we asked Mom to put out all the lights in the house.

Back then, there were no clothes dryers, and everyone hung their laundry outside to dry. On this particular November day, it had rained and Mom had to bring the wash inside to hang in the dining room to finish drying.

As we listened to that night's show, I glanced into the darkened kitchen and noticed my father's long johns starting to move slightly. Suddenly they began to jump around wildly, and we children screamed in fear.

Mom quickly turned on the lights, and we all laughed. We had been terrorized by our cat, who was playing with the legs of Dad's long underwear.

I can remember quite clearly that the next time we wanted to watch our favorite Friday night program, we asked our mother to please leave a small lamp on!

—*Elizabeth Steiner*
St. Paul, Minnesota

Radio Mystery Provided Special Time with Dad

THERE WERE several good mystery programs on the radio when I was about 8 years old, but Dad and I had a favorite—*The Flo Gardner Mysteries*.

After supper, Dad would sit in the rocking chair in front of the radio, smoking his pipe and reading the paper. As soon as the *Flo Gardner* theme song started, pipe and newspaper would be put aside, and I'd crawl up on his lap.

The program held us both spellbound (I later found out the name of the theme song was *Death*). When I got scared, Dad would hold me a bit tighter, reassuring me that everything would turn out okay and that Flo would be back again next week.

—*June Johnson*
Eau Claire, Wisconsin

Oil Can Silenced Famous Squeaking Door

ONE OF OUR neighbors in Rockville Centre, New York was a kindly senior citizen named Stuart McQuade. He was loved by all the neighbors, kids and adults and alike.

For many years, Mr. McQuade worked for NBC Radio in New York City as a sound effects man. One of his responsibilities (he told me so himself) was handling all the sound effects for the popular radio show *Inner Sanctum*. I was proud to know someone so important.

Remember the door that squeaked at the beginning of each show? Mr. McQuade *built* that door, and it took him a long time to get it to squeak just the way he wanted it. He operated it lovingly each week on the live broadcast.

One day he came to the studio on the day of the show and found that a well-meaning maintenance man had oiled the door's hinges so it wouldn't squeak!

Mr. McQuade spent most of the day frantically trying to remedy the situation. He was much relieved when he got the door squeaking properly again.

—*Paul Williams, Apopka, Florida*

ENID THE FLOOR SHOW. Kathy Shrake (below left) of Lakewood, Wisconsin recalls fun in '53 when this photo was snapped. She and sisters Joanne (center) and Sharon spent hours reading Classics Illustrated Comics and listening to radio favorites *Mr. Keene, Tracer of Lost Persons, FBI in Peace & War, Duffy's Tavern, The Life of Riley, Cisco Kid* and *Jack Benny*.

Broadcast Over the *Scarewaves*

She Was Thrilled to Meet Voice of "The Shadow"

IN 1939, I started working as a secretary for Rothschild Bros. Hat Co. and Stetson Glove Co. in Chicago, Illinois. (Those were the days when all men wore hats and ladies wore gloves or else we weren't properly dressed!)

One of the salesmen for these companies was Mr. Morrison, and one day his son came in to buy a hat. Imagine my delight to learn he was Brett Morrison, the man who played "The Shadow" on radio! Even before I was introduced to him, there was no mistaking his distinctive voice. I'd always been a fan of the show, but I was an even bigger fan after that.

—*Dorothy Cole, Mesa, Arizona*

Young Fans of "The Shadow" Listened in Rapt Silence

MY SISTERS and I listened to *The Shadow* in complete silence—it was one of the few times we didn't speak. We'd hurry through homework, chores and dinner to get to our favorite spot in front of the Philco by 7 p.m.

The radio sat on a table in our living room, allowing us to get as close as possible to the speaker and muffle any sounds from the kitchen. With the shades drawn, the only light came from a small low-voltage lamp that gave the room an eerie glow. A perfect setting.

"Shush, here it comes!" my oldest sister commanded as soon as she heard the music. From then on, we hardly dared to breathe.

Lost in our own imaginations, we were transfixed, and when the program was over, it took a few seconds to regain our composure and get back to reality. Afterward, we girls relived the episode and excitement, chattering like magpies.

Between weekly shows, our imaginations worked long and hard. Then on Saturday nights, shortly after dusk, we'd gather in the narrow confines of the dimly lit second-story stairwell to make up our own spooky stories.

My only regret is that we failed to record those tales for posterity!

—*Mary Elizabeth Martucci South Bend, Indiana*

Youngster Thought Characters On Radio Could See Her

ONE NIGHT when I was about 8 years old, my cousin Marie and I were listening to *Inner Sanctum* on my family's black Emerson radio.

Just as Marie opened the door to the refrigerator, a voice from the radio said, "Don't open that door". We were scared silly, and from then on, I thought the people on the radio could see us.

—*Joyce Christian Fayetteville, North Carolina*

Radio Howl Brought Out "Beast" in Family Pet

IT WAS 56 years ago, but I remember it as though it was yesterday. Dad was away on a business trip in Philadelphia, and Mother and I were sitting on the couch listening to a scary radio program called *The Witch's Tale*.

On this night, the story featured a howling dog, and at just the moment the radio dog howled, our German shepherd burst through the drapes of the adjoining room with her eyes glowing from the reflected light of our dim living room lamp!

Needless to say, our hair stood on end and we both jumped about a foot off the couch!

I also remember a program called *Grand Central Station, Crossroads of the World*. They had some great stories about

WOULD SOMEONE P-P-PLEASE TURN ON THE LIGHTS? This photo of her captivated nephew and niece was shared by Betty Mochnick of Sun City, Arizona. "My husband joined the Coast Guard in 1942 and was stationed in Seattle," explains Betty. "I stored our furniture before moving out there, but gave the radio to his sister for her family to enjoy. She sent us this picture of Stan and Norma listening to their favorite program, *The Shadow*."

MYSTERIOUS ORIGINS. Wooda Carr of Fort Wayne, Indiana still has a copy of this pulp mystery magazine upon which radio's *Detective Story* was based in 1930. The program was introduced by a narrator called The Shadow, who had a penetrating voice and macabre laugh. His popularity with listeners led to *The Shadow* airing from 1937-1954. This Shadow was amateur criminologist Lamont Cranston, who could hypnotically fog men's minds so that they couldn't see him. The program started with Orson Welles as Cranston and Agnes Moorehead as Margo Lane, his assistant and the only one who knew his real identity.

The kitchen was the hub of our home. During winter, Mother had her rocking chair in there, so she could sit and shell peas or mend our clothes. In the evenings, we kids gathered around the kitchen table to do our homework and listen to *The Inner Sanctum* with its well-known squeaking door.

One night, Mother Nature made a particularly exciting episode even more thrilling by sending us a thunderstorm. The climax of the story was imminent and the famous door began to squeak. Just then, our kitchen door opened and a mysterious figure in a white sheet glided into the room.

You've never seen three children—nor their mother, for that matter—scream so loudly or move so fast! Of course, it was only Daddy, seizing the moment to bring a little excitement to our quiet country life.   —*Janice Hulsizer*
Florence, Alabama

Daughter Enjoyed Sharing Shows with Parents

MY FAVORITE radio show was *Inner Sanctum*, with the squeaky-creaky door that sent chills up my spine. Dad loved the news with Gabriel Heatter, his favorite newscaster, and no one ever missed *The Lone Ranger*. Even little girls loved that program.

Mom would darn socks or catch up on mending during our favorite daytime shows. I'd dampen the clothes with the sprinkle bottle and Mom would iron while we listened to *Grand Central Station* and *Stella Dallas*.

I can still see my mom and dad in my mind's eye, enjoying those programs. I enjoyed them, too, because it meant quiet time with my parents.   —*Geraldine Karl*
Selden, New York

"Lights Out" Brightened Scary Sunday Ritual

GROWING UP on a Vermont dairy farm in the 1940s, we had a Sunday night ritual we still enjoy reminiscing about.

My brothers, sisters and I would line up our chairs on either side of Mom and Dad in a semicircle in front of the wood-burning stove in the kitchen. The lights would be turned out and the radio, which sat on a wall shelf behind us, was turned on.

The opening of the program began with the ominous voice saying, "Who knows what evil lurks in the hearts of men? The Shadow knows!" followed by a blood-curdling laugh. We'd listen to *The Shadow* and let our imaginations run away until the show closed with "The weed of crime bears bitter fruit…the Shadow knows."

Right after that, the lights would be turned on again and Mom or Dad would announce bedtime. It was scary, but we all loved it.   —*Martha Hyne, Bakersfield, Vermont*

people just in on the train. The show started with the sound of a steam locomotive coming into the station, and my perfectionist dad always said that no steam engines were allowed into the city, only electric!

I guess during "radio days" your imagination really worked overtime.   —*E.W. Tanner, Harriman, New York*

Mischievous Dad Added To Show's Scary Thrill

MY DAD worked the late shift, so we children learned to be quiet while he was sleeping.

MESMERIZED by the screen of this 1950s set, how much do you bet these boys grew up to tell *their* kids not to watch so much TV!

"Winky Dink" Viewers Helped Hero Out of Jams

A CLEVER SHOW in the 1950s was called *Winky Dink*. The gimmick was that you sent away for a clear plastic sheet to fit over your screen. Then you could draw on it with the "official" crayons to help Winky in his adventures, like filling in a bridge when Winky needed one.

Unfortunately, patience wasn't one of my virtues. The screen took 5 weeks to arrive, and Winky needed my help! So when my father turned on the set for a baseball game, he was not amused to find a red and blue barn where left field was supposed to be!

Looking back, my friends and I managed to clock in an enormous amount of time in front of the tube, yet still read and play baseball, tease girls and drag ourselves to school. I'd cringe when my father lectured me on how different and how much better his boyhood was, but looking at the way kids are today, I understand how he felt. Sometimes I even miss Howdy!

—*Harold Callahan, Dayton, Ohio*

Family Fell Under TV's Spell

By Cookie Curci-Wright, San Jose, California

AUNT ANN and Uncle Pete lived on a small ranch outside of town, and their house was always full of relatives. Each room of the big house seemed to bustle with activity.

The men gathered around the big oak dining room table for their weekly card game while Grandma Maria and the ladies worked and talked in the kitchen, preparing that night's dinner.

My grandfather, "Papa Tony", could always be found in a comfortable old rocker on the back porch, watching me and my cousins play for hours on the tree swings he'd built.

When Aunt Ann and Uncle Pete bought a TV, everything began to change. Most of the rooms were quiet and empty, except for the room that held the TV. It became filled with relatives young and old, staring through the darkness at a flickering black-and-white picture on a 10-inch screen. Everyone had fallen completely under television's spell. Everyone, that is, but Papa Tony.

A Passing Fancy

He stayed outside on the porch in the evenings, content to rock and enjoy the night air with a small glass of his homemade red wine and his dog, "Tippy" by his side. Television was just a passing fancy, he figured. Things would soon return to normal at the ranch. Besides, he suspected this glowing "box of light" was somehow going to damage our eyesight.

Years later, Edward R. Murrow took his cameras to Venice, Rome and Naples, broadcasting glorious scenes of Italy back to America. *Now* Papa Tony was impressed. This wonderful device could bring the sights and sounds of his beloved old country directly into his living room!

INTO OUR LIVING ROOMS and into our lives came the TV, which even looks to have "posed" with the family in this 1950 photo.

Before long, Papa even talked Grandma into setting up TV trays so he could watch his favorite adventure shows, *Rin-Tin-Tin* and *Flash Gordon*, during the dinner hour.

A short time later, Dad bought us a television, a beautiful mahogany Packard Bell. I knew we wouldn't be going to Aunt Ann and Uncle Pete's so often anymore. Now we'd be spending more time at home in front of our own TV, with our own TV lamp, TV trays and, eventually, our own TV repairman.

We were now a '50s TV family. A new and exciting world awaited us, and we were anxious to become a part of this wonderful adventure. ❧

'Pay-Per-View' Is Nothing New

By Marjorie Baker, San Antonio, Texas

PAY-PER-VIEW TELEVISION wasn't invented in the '90s. We enjoyed it in the early 1950s with our first set.

In those days, Zenith, Bendix and other manufacturers made televisions with a coin collection box on the back. A quarter slipped into the box would buy several hours of programming.

Each member of the family tried to save up quarters to watch favorite programs. In our household, the No. 1 priority was Dad's wrestling matches, while *Kukla, Fran and Ollie* and *The Lone Ranger* took top billing for us kids.

Other favorites included *I Was a Communist for the FBI*, *The Hit Parade*, *What's My Line?* and *The $64,000 Question*. There were family shows, too—*I Love Lucy*, *Ozzie and Harriet*, *The Life of Riley* and shows featuring comedians Red Skelton and Jack Benny.

Invariably, the meter would run out at the most crucial part of a program, sending us on a frantic search for more quar-

ters. It was so frustrating to be in the middle of a show and then be unable to come up with the money to watch the ending.

I was talking to a friend who was a distributor of metered televisions back then, and he said this was a common problem. His company received many phone calls from viewers wanting to know the outcome of a program—especially *Queen for a Day* and *As the World Turns*, Mother's favorite daytime shows.

One reason that pay-per-view didn't last is that too many people learned ways to activate the meter without putting in money. When the box was opened and the funds were insufficient to make the payment, those people often lost their televisions.

When I told my brother about this recently, he admitted that he sometimes used a clothes hanger to trip the meter on our TV. I wonder if that's the reason why we didn't have our set longer! 🌀

"We Had Lawn Spots for The Sullivan Show"

MY SISTER and her husband were the first in our community of Luther, Texas to buy a television set in the 1950s. The nearest station was about 100 miles away, so the reception was a little snowy, but we didn't mind.

On Sunday nights, the whole family gathered at their house and spread blankets on the grass. My brother-in-law put the TV in the window, and we had our own private drive-in theater.

That's where we first saw the Beatles and Elvis Presley, on the Ed Sullivan show. We hardly ever missed it, unless it rained—and in West Texas, it rarely did!

—*Louise Stanley*
Big Spring, Texas

SADDLED NEXT TO THE SET, Julia Mahoney watches the family's first TV, which only got one station. Ann Follansbee of Milwaukee, Wisconsin shared the 1953 photo of her grandmother.

Favorite Shows Served Up with Special Supper

WHEN GRANDMA came to live with us in 1954, she brought her television with her.

On Thursday nights, she'd cash her paycheck and stop by the store to get all the fixings for homemade hamburgers, plus potato chips and Cokes. How we loved those suppers she made for us!

We enjoyed our meal while watching *Rin-Tin-Tin* and *Dragnet* on TV. We had a houseful of people, but that was the one night of the week it was absolutely quiet. The only sound came from the television and the fire popping in the wood stove that heated our tiny living room.

—*Annie McCoy*
Cartersville, Georgia

HAVIN' A BIG TIME on the midway at the Indiana State Fair, these lads perched atop a gentle beast are in for pure wonderment. With the music of the carousel and aromas of cotton candy and fried delicacies (guaranteed to spoil supper) in the air, this memory from yesteryear surely lasted a lifetime.

Chapter Seven
On with the Show!

State fair, showboats, Chautauquas and the big top
were just a few of the dazzling events we enjoyed.

It's almost impossible for recent generations to imagine a time when you couldn't have dazzling entertainment at the flick of a switch. Exciting diversions were fewer and farther between in the pre-television days, so you often had weeks of delicious anticipation before the actual event came to town.

What a day it was when billboards were papered with posters announcing the circus was coming. Elephants! Lions! Death-defying aerialists! Peanuts and cotton candy! Clowns! Time crawled by.

An annual event was the county fair with its rides and barkers and harness races and night-time grandstand show. And if you were a 4-H kid with a prize calf to show or a homemaker with an entry in the quilt competition, you spent weeks getting ready for the fair.

Then there were the traveling tent shows...the Marguerite Bryant Show in Pennsylvania and New York, "Goofy Goffs Comedians" in Texas, and dozen of others. They featured comedians, melodramas, an orchestra, and quite likely a magician and a trained animal act.

If you lived along the Ohio River, you could enjoy the *Majestic* showboat, which was a regular theater built on a barge and pushed by a tugboat. One of the members of the show, Lanya Bump, recalls that many of the places they played weren't even towns, just landings on the river. The only advertising was a huge steam calliope mounted on top of the showboat. It could be heard 20 miles away and was all the notice needed to draw a crowd at night.

Crowd Was Under Their Spell

There also were traveling medicine shows that provided free entertainment in return for a chance to sell "magic elixirs" to the crowd. Believe it or not, the show wasn't half bad, either!

I also remember attending a Chautauqua one summer. It was in town for a week, and the programs were held in an enormous tent. The audience sat on wooden benches and the bare ground was covered with sawdust. Oratory was a much-admired skill in those days, and you got to hear a lot of it at a Chautauqua—inspirational speeches, patriotic speeches, plus poetry and readings from the classics. There was also, as I recall, music and lighter stuff, but the programs were considerably more highbrow than tent shows.

The monster event of the '30s was the Chicago World's Fair. There hadn't been one of that scope since the St. Louis Exposition at the turn of the century, so people came from all over the United States. Its theme was "The Century of Progress".

There were lavish corporate exhibits filled with a glimpse of the exciting products that were in store for us. An outdoor amphitheater featured frequent performances by "The A&P Gypsies" from the popular radio show sponsored by the grocery chain.

The midway was the biggest and most exciting anyone had ever seen, and an aerial tramway gave you a knee-knocking view of the grounds from a dizzying height. Our family went there for a full day and didn't begin to see it all. The Century of Progress was so successful that New York staged its own exposition in 1939.

Nowadays, I can get 3 hours of pretty good entertainment any night of the week. But when I had to wait a month for 3 hours of entertainment, it somehow was more thrilling and memorable. Mom was right—anticipation is a big part of enjoyment.
—*Clancy Strock*

Her 'Wild' Uncle Volney

By Joanne Rains, Cincinnati, Ohio

IT WAS SUMMER 1933, and my 7-year-old brother and I were sitting inches away from a snarling lion, waiting for our uncle to take our picture.

In a cage right behind us was "Leo", the world-famous MGM lion. Our adventurous uncle had raised and trained Leo, and they'd performed together all over North America on promotional tours for MGM. Uncle Volney would pull into a small town, set up Leo's ornate cage in front of the theater and have him roar on cue. His roar carried so far that people came from all directions.

Now Leo was the main attraction at the Chicago World's Fair, and we were close enough to hear every growl.

Just the day before, we'd been safe at home in St. Louis—until Uncle Volney and Aunt Eloise dropped in.

"We stopped by to take you to the World's Fair," he said. "We have to make the jump back to Chicago tonight, so we leave right after supper."

Mother didn't even hesitate. "We'll be ready," she said.

We were always ready for excitement when Uncle Volney showed up. As a teenager, he "rode the rails" just to see the country. He trapped wild animals in South America and Africa, then trained them for carnivals and circuses. He'd been mauled by a tiger and injured by an angry elephant.

Started with a Scare

In Chicago, we took the streetcar to the fair. As I ran up the wide promenade, an earth-shattering screech stopped me in my tracks. I looked up and saw a gigantic monster coming right at me! There was nothing to do but run for it. Behind me, over the creature's terrible roar, I heard Mother calling, "Joanne, wait!"

When the others caught up, Mother explained I'd just seen one of the life-size dinosaurs at the Sinclair Oil display. Taking my hand, she walked me back to show me how harmless they were.

Uncle Volney took us to the MGM display after lunch. The building looked like a huge straw hat, with giant cutouts of MGM stars around the brim. A big sign on the crown read "Hollywood".

Next door was Leo, in a cage surrounded by artificial rocks and tropical foliage for a "jungle effect". A picket fence kept the viewing public about 10 feet from the cage.

At Uncle Volney's signal, Leo let out a series of roars that seemed to shake the ground. "You can hear Leo all over these fairgrounds," Uncle Volney said proudly. "It really brings in the people."

Uncle Volney took a few pictures of us standing in front of the fence, then announced, "This time I'll get the punks" (his generic term for children) "with Leo." Before we knew it, we were *inside* the outer fence, on the rocks in front of Leo's cage.

"We're awfully close to this lion," I whispered to my brother. We looked back and saw Leo's enormous yellow eyes staring right at us.

"He doesn't *want* us here," my brother whispered back. "Listen to him growl. He's making mad noises. But we can't show we're afraid."

My brother sat rigidly,

NICE KITTY! Though her brother, Volney (right), is all smiles, Joanne Rains (holding her cousin Ellis) was so nervous that she stuck her tongue out at her fearless uncle, who insisted on taking this shot near the MGM display at the 1933 World's Fair.

but I crouched, ready to spring down if I had to. It didn't help that Uncle Volney seemed to know everyone at the fair and was interrupted continually by people who wanted to chat!

While we waited, Leo sniffed at us, growled, licked his lips and shook his golden mane. But he, too, sat still, waiting for his trainer and friend to release him.

When someone gave me Uncle Volney's 7-month-old son to hold for another picture, the baby took one look at Leo and did the only sensible thing. He screamed.

I was normally a well-behaved child myself, but when Un-

Tamed the MGM Lion

cle Volney finally clicked the shutter, I stuck out my tongue. (I was shocked no one scolded me for such behavior to an adult.)

Uncle Volney offered to let us go into the cage with him to pet Leo, but we politely declined. He went in alone, and we watched as he romped with Leo and hugged him. I'm sure those two loved each other. With Uncle Volney, Leo was as affectionate as a pussycat.

After the fair closed, Leo lived in a special cage on the MGM lot in Hollywood. Later, MGM moved him to a zoo in Pennsylvania so Uncle Volney could visit him often.

In 1934, our family moved to Uncle Volney's farm in New Jersey. My father cared for the wild animals while Uncle Volney toured the country, promoting movies.

One day as I walked home from school, I saw Uncle Volney digging a deep hole in the front yard. It was a neat rectangle at least 5 feet deep and just as long. Uncle Volney stood at the bottom, digging with a pickax and shovel.

A Sad Task

"Hello, Uncle Volney," I said, standing at the edge of the hole.

"Hello, Joanne," he replied without looking up.

"What are you doing down there?" It was a bold question since Uncle Volney was very closed-mouthed about his business. He ignored me.

"Why are you digging this hole?" I persisted.

"I'm going to plant some flowers," he answered.

"But it's too cold to plant flowers, and your hole is too deep," I reasoned.

Now, a man who'd spent a good part of his life in a cage with wild lions and tigers had no trouble dispatching a curious fourth grader. His icy stare sent me scurrying to the house. When I returned from school the next day, our front yard contained a nicely mounded grave marked with a large metal stake.

"It's Leo," Mother explained. "He died a few days ago, and since your Uncle Volney trained and loved him, MGM officials shipped his body here by train. It came today, and Uncle Volney buried Leo. He feels sad, so don't bother him."

I delighted in telling my classmates, "You know that lion that roars at the beginning of the movies? He's buried in *my* front yard." When they looked at me in disbelief, I added, "If you don't believe me, come to my house and I'll show you."

When we moved back to St. Louis. I tried to tell the kids there about the famous lion in my front yard, but they thought I was making it all up.

Now, after all these years, Leo's famous again. My late uncle's farm is being sold, and a small dedicated group is trying to preserve Leo's grave. Leo is still buried in what was once my front yard. For a short time, I was very close indeed to that world-famous lion. 🎋

DYNAMIC DUO. Volney Phifer had no qualms standing next to a caged lion while on tour in the '30s. The MGM trademark, Leo was more like family.

A TIGER FOR TOURING. Volney holds his son, Ellis, with wife Eloise standing at his left. They're surrounded by the Page Kiddie Band—all helping Leo promote MGM studios in 1933.

AH...SETTING UP THE BIG TOP! A team effort made quick work driving in stakes for Ringling Brothers and Barnum & Bailey Circus.

Archive Photos/Thornton

about everything a boy could've ever wanted to do.
—Ermil Pitt
Allen Park, Michigan

Family Had Ringside Seats For Circus "Parade"

THE ONE NIGHT of the year we were allowed to stay up late was when the circus came to town.

The circus train arrived at the south end of town, then the whole procession traveled to the show grounds on the east end of town—right past our house!

We'd get up early and head for the porch, where we'd sit and watch the caravan travel down our street. We saw all the elephants, the cages holding the wild animals, the cotton candy wagon and wagons carrying the rides.

That afternoon, we'd go to the circus with our parents. When we returned home that evening, we sat on the porch and waited for the wagons and animals to pass again on their return to the train yards. By the time the last elephant lumbered past, it was usually after midnight.

What great days those were—I think I probably enjoyed the "parade" past our house more than the actual circus!
—Lillian Scieszka, Lansing, Michigan

"Pocket Omelet" Nearly Cost Boy Trip to Circus

WHEN I WAS 5, the grain elevators in Colusa, Illinois were home to some chickens no one seemed to own. The eggs were free to anyone who wanted them.

One morning after church, a friend and I went there to look for eggs to sell. We had nothing to carry them in, so we put them in the pockets of our Sunday school suits. Well, you guessed it—before I got home, I had a pocketful of scrambled eggs!

I emptied the mess as best I could and quietly hung my suit in the closet. Later that week, my folks decided to go to the circus in Burlington, Iowa. Everybody was getting ready to go—me included—but when I went to get my suit out, it dawned on me that I had a big problem.

When Mother noticed that I wasn't getting ready like the rest of the kids, she asked what was wrong. I told her the most unbelievable lie you could imagine: I told her I *didn't* want to go to the circus!

Well, Mother hustled me inside, got out my suit and discovered that smelly "omelet". Once she'd washed and ironed my suit—and given me a good lecture—I was filled with glee. I was going to the circus!

We rode in our horse and buggy to a livery in Dallas, Illinois, took a train to Burlington, then boarded a streetcar to the show grounds. There was even more excitement on the way when our streetcar jumped the tracks. Eventually, a bunch of men were able to lift it back on.

I don't recall much about the circus itself, except that it lasted longer than expected and there was a big crowd back at the streetcar stop afterward. By the time we finally reached the depot, our train had left.

So, with three other families, we hired a big boat to take us down the Mississippi River back to Dallas. It had been a hot day and everyone was tired, but the Mississippi was refreshingly cool and the water smooth as glass. Our boat was in the shade as the sun dipped behind the bluffs. At dusk, we landed at Dallas, found our horse and buggy and went on home.

What a day! I felt like I'd done just

'Armed' with Mama's Quick Thinking, We Made It Into the Circus

By Neva MacMaster, Williston, North Dakota

BURSTING THROUGH the screen door and dumping a small bag of groceries on the kitchen table, I gasped, "Mama, guess what's going to happen?"

"Must be something exciting," said my mother, lifting her flour-covered hands from the dough she was kneading.

"It sure is! The circus is coming to town a week from Saturday," I explained. "There's a big poster about it down at the grocery window."

"Well, won't that be a thrill!" Mama agreed. "There hasn't been one here since before the war. I'll talk to Papa—maybe all five of us can go."

The year was 1919 and the month was June. World War I had ended the November before and the country was getting back to normal. For a 10-year-old like myself, circus day was like Thanksgiving, Christmas or the Fourth of July.

The anticipation was almost more than I could bear. On the day of the circus, Papa had a business appointment in a neighboring town, so it was just Mama, me and my brother and sister.

In the past, admission had always been 50¢ for adults and 25¢ for children, so Mama took two silver dollars from her purse. That would cover tickets for her and three children, and leave 75¢ for treats.

There was a long line at the ticket booth. As we moved slowly forward, I quivered with impatience. Then, as we inched closer, my heart sank. A sign said admission was $1.25 for adults and 75¢ for children. We didn't have enough money! Tears welled in my eyes.

"Don't panic," Mama said. "There's small print at the bottom of the sign. We'll stay in line until we see what it says."

As we moved closer, we read the words: "Babes in arms admitted free."

"Do you think you could carry Louise?" Mother asked me after she'd thought a minute. "She only weighs 23 pounds."

Did Mama think *she* was going to carry 5-year-old Henry? He must've weighed 50 pounds! Besides, neither

SEATED RINGSIDE, these boys (inset) got to gaze at "the greatest show on earth", and thanks to a Mother's ingenuity, Neva MacMaster saw sparkling performers like those rehearsing above.

child was a baby. "We've come this far," Mama replied. "We're not giving up that easily."

I could barely tote my 2-year-old sister, and Mama lurched along with Henry before plunking down her two silver dollars in front of the ticket seller.

"One adult and one child's ticket," she said.

The man's cigar stub almost dropped from his mouth. "You can't get by with this, lady," he growled. "The sign says 'babes in arms'."

"These are my babies, and we're carrying them; and besides, that's all the money I have with me."

Gradually, a wry smile twisted the man's face. "Well, why not?" he said. "If you've got the nerve to ask, I'll be a good enough sport to let you in. Go ahead."

My heart pounding, we started toward the entrance gate. We'd only gone two steps when the ticket seller hollered after us, "And lady…if you get tired, put the kid down and let *him* carry you!🎪

Teens' Olympic Trek Was Quite an Event

By Hal Roberts, Milwaukie, Oregon

IN EARLY JULY 1932, my neighbor, Lew, my brother and myself were sitting on our back porch in Jennings Lodge, Oregon, reading about the 10th Olympic Games, which were about to start in Los Angeles.

Right then and there, we decided we were going. Although the Great Depression was raging and I'd just been laid off, I still had a few dollars left in the bank. Besides, this was a once-in-a-lifetime opportunity.

Lew and I wanted to hitchhike to Pasadena and stay with my aunt and uncle. Mother didn't like that idea, but suggested if we took my 13-year-old brother, Hugh, she would talk Dad into loaning us the car. My nephew, Jerry, also 13, was visiting us and wanted to come along, too.

AN OLYMPIC TRIP in Dad's 1930 Chevrolet is one Hal Roberts (right), his brother, Hugh (center), and nephew, Jerry, won't forget.

The first thing Dad said was that he didn't think the tires on our 1930 Chevrolet would make the trip. I bought two new ones and took another $100 out of my bank account for expenses. Lew scraped together $25 or $30 and Hugh and Jerry brought a little cash, too.

We left at 5 a.m. on July 27, driving narrow twisting roads and steep hills. Our top speed was about 40 mph. That evening we arrived at a cousin's home in Gerber, California, after traveling 530 miles. In 1932, that was a *lot* of driving.

After arriving in Pasadena a couple of days later, we drove to Los Angeles to buy tickets. We told the clerk we were strangers from Oregon and asked for the best tickets possible for 3 days of events. All the seats were great,

and the most expensive ticket, for track and field, cost only $2.

We saw some excellent wrestling matches, but the track and field events were probably the highlight of the entire trip. The athletes competing at Olympic Stadium were among the greats of the day.

We saw Mildred "Babe" Didrikson set a world record in the 80-meter hurdles and the javelin, then watched the great Glenn Cunningham and two other Americans qualify for the 1,500-meter run.

We saw American John Anderson set an Olympic record in the discus throw, winning the gold. Teammate Henri Laborde won the silver. In the pole vault, all the top four finishers

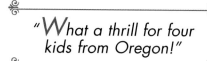

"What a thrill for four kids from Oregon!"

broke the previous Olympic record, with Americans finishing first and third.

Americans swept the men's 110-meter hurdles—the first time in Olympic history that three athletes from the same country finished 1-2-3. It happened again in the 200-meter run, with Eddie Tolan setting an Olympic record to win the gold, and two of his teammates tak-

OFFICIAL PROGRAM
XTH OLYMPIAD · LOS ANGELES · U.S.A.

OLYMPIC GAMES

JULY 30 1932 AUGUST 14

CALL TO THE GAMES OF THE XTH OLYMPIAD

LOS ANGELES CALIFORNIA

OLYMPIC PARK   **10ᶜ**   WEDNESDAY AUGUST 3, 1932

LOS ANGELES hosted the Olympic Games in '32, as shown on official program at left. Hal bought $2 tickets (below) to enter the games. At right is Olympic Stadium, where three American flags fly for U.S. athletes who placed 1st, 2nd *and* 3rd in the 110-meter high hurdles (a world record).

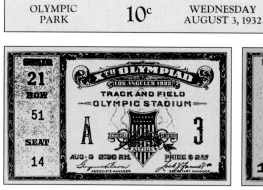

ing silver and bronze. The crowd roared when these trios received their medals as three American flags flew overhead.

What a thrill for four kids from Jennings Lodge, Oregon! "Never enjoyed track and field events so much," I wrote in my diary.

After seeing yet another American medal sweep at the diving finals, we started for home Aug. 8 and arrived Aug. 15. We'd spent $35 on gas and oil and put 3,113 miles on the Chevrolet.

Twenty years later, I learned that one of my employer's clients was a former Olympian. When I asked the strapping fellow what year he'd participated, he replied, "1932, Los Angeles".

I couldn't wait to get home and look at the program I'd bought years ago for a dime. Sure enough, in the track and field events, there was "H. Laborde"—the man we knew as "Herc". He'd never seen a program, so I loaned him mine to show his wife and friends.

A lot of water has gone under the bridge since then, but none of us ever regretted that trip, which gave us so many fine memories. ❧

GOLD MEDAL POSES were struck by Hal's traveling companions in the top photo, taken in the park outside Olympic Stadium. The group also enjoyed Olympic high-diving performances (above).

Showboat Shook Up the Town

By Marie Freesmeyer, Jerseyville, Illinois

IN THE 1920s, we were lucky to be on a river port because the showboats stopped there two or there times a summer. The melodramas and vaudeville drew crowds from miles around.

My parents considered showboats in a class with dance halls and taverns, so I was not given permission to see one of these shows until several years after I first began begging to do so! For many years, I had to be content with listening to the calliope and only dreaming of going to the show.

Just after my 14th birthday, I saw the posters in town advertising the coming of the *Cotton Blossom* showboat. It took days of coaxing, but Mother finally said I could go with one of my brothers.

My brother and I were hoeing sweet corn when we heard the sound of the calliope. "Here comes the showboat!" I exclaimed. Stopping work, we leaned on our hoes to listen.

Couldn't Wait

I sure didn't dawdle while doing my chores that evening. Afterward, I slipped on my best dress and put my hair up to make me look older. I probably should've put more pins in, though, because my brother drove his Ford roadster so fast that the wind pulled a few out.

When we arrived in town, we found a parking space near one of the hitching racks and quickly joined our peers, who were watching a man play the calliope on the top deck.

Soon it was time to join the crowd lining up to board. Our tickets cost $1.50 each. That was half a week's salary for some of the boys and girls who hired out. But just walking into that spectacular room and being ushered up the aisle to a lush velvet seat made it worth the price.

I was on the edge of my seat through the entire first act. We were able to quickly detect the villain and were given clues as to budding romances. Yet, the show kept us in suspense until the very end.

Between acts there was a brief vaudeville show, and the actors told some jokes about prominent citizens of our community.

Then it was back to the play. All too soon, the villain was apprehended, the romantic problems were resolved and the curtain came down. Our drive home was slower than the one to town.

For days afterward, my brother and I talked about the evening's events. In following years, I enjoyed shows on the *Cotton Blossom* and another showboat, the *Goldenrod,* but the thrill was never quite the same as that first time. ❧

Sincerely Your Friends
Jimmie Martin
King Rector *And*
Neale Helvey

IT'S SHOW TIME, FOLKS! Mary Jane Lowry of Blossom, Texas remembers these actors—Jimmie Martin, King Rector and Neale Helvey—from the Doug Morgan Show, which brought plays and other attractions to small towns in the late 1920s and early '30s. "How we loved those 2 or 3 days of entertainment from the outside world," Mary Jane recalls.

Dad Had the Cure for Star-Struck Teen

By Jean Amundson, La Crosse, Wisconsin

RADIO PERFORMER Hugh Studebaker was my dad's best friend. They'd performed together in Chautauquas in the early 1920s, but Dad guarded those memories carefully. The only time I heard about his show business days was when "Uncle Studie" visited.

He didn't visit often, but we listened to him faithfully on *Lux Radio Theater*, *Captain Midnight* and *The Guiding Light*. He also starred as Dr. Bob on *Bachelor's Children*, a popular soap opera.

Whenever I asked Dad why he hadn't continued in show business like Studie, he'd just say you needed more than a good voice and piano lessons to succeed. "Studie had it all," he'd say. "Besides, I've had enough of show business."

But *I* hadn't. By 1943, when I turned 15, I'd been in a few plays myself and was dazzled by radio and Hollywood. Dad said I was star-struck, and he *wasn't* pleased.

Mom spent weeks polishing and cleaning for Studie's visit that year. "Studie's a friend, not the president," Dad protested. "That's the way I want him treated." He insisted Studie's visit be kept quiet, too. "No picture-taking. No autographs. And no questions about Betty Grable!"

During Studie's visit, our house was filled with music and laughter. Dad and Studie sat at the piano, harmonizing on *Lida Rose*. Studie tapped out a beat on one knee with spoons while Dad did a soft-shoe. Mom and Studie's wife, Chic, danced the Charleston. I'd never seen Mom and Dad act like this!

As Studie was leaving, he asked if I'd like to visit him in Chicago. "Yes!" I blurted. "Can I meet Betty Grable?"

Trip "Burst Her Bubble"

When Studie met me at the train station that following summer of '44, he looked shorter and tired—not at all glamorous or like a radio star. He'd just finished *Bachelor's Children* and had to rehearse for *Captain Midnight*, which aired in an hour, so we took a cab to Radio City.

I felt so important rushing past the security guards to the elevator. The studio was filled with microphones, cables, equipment and people. I was given a chair and told to sit quietly. When the "On the Air" sign lit up, I was not to move, cough, sneeze or clear my throat. I hardly breathed.

Studie played a police officer and had only a few lines, sharing his mike with three other actors. The sound effects man was more fun to watch, slamming doors, turning a handle on a siren and firing guns on cue.

Before I knew it, *Captain Midnight* was over. We caught another cab to Studie's classy apartment building on Lake Shore Drive. Chic greeted us, and a maid brought in three crystal goblets on a silver tray. Mine was filled with milk.

From then on, all we did was rush everywhere. We went

"UNCLE STUDIE" (Hugh Studebaker) hams it up below. To Jean Amundson (above), he and her father (on the left in Marion Quartette photo at right) were stars.

to the theater to see *Oklahoma!* (positively great), then had a late supper in a private room at a Chinese restaurant. There was little time for all my questions, because important-looking people kept coming up to Studie and Chic to chat.

One lady hugged Studie, pecked his cheek and asked how he was. "Hello, Betty," Studie said, winking at me. "I'd like you to meet my special guest. This is Jean from La Crosse."

"La Crosse? Where's that?" the blond asked. I reached out to shake her hand but got no response. "I have to run," she said. "I'm flying back to Hollywood early." With one last look at me, she said, "I'd really do something about that hair, dear," and left.

"*That's* Betty Grable?" I asked in amazement. "It doesn't look like her."

"That's the real Betty," Studie replied. I was deflated.

When my whirlwind tour ended, I still thought Studie was wonderful, but he and Chic were just ordinary people despite their celebrity status. Show business no longer seemed so glamorous, and I was glad to be heading home to La Crosse. I later learned that Dad had thought I was becoming far too serious and planned that trip to discourage me from pursuing an acting career. It did! ✄

NEITHER GUN-SHY nor camera-shy, Chautauqua actors Harold Catlette and Hugh Studebaker (left and below) kept audiences roaring with their country bumpkin antics. Jean says her father performed with the duo in the 1920s before giving up show business.

STAGE CHRISTENING. Huberta Swensen was a lady-in-waiting and her brother a knight for a children's pageant at an Idaho Chautauqua in 1916. Her brother later adopted the stage name of Michael O'Rourke and became a renowned puppeteer.

Chautauquas Inspired Many Young Performers

OUR IDAHO TOWN had few cultural activities or outside attractions in the early 1900s, so when notices of the annual Chautauquas were posted, the entire population came to life.

We lived for the day when the enormous tent went up. Schedules would then be posted for children's morning sessions. Afternoon and evening programs featured musicians, well-known orators and actors. We lived and breathed Chautauqua.

The year I remember best is 1916, when my brother and I had parts in the children's pageant. Proud parents, relatives and friends watched from wooden seats padded with cushions they'd brought from home.

My brother went on to become a famous puppeteer, using the professional name of Michael O'Rourke. As half of the team of Walton and O'Rourke, he performed for 35 years for MGM in Hollywood and in theaters and royal courts around the world.

Chautauquas were an inspiration for many young people when radio and television were nonexistent and only a few people had windup phonographs. I've often wondered if taking part in that children's production inspired my brother to succeed in the competitive world of show business. —Huberta Swensen, Seattle, Washington

Trips to State Fair Gave Her a Lifetime of Memories

By Catherine Baermann, Milwaukee, Wisconsin

THE FIRST TIME I remember going to the state fair was in 1934. I was 10 years old and can recall Mom packing a lunch in a big paper shopping bag with cord handles. In a second bag, she packed sweaters in case the weather changed later in the day.

From our home in central Milwaukee, we traveled to the fairgrounds by streetcar. All the way there, I thought about the roller coaster, my favorite ride.

Once inside the gates, Mom zeroed in on a shady spot near the roller coaster to put down our lunch and sweaters. Then we found a clean picnic table, which she covered with a freshly ironed tablecloth.

After that, my 4-year-old sister and I were allowed to roam the grounds until lunchtime. Mom stayed with the lunch, usually crocheting or doing embroidery. When we came back to eat, it was just wonderful to sit and gaze up at the roller coaster while munching a sandwich and drinking warm lemonade.

I knew that I'd soon be riding on the thrilling maze of wooden magic we were now seated under. Soon, *my* screams would be the ones other people heard.

When lunch was over, we'd walk with Mom to see some of the exhibits (she didn't have to sit and guard our lunch anymore). I guess the rides must not have been very expensive, because I rode all of them. And we all went on the merry-go-round—even Mom.

Our routine didn't vary until 1938, when Mom brought along bottles of pop instead of lemonade. In the afternoon at about 3 o'clock, we'd have a hot dog and wash down the dry bun with an ice-cold root beer.

The next year, I went with a girlfriend. We stayed until dark and went on the rides after all the lights were turned on. There were no more noon

> *"The rides mustn't have been expensive— I rode them all..."*

lunches under the roller coaster (and no little sister tagging along!). We'd even venture over to the pavilion where famous bands played—although we didn't realize they were famous at the time.

In 1940, when I was 16, I got dressed up in stockings and high-heeled shoes and wore a picture hat. It wasn't too appropriate for going on rides, but it was fun for walking around and flirting with the boys. I felt so grown-up!

The next year, a date took me to the fair. What fun! We walked around holding hands and even kissed in the Tunnel of Love. Bob was so much fun to be with. He lost his comb, a package of gum and lots of change out of his pockets when we went on the Loop-O-Plane. Later, we danced to a band.

Little did I know that another young man on the dance floor that night would become my husband, and that someday I'd bring my own children to the state fair every summer, just as Mom had once taken me.

J.C. Allen and Son

FERRIS WHEELS AND HOMEMADE MEALS. When Catherine Baermann and her mother and sister joined the throngs at the state fair back in the mid-'30s, they took along a shopping bag full of lunch and lemonade...and took home many happy memories of fun times.

Baby Parade Entries Took Exposition's Top Honors

IN Rochester, New York back in the '20s, one of the big events of the year was the Rochester Exposition held every September. I have precious memories of it even today.

There were horse shows during the day and open-air pageants and band concerts at night. In a large building called Exhibition Hall, many companies had booths displaying their products. The one I remember best is the glass case where a man would make life-size sculptures out of butter. How we kids marveled at his skill!

So Many Attractions

Our real hero, though, was Daredevil Oliver, a diver who slowly climbed a ladder to a platform high in the air. At the top he would pause for a few moments (as if praying), then dive toward the little tank of water below. We always held our breath till he hit the water safely.

On the midway, we rode the merry-go-round, Ferris wheel and a ride called the Caterpillar. We let the man with scales guess our weight. If he missed by more than 3 pounds, we could win a Kewpie doll. When we got hungry, we bought a Coney Island hot dog and a root beer.

But for our family, the most important attraction was the baby parade. Dad would decorate my wagon, and I sat in it while my sisters pulled it along the parade route.

One year, our Gold Rush-era "covered wagon" won first

CAPTAIN OF THE KIDS. During Rochester, New York's baby parade in the '20s, Gerald Palmer (at left above) won a prize for his Captain Kidd impersonation. His sisters participated in the annual event, too.

prize—a $25 savings account. Another year, I won as Captain Kidd. One of my sisters won a prize in the doll carriage division for her "old woman in a shoe" entry.

Even if they didn't win a prize, each child who entered received a silver teaspoon with "Rochester Exposition" and the date engraved on the handle. Seventy years later, my sisters and I still have our spoons.
—Gerald Palmer
Charlotte, North Carolina

QUEASY RIDER. Anita Champeau preferred playing bingo and eating ice cream to enduring rides like this one.

$1 Bought a Full Day Of Fun at the Fair

THE Oklahoma State Fair always had one day when school kids got in free. On that day, Mother would give my sister, brother and me a dollar each to spend.

The rides made me too queasy, so I used my dollar to play bingo, buy soft pineapple sherbet and try my luck tossing embroidery hoops for prizes.

I looked at cows and ribbon-winning cakes, pies and cookies, examined handicrafts and watched a man slice, dice and curl vegetables.

When I came home, I had a free shopping bag full of advertising pencils, yardsticks, pins and political propaganda. I loved it!
—Anita Champeau
Norman, Oklahoma

Long Ferris Wheel Ride Added to Fair's Magic

FOR FARM FOLKS, the prize-winning livestock, fruits, vegetables and crafts were the "meat and potatoes" of the county fair, while the midway and grandstand shows provided the "icing on the cake"—especially the "Million-Dollar Stock Parade". Every animal except the swine was led in a big parade before a grandstand full of people.

After I'd fallen in love, though, nights at the fair took on a different mood. As my girl and I walked the midway, the lights seemed brighter, with more sparkle. The music on the old merry-go-round sounded great.

One night, there were very few people on the midway. Everyone else was in the packed grandstand, watching a stage show. We were the only riders on the Ferris wheel and must have ridden a full 10 minutes before the operator slowed it down and asked, "You want off?"

We both hollered, "No!", so he put it back up to normal speed and let us ride.

From high atop the wheel, the grounds below looked like a fairyland with all the twinkling lights. On the grandstand stage, we watched girls dancing in pretty costumes, as if performing just for us.

Two more times the man asked us if we wanted off, and each time we shouted back a firm "No!"

When the grandstand show ended and thousands of people poured out onto the midway, the operator stopped to load the Ferris wheel with riders. As we got off, we thanked him.

"I knew you were enjoying it," he said with a grin.

That we did.

—*Bob Witkovsky*
Bay City, Michigan

Archive Photos

THE FIRST SHRIEKS of delight from riding a Ferris wheel were heard at the World's Columbian Exposition in Chicago in 1893. That's when thousands of kids and adults waited in line for a chance to board the huge "bridge on an axle", invented by George Washington Gale Ferris.

'Should I Risk That Last Nickel?'

By Annette Oppegard, St. Paul, Minnesota

THERE WAS one event my family looked forward to each fall with eager anticipation. That was the county fair. For one day, my parents would leave the farm work behind, pile all five kids into the car, and let us catch a glimpse of the razzle-dazzle world of sideshows, daredevil acts, celebrity performers and fireworks.

The most memorable trip was when I was about 7. Dad gave each of us a quarter to spend, and we knew no more would be forthcoming. We'd have to choose carefully how each nickel was spent.

My first nickel went for a ride on the merry-go-round. The music cast its spell on me and I wished the ride would never end. My second nickel went for a big glob of grape cotton candy on a stick. I relished every mouthful.

Now I only had three nickels—my money was going fast! After listening to the barkers along the midway, I gave up another nickel to see the fat man.

Then I saw a girl with a big ice cream cone and just *had* to have one. How I loved that luscious strawberry ice cream!

Now only one nickel remained in my pocket. Soon it would be time to go home, and my special day at the fair would be over for another year. I had to make that nickel count!

I weighed the possibilities. A tall glass of lemonade would taste good, and the hot dogs smelled yummy. Then I saw a stand with rows and rows of teddy bears and a man who spun a big wheel after you paid him. If the number you picked came up on the wheel, you'd win a bear.

How I longed for one of those bears. But I'd have only one chance, and the nickel would be wasted if I didn't win. Was it worth the risk?

I decided I'd always be sorry if I didn't try, so I gave the man my very last nickel, picked a number and held my breath. The wheel spun around and around and around, slowed down and finally stopped…on the exact number I had chosen!

I couldn't believe my eyes. Had I really won? The barker said, "A winner here! The little lady wins a bear." When he placed the soft cuddly toy in my arms, I was the happiest girl on earth.

I cherished that bear for many years and still tell my grandchildren the story of that last nickel and how much happiness it brought me.

Unique Sights and Rides Left Her Queasy

By Cookie Curci-Wright, San Jose, California

THE FUN HOUSE on the boardwalk in Santa Cruz, California is gone now, but it was home to many thrilling, unique rides during its heyday in the 1940s and '50s.

Among my favorite amusement rides was the notorious fun house slide. I was both terrified and attracted by its grand dimensions, its high wooden slopes and deep, deep dips. That scary ride had claimed my stomach on more than one occasion. But, despite my fears, I was drawn back again and again to its sleek mountainous peaks.

Goaded by my older brother and his pals, I'd reluctantly

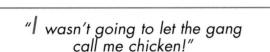

"I wasn't going to let the gang call me chicken!"

take a gunnysack at the bottom of the steps. Once it was in my hands and I began climbing the narrow walkway, there was absolutely no turning back.

I had reason to be afraid. Amusement rides didn't adhere to the stringent safety rules that they do today. That highly polished, inlaid oak wood slide had the potential to cause injury.

In fact, the last thing riders saw before shoving off was a bold warning sign: "Keep your hands and feet on the sack at all times—you could suffer a severe skin burn or even a

Circus Pass Still Hasn't Expired

THERE wasn't much excitement in our small town, until one day in 1936 when flyers were nailed on posts around town announcing the Tom Mix Circus was coming to Fresno County.

It seemed like an eternity waiting for the day when the trunks and tents arrived. Of course, all the talk at home was "when can we go see it?"

Then at the dinner table that evening, my father really got our attention when he said to Mom, "I wonder if 'Fats' Turney is still working for Tom Mix?" (Now Dad *really* had some questions to answer.)

We found out he'd worked with Fats in the oil fields years before. Dad said he'd see if his old friend was still working for Tom Mix.

We drove to the circus site that evening, and after a few inquiries, found Fats. Mom and Dad talked with Mr. and Mrs. Turney for a long time and found out Fats was treasurer for the circus.

When we started to leave, Mr. Turney gave Dad an envelope, saying, "Here's a present for you." It contained a lifetime pass to the Tom Mix cirus. *Wow!* We used it the next day and had a glorious time, but that was the only time the pass was ever used.

—*Allen Fritzie, Stockton, California*

28

The only string to this here pass is that you and your family use it often and have a rip-snortin' good time in the bargain.

Tom Mix

broken leg if your rubber heel catches the side of the slide!"

Sitting at the top of the slide on my gunnysack, I invariably lacked the fortitude to push myself off. But my big brother was *more* than happy to give me the shove that would start my descent. Careening down the slippery slopes, I

soon reached speeds that filled me with a delicious combination of sheer terror and wild exhilaration. Up and down, faster and faster I went.

By the final drop, I was almost airborne. Then I was deposited abruptly, but safely, into a soft pile of waiting sawdust. When I stood up, I was visibly shaken and breathless, prompting the ride attendant to offer his usual advice.

"You'd better go back up again, little lady. I think you left your stomach up there!"

He was right, of course, but I'd rather die than admit the old slide had gotten the best of me. So I just swallowed hard and prayed I didn't look as green as I felt.

Clutching my gunnysack in both hands, I bravely followed behind my older brother and his pals as they made their way to the walkway that led back to the top of that stomach-churning ride. Although my hands and knees were trembling with fear, I managed a queasy smile and faked a look of confidence as I made the dizzying climb. I wasn't going to let the gang call me chicken!

Besides, I knew that my stomach was still up there *somewhere*.

That fun house also had a gigantic wooden barrel that spun around and around. The object was to walk from one end to the other without falling—a feat I found impossible to master. Sometimes there was a massive pileup and all of the riders would be tossed, turned and churned inside the enor-

mous barrel like a great big washing machine full of kids.

The spinning top was easier. We'd pile onto a big flat wooden disk, and the attendant would start it spinning. As it went faster and faster, kids began rolling off. The trick to staying on was simple—get on first and sit squarely in the middle. The last ones on were always the first to roll off.

There were also funny mirrors that distorted our faces, gusts of air that blew up our skirts, and loud bells and horns that lifted our spirits. All were part of the fun house mystique. These unusual amusements were big entertainment and a special part of my childhood. 🍂

DANCING DUO wore patriotic WAVE and WAC uniforms in 1943 to perform in the Woodruff High School dance follies. Phyllis Heberling (WAVE at right) of Virginia Beach, Virginia says she looked forward to the follies more than any other event in her hometown of Peoria, Illinois. She and friend June were coached by a popular local dance teacher on their dance steps, enabling them to put on performances their sophomore and junior years. The partnership ended when Phyllis and her family moved East with her dad's WWII job.

Amazing 'Cookie' Performed Cow-lossal Feats

By Phyllis Roelfs, Waverly, Iowa

FOR 6 marvelous, exciting years, my summertimes meant going to fairs, parades, carnivals and centennials with Grandpa Ted and his amazing cow, "Cookie".

From the time Cookie was born in the early 1950s (she was named after the daughter in the *Blondie* cartoon strip), Grandpa singled her out to be special. We kids had to stay away when he worked with her in the pasture behind the barn.

The mystery of what was going on back there was almost unbearable for us. Before long, however, we learned how all those hours and days had been spent. It turned out that Grandpa had been training Cookie to do the most amazing tricks you could ever imagine!

She could gallop, pace, trot and canter just like a horse. She could stand atop a 3-foot-tall metal barrel and, at Grandpa's command, twist and grind in a complete circle. (I always worried about her falling off, but she never did.)

Word of Ted Reiling's amazing cow quickly spread throughout northern and central Iowa. The pair was asked to appear at county fairs, city celebrations—anywhere entertainment was needed.

Cookie's most popular trick was "udderly" amazing. Grandpa would ask Cookie if she felt sick, and she'd flop onto the ground, throw her head back and groan. Grandpa would naturally check her over, acting puzzled.

Then Grandpa would say, "I know what you need, Cookie. You need a shot of penicillin!" He'd then "inject" her with a realistic-looking spring-loaded syringe. But Cookie stayed on the ground yet, tossing her head and moaning.

At last, Grandpa would announce that what Cookie *really* needed was a *beer* (or a soda if they were appearing at a church event or picnic). Someone in the crowd would hand him a bottle and he'd tip Cookie's head up and start to pour it down her throat.

Instantly, she'd jump to her feet as the crowd roared with laughter and cheered! It was truly astonishing that Grandpa could train a "dumb" animal to do this.

I loved the outdoors and spent many a summer vacation with Grandpa on his farm. I was the tomboy in our family and craved the special attention he gave me. He'd let me tag around behind him while he did his chores and always listened respectfully to what I had to tell him.

One memorable day, Grandpa asked if I'd like to try jumping rope on Cookie's back. I was a gutsy 7-year-old, so I was delighted by his confidence in me. After I let him boost me onto her back, I quickly learned that if I stayed on Cookie's rear haunches, I had plenty of room to jump.

With practice, I could crisscross my arms at the same time. Oh, the talent I possessed!

After several days of training, Grandpa asked me to try jumping on Cookie while she stood on top of the barrel! I was a little apprehensive, but I didn't want to disappoint Grandpa, so I gave it a try. It was a thrill being so high in the air, and jumping was no problem at all. It was then that Grandpa

asked if I'd like to be part of his "act". I was so excited I could barely believe it. Grandpa wanted *me* to travel all over the state with him and be one of the stars of his show!

I was just a little wisp of a girl, but I felt like a celebrity in my big white cowboy hat and sequined blouse and skirt. I loved running out to Grandpa during a show to hand him the syringe or the bottle of pop. When I jumped rope on Cookie's back, the crowd would gasp in amazement. A star was born!

We used a big white enclosed truck to transport Cookie around the state. Between the back section and the cab was a sliding window, and I don't know how many times we'd be driving down the road when I'd look back and see her big black eyes looking out of that window.

We'd slide the window open and I would scratch her nose. I loved her so!

The years went by and Grandpa and I and Cookie had so many smiles and memories together. Grandpa never *told* me he loved me (that was just never said in our family), but I knew he loved me as much as I loved him.

Then one day, when I was 18 and away at school, I received a large envelope in the mail from Grandpa. Inside was a color photo of Cookie with Grandpa by her side (left). There was also a short note that read, "Phyllis, this is the last picture taken of Cookie before we had to put her to sleep. I thought you'd like to have it."

Never in my young life had I felt so sad. I still have to wipe tears from my eyes when I remember all those years we spent together …my grandpa, me and a gentle beast named "Cookie the Cow". ❧

BOVINE OVER A BARREL. Phyllis Roelf's grandfather spent countless hours out behind the barn training a lovable cow named "Cookie". Ultimately, his efforts were so successful that Cookie could balance herself on a barrel while 7-year-old Phyllis climbed atop her and jumped rope on her back (right).

LITTLE GEM. Sister Ruth Kaltenbach's family won the grand prize in the 1910 Asbury Park (New Jersey) Baby Parade for this entry, titled "Our Jewel". Ruth, now of Tampa, Florida, sat in the "ring" while her sisters pulled the float. Also pictured are their mother and aunt. The girls received a brass loving cup for their efforts, and they even caught a glimpse of parade queen Mary Pickford!

GRANDMA'S MAKIN' PIE! Baking might not seem like such a hot activity in today's fast-paced world of televisions and VCRs, but years ago when families did so much together, even a household chore could be thoroughly enjoyed—particularly if you got to eat the fruits of your labor. These kids certainly don't appear to be deprived without video games!

Chapter Eight
Fun Was Always Close to Home

Pulling pranks, throwing parties, putting on a backyard show...with family, friends and neighbors near, good times were never far away.

elevision has a lot to answer for, both good and bad. But more than anything else, I blame it for the virtual extinction of family get-togethers. I'm not talking about the traditional big holidays, because those are well-rooted family traditions. But what we don't do much anymore is just get together for no reason at all.

My mother's side of the family was particularly fond of Sunday get-togethers. It was a big tribe and everyone took their turn at hosting the gatherings, but my recollection is that during the summer months, they more often than not took place at our house.

For one thing, we had the only ice cream churn. It was the jumbo size that made 3 gallons at a crack. Best of all, we had a herd of dairy cows on our farm, so the custard was made from pure cream. Fortunately, calories hadn't been invented yet, so we feasted in guilt-free bliss.

We also had chickens, a huge garden, long rows of sweet corn in the field and a big red rasberry patch. Consequently, summer Sundays usually saw the family gathering at our place ...so frequently, Dad sometimes grumbled about the "seven-day locusts descending again".

Even Arguments Were a Pleasure

Those Sunday gatherings of the Stevens clan were warm and wonderful. The men argued about politics, shared their worries about the Depression and drought and speculated on what the goings-on in Europe portended.

They were a diverse group—a farmer, a carpenter, a house painter, an engineer for a farm machinery company and my retired grandfather—which made for lively discussions.

The wives were equally interesting, and included a former schoolteacher, a nurse, a hat designer and a one-time bookkeeper. So their conversations ranged far beyond exchanging recipes and discussing soap operas.

See what was going on? Golly, *people were talking with each other!* They entertained and informed each other. Nowadays, we turn on the television to be entertained and informed. There's just a lot less "getting together" going on.

And it was more than gatherings with the kinfolk. Years ago, it wasn't regarded as unseemly to just "drop in". You might be out for a walk or a drive and on the spur of the moment say, "Hey, let's stop and see if the Smiths are home." If they were, you were sure of a warm welcome. You hadn't interrupted a gripping segment of *Home Improvement* or *Murphy Brown*.

Jimmy would be sent running down to the corner grocery for a quart of ice cream while fresh lemonade or iced tea was being made in the kitchen. Drop-in company was a welcome break, not an awkward intrusion. There was catching-up to do and gossip to swap. Most of all, it was fun to just *visit*.

Now turn the page and enjoy a wonderful collection of memories about the days when the good times with friends and family were never far from your own front door. —*Clancy Strock*

I REMEMBER Grandpa's barbershop and Grandma's beauty parlor the way I remember childhood celebrations, adventures and holidays. Visiting them was like a combination of all three.

The shops adjoined each other, but their atmospheres were as different as night and day. Grandma had a parrot, tasseled lamp shades, lotions, potions, bouquets and china teacups.

Grandpa had a calendar, whirly-go-round barber chairs, clippers that hummed and tickled our necks and a razor strap that sang with him.

Whenever a customer asked, "How much?", Grandpa would answer by singing, "Shave and a haircut—two bits!" When he said "two bits", he snapped the razor strap with two loud cracks, and everyone laughed.

If my sister, Gloria, or I asked, "What's two bits, Grandpa?", he'd reply, "More than a little bit." And again the customers would laugh in agreement.

I don't remember ever seeing an unhappy person in Grandpa's barbershop, and if someone wasn't satisfied with their haircut, he wouldn't take their money.

Grandpa loved kids and always had time for us. When there were no customers, we sat on the footrests of the barber chairs and dug our heels into the linoleum floor to make a human spin machine. Every now and then, Grand-

'Shave and A Haircut ...Two Bits!'

By Glenda Barbre
Rhododendron, Oregon

CHRISTMAS WINDOW display included the then-popular combination of Christmas photos and cards—and a sign advertising "Private Booth for Ladies" Note the clever cottonball snowfall.

pa would give the chair an extra quick spin, and we'd scream with excitement—until Grandma came over from her side to say we were disturbing "her ladies".

In Grandma's shop, where ladies had their hair done in private booths, we were models of feminine propriety. After one ride in the barber chair at near lift-off velocity, I remember going to "Grandma's side" and trying to rub the scuff marks off my new patent-leather shoes so I wouldn't get Grandpa in trouble.

Grandma specialized in the marcel hairstyle. It looked like a bunch of tiny waves that had frozen all over the lady's head.

Women sat with pinchy-looking metal clamps hooked to electric cords that dangled behind her. A customer getting a permanent looked like she was hooked up to enough voltage to light the city of Portland.

Between customers, Grandma would curl our hair. Sometimes she just used a hot curling iron, but other times she would do a major production. There was the shampoo and metal curler day; the ringlet day; the big bow day... when we were turned into cute little replicas of Shirley Temple.

Grandma believed in taking care of the whole person. She was full of diet advice and homemade remedies, and the only reading material she allowed were "good books" that would uplift the spirit. Grandma also used a strange con-

GRANDPA treated every customer special, Glenda Barbre remembers.

MOTHER'S MARCEL. Glenda's mother, Margorie, models a popular hairstyle of the day. A licensed beautician, Margorie sometimes worked with her mother in the shop.

traption called The Violet Ray to treat arthritis. It was shaped like a giant vegetable spoon, and the "ray" zipped in a crimson circuit with a crackling sound like static electricity gone berserk. When I was little, I thought it was magic. As I got older, I wondered if it was illegal.

Even Grandpa didn't dare to question some of Grandma's beliefs. If your bangs were too long, you might get eyestrain and need glasses. Too-thick hair could cause a headache. All of her granddaughters had bangs cut above their eyebrows, and she constantly kept at my hair with the thinning scissors.

She knew how to have healthy hair and a good complexion, too. Parsley, and lots of it. (Everyone had to eat that little sprig on their plate put there for decoration when we were out to lunch with Grandma.) She also believed that if she ate enough of it, she wouldn't need glasses someday.

She believed in gelatin for hair and

nails and wheat germ in our orange juice so we wouldn't catch colds. The days in Grandma's salon were filled with health instruction.

Sometimes those memories come back when I'm having my hair done…I hear the laughter of Grandpa and his customers…I watch two little girls spinning delightedly in the barber chair as Grandma calls from the next room, "Hayes, what's going on in there? After I'm done with Mrs. Hendricks, send the girls in here. I'm going to curl their hair and cut their bangs"…and I watch Grandpa's next customer settle into the barber chair. "How much is this haircut today, Hayes?"

"Shave and a haircut," Grandpa sings, "two bits!"

GRANDMA'S GIRLS. Glenda and Gloria had their hair done in the beauty shop for this photo. Glenda (left) recalls, "I wasn't old enough for a permanent, so Grandma took some sticky stuff and water and rolled my hair on her fingers."

A VIEW OF GRANDMA'S SALON reveals the mischievous side of Glenda's dad, Lloyd Jenkins, who glued a picture of his own face over a customer's.

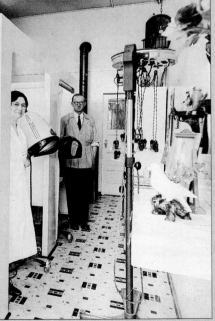

CURLY TOP. Sister Gloria posed with Grandpa and Grandma after her first permanent, which she didn't like until the curls relaxed *3 months* later.

PRIVATE BOOTHS were considered the proper place for a lady to have her hair done. "Grandpa is back by the stove," Glenda reports, "always the proper gentleman. The customer is reading *Faith*, one of the uplifting books Grandma kept on hand for her clients. My dad designed the booths, including the vanity tables in each one."

The Pranks We Pulled

Gramps Broke the Record for The 'Sitting Broad Jump'

Eric R. Berndt/Unicorn Stock Photos

By Clellon Callahan Sr., Orient, Ohio

GRANDPA USED tobacco in every form, and his pipe was so much a part of him that he grew absentminded about it. Sometimes he even searched for it when he had it in his *mouth*.

My grandma, on the other hand, frowned on the use of tobacco and induced Grandpa to offer $100 and a gold watch to any of us kids who abstained until the age of 21. My Uncle Roger came closest to winning. He didn't use tobacco until he was 9!

One day, when Roger and I were home alone, he filched some of Grandpa's tobacco and invited me to the small outbuilding between the house and the barn to watch him smoke.

He clumsily rolled a monstrous, unwieldy cigarette, using a page from the handy Montgomery Ward catalog for a wrapper. With every puff, the paper burst into flame, filling the wee building with smoke.

When Roger invited me to "try a puff", I coughed so hard that tears ran down my cheeks. I was only 6, but I knew I'd be branded a sissy if I fled, so I stayed. When the smoke cloud made breathing difficult, I put my face close to the crescent-shaped opening in the door and sucked in a breath of clean air.

Then we heard the sound of a car. Since Grandpa didn't own one, we weren't alarmed—until it came roaring into the yard.

"There's Grandpa!" I whispered hoarsely. Roger turned and flicked the huge cigarette into one of the oval openings on the wooden seat, and we ran to the house.

Grandpa waved at the neighbor who was dropping him off, but he seemed agitated. Roger and I watched, pop-eyed with fear, as he strode straight for the little outbuilding. Tiny strings of smoke still floated lazily around it.

To our amazement and relief, Grandpa showed no reaction as he stepped inside. He seemed to have more pressing things to think about.

An instant later, Grandpa crashed out the doorway as if propelled from behind by some gigantic unseen power. It was the world's greatest broad jump—and he did it from a sitting position. I'm sure he would've shattered the record for the 100-yard dash, too, if his feet hadn't been tangled in his bib overalls.

Roger ran outside and grabbed a bucket. By the time Grandpa had pulled up his suspenders, the fire in the little building was out.

When Grandma returned from town, she noticed Grandpa was walking with the stiffness and care of a man who'd sat on a bumblebee. "What in the world is the matter with you?" she asked.

"I got singed," Grandpa said, "in the outhouse. The paper caught fire under me."

"I knew it was bound to happen," said Grandma, shaking her head. "You go around dumping ashes and fire out of that pipe without even knowing what you're doing! It's a wonder you haven't burned down the house around our heads before."

"But I don't *think* I was smoking when I went in," Grandpa protested.

"You smoke so much you don't know whether you're puffing on that pipe or not!" Grandma retorted.

That evening, Grandpa carefully placed a soft pillow on his favorite chair before settling in for his after-supper pipe. Roger and I never did tell anyone how Grandpa *really* got singed—until now. ❧

Old Habits Die Hard

ONE OF my dad's favorite theories was that "old habits and actions become so automatic they prevent you from thinking for yourself". Since he also delighted in pulling a good joke, he often employed this method to prove his point.

One ongoing illustration was at our rustic cabin in the Montana Rockies where we often entertained visitors. In the outhouse there, Dad installed a square box with a long chain and a sign that read, "Pull chain to flush."

When the chain was pulled, a loud bell inside the box clanged and echoed across the mountains.

Over the years, that bell sounded many, many times—much to the chagrin of our red-faced guests. But they ultimately had to laugh at the unique way Dad proved his point!

—Betty Simmons
Brownwood, Texas

Grandma Started Halloween Legend...or Did She?

MY FIRST experience with trick-or-treating was the year the Hartley boys showed up at our door with open pillowcases, asking for treats. This was a new concept and nobody knew what they wanted, so they had to explain.

Not being prepared, Grandma shared our cache of fried cakes and apples with the boys, who left happy with their booty.

Grandma lived on the second floor of our big farmhouse, and we kids made frequent trips upstairs to visit her.

As we started up the stairs one Halloween, we came upon a "ghost" in the hallway. I realized it was only Grandma's hall tree draped in a sheet, with a cheesecloth mask, but a flashlight set in the base gave it a real ghostly look.

Squealing partly with fear, partly with delight, we rushed back to tell everyone about the ghost in the hall. By the time we managed to drag them there to see it, it was gone.

Later, when she showed up with her fried cakes, Grandma firmly denied she'd had anything to do with our "visitor". Maybe we *had* seen a ghost!

Now I have five grandchildren of my own, and the old-fashioned hall tree ghost has become a Halloween legend.
—*Arlene Shovald, Salida, Colorado*

Students Privy to Plot

IN OUR TOWN, the Halloween custom was to take everything not nailed down and deposit the items at the high school football field. Everyone knew they'd be able to find their possessions there and tolerated this custom—except the local gas station owner.

One year he made *such* a fuss that our principal made every student promise not to take a single item from the station. So we all promised...then plotted our revenge.

On Halloween night, one boy borrowed his uncle's truck, and the rest of the students showed up to help. When morning came, not so much as a tire rack was *missing* from the gas station.

It had taken us hours, but there blocking the pumps sat the scroungiest old abandoned outhouse we could find. It didn't improve the station owner's disposition when the whole town thought the prank was hilarious!
—*Shirley Cook, Oroville, California*

STRAPPING YOUNG 'BOES. Jeri Oscarson of Austin, Minnesota shared photo of Dad (left) and friend en route to a Halloween hobo party in 1910.

Grandpa Had Last Laugh

MY GRANDFATHER lived on a farm near Seward, Illinois in the 1900s. He was a jolly old man who loved a good joke, and everyone knew it.

One Halloween, he heard someone outside. He peeked out the back door, then snuck out (it was a moonless night) and quietly joined the men who were huddled in the dark around his machine shed.

It was hard work, but the strong young men and my grandfather finally got his big wooden-wheeled farm wagon on top of the shed. When they'd finished, one of them whispered, "Ol' Henry's going to be real surprised when he sees this in the morning."

Grandfather said loudly, "Oh, I don't *think* so, but we did a *real* good job."

The men were so shocked that they offered to take the wagon down right then and there. But Grandpa told them to go out and enjoy the rest of their Halloween night.

The next morning, everyone came back and helped get the wagon down, amid lots of laughter. No one was more amused than my grandfather. He surely got the last laugh.
—*Lois Ihne*
Rockford, Illinois

Prank Had Happy Ending

ON HALLOWEEN night in 1953, my girlfriends and I were out trick-or-treating. As we walked along in the dark with our paper sacks, some boys across the street started shouting at us. We just giggled and went on to the next house.

A woman opened the door, and just as she held out a basket of candy, the boys threw *raw liver* at us. I was bending over the candy basket, and the piece of liver aimed at me sailed right over my head and into the woman's living room!

"Friends of yours?" the woman asked sarcastically.

"No," I said. "I've never seen those boys before."

I could tell she didn't believe me when she asked me to pick up that disgusting piece of meat and throw it outside. Afterward, we girls walked down the street saying, "Boys are sure yucky!"

Three months later, at a Valentine dance, I spotted the "yucky" boy who'd thrown the liver at me. I went over to give him a piece of my mind, but when I looked into those brown eyes, I gave him my heart instead.

Two years later, we were married. And every year since, on our anniversary, I've fixed my darling husband a special meal—liver and onions!
—*Diane Arnold*
Long Beach, California

OUT-AND-OUT FUN. Tipping over "the house out back" was the preferred prank of yesteryear funsters.

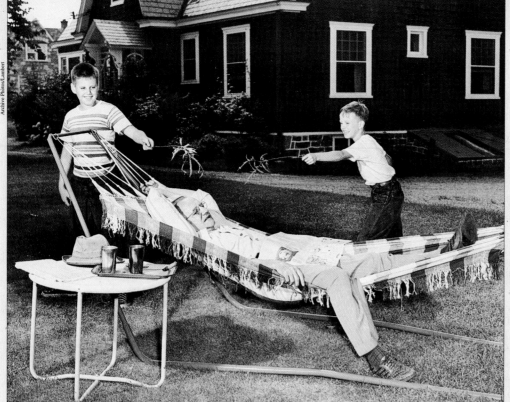

A GOOD PRANK could easily tickle our fancy, and in the good old days, we found loads of fun and plenty of "victims" right in our own backyards.

Fake Cake a Tough Customer

THE 24-year-old bank teller who worked in the cage next to me had a birthday coming up. Being 32 years old and a 15-year veteran teller, I decided to make it memorable for the young guy.

I just happened to have on hand a round cake of pork cracklings (pork rinds left after lard was rendered at hog-killing time). The cracklings had hardened, so I spread white frosting all over them, then made a regular cake and decorated it the same way.

At quitting time the next day, I gave the teller his cake. He was thrilled and called for everyone to come share it. Of course, this was the "cracklings cake"—and it was impossible to get a knife through it.

I finally took pity and gave him the real cake. He good-naturedly chased me around the bank for a while, then we all sang "Happy Birthday" and enjoyed his treat. —*Verla Slocum*
Altoona, Florida

Cousins Made the Switch

YEARS AGO, before we had church buildings, "fire and brimstone" preachers would visit our part of Louisiana for outdoor revivals. The younger kids usually fell asleep during the services, so their parents would put them on a mattress in the back of the wagon.

One year, my little sister was being a pain in the neck, so with a cousin providing the muscle, we switched her with a sleeping child from another wagon. To protect ourselves from detection, we switched some kids in other wagons …about five in all.

When the service ended, Dad and Mother got in the wagon, counted sleeping bodies and left. Only when we got home did Mother notice she had three boys instead of two boys and a girl! She was sure Dad had put my sister in the wrong wagon.

Daylight the next morning found many a farmer making the rounds, asking, "Say, do you know whose kid this

---

5¢ Bought Years of Fun

WHEN WE were kids, 5¢ really went a long way. In fact, we got *years* of enjoyment out of a single nickel!

Dad soldered a nail to the back of a nickel and hammered it to the dining room floor. Then we'd watch with glee as unwary visitors tried in vain to pick it up!
—*Virginia Erk*
Stanton, California

---

is?" or "Do you know anyone who has an extra young'n around?"

My poor parents never found out about my small part in that caper. At last, I have that confession off my chest!
—*John Normand*
Vinton, Louisiana

Pair's Joke Was a Bell-Ringer

ONE SUMMER evening in the '50s, my wife and I were talking to some friends as we watched a neighbor across the street paint his front stoop.

When he was finished, he draped a lawn chair frame over the railing to keep people off the porch and went back inside his house.

I turned to my friend Chuck and asked, "How do you think Ralph would react if he heard his front doorbell ring about now?"

Chuck smiled broadly and said, "Let's find out."

Armed with a rubber-tipped clothesline support, we crossed the street and waited at the edge of his stoop. The windows were open so we could hear Ralph wash up, turn on the TV and settle back in his recliner.

At that point, bracing the support pole on the railing like a pool cue, we reached over and rang the doorbell. The recliner came down with a crash!

In three thundering steps, Ralph crossed the floor and tore open the door. The rage on his face changed to surprise, then amusement, as he gradually realized what had happened.

"Bless you guys," he said, laughing. "All I could picture was some salesman standing here and how I was going to kill him for walking on my new paint!"

For years afterward, Ralph told friends it was the best prank anyone had ever played on him. —*James Glander*
Rockville, Maryland

Chickens Had School Clucking

EVERY MONDAY, our public high school had a chapel service, and each week a different pastor lead us in singing hymns, a prayer and a short lesson.

The year that Halloween fell on a

Monday, the student roll-taker opened her desk at the start of the service and a big white leghorn rooster flew out!

The rooster flew out the door and down the stairs before he was caught—right in front of the superintendent's office. The superintendent was livid and stormed upstairs to yell at us.

The service continued, and the roll-taker sat down at the piano to play a hymn. But something was wrong—the piano just didn't sound right. She lifted the top to peek inside—and two more white chickens flew out! They took the same route as the first, flying right past the superintendent as he descended the stairs after the first incident.

Most of us had chickens at home, and several of us seniors were called to the office for questioning. Luckily, my family had Rhode Island Reds—*whew!* We never did find out where those three chickens came from.

—*Annie-Laurie Robinson*
Williamston, Michigan

Gutter Balls? No Problem!

IN 1944, I belonged to a bowling league. We were all poor bowlers, but I was the worst. One night, I had a hard time just keeping the ball on the alley.

After several frustrating turns, I again walked to the line, wishing I could roll a strike or at least a spare. Then I noticed there were no pins at the end of the alley.

The helpful pin boy had set them up in the *gutters* on both sides of the alley! We all had a good laugh! —*Anareba Rinner*
Jamul, California

This Prank Stank!

IN THE LATE 1930s, when I was still in high school, a friend and I decided to pull the prank of all pranks. We bought a jar of Limburger cheese, and, armed with a toothbrush, proceeded to spread it on the door handles of *every store* in Elk City, Oklahoma.

It was the talk of the town, and a write-up in the local paper even called it the year's best Halloween prank. But you can bet we didn't let *anyone* know we were the ones who did it.

—*Glen Fergason, Antlers, Oklahoma*

Payday Trick Tore Him Up

ONE SATURDAY in the early 1940s, Dad hired me and a pal to set out Bermuda grass sprigs in a new pasture. When we finished, Dad gave us a dollar bill and told us to have Mr. Jones over at the country store "tear it in half" for us.

We walked about 2 miles across the fields to the store. When we told Mr. Jones what Dad had said, he replied, "Sure, I can do that"—and tore the bill in two!

"But, Mr. Jones," I exclaimed, "that's not what I meant. We want a half-dollar each!"

He replied, "Well, that's what you got."

Mr. Jones was teasing us, of course, but we took this very seriously. We had plans for that money—a Woozie root beer, a Big Peanut Patty and a bag of Bull Durham, for starters.

Finally, after everyone in the store had a good laugh, Mr. Jones took back the pieces of the bill and gave us 50¢ in coins. For years afterward, whenever we saw him, he told us he still had that taped-together bill in his wallet.

—*Paul Reagan Sr.*
Gun Barrel City, Texas

Eggs Became "Bombshells"

"CONFETTI EGGS" were the star of our school's Halloween carnival held outside in the playground area every year. We visited the rickety wooden booth to buy as many of them as we could afford, then threw them at everything—and everyone.

A group of volunteer mothers made these harmless bombshells by carefully removing the raw egg, then filling the intact shell with a handful of confetti. A strip of tape kept the paper from falling out of the tiny holes at either end.

When thrown at any-

thing solid, the eggs instantly shattered, releasing a fluttering shower of confetti.

The eggs sold two for a nickel, but two eggs were *never* enough. Those of us with enough money visited the confetti-egg booth many times. (After all, it *was* for a good cause, raising funds for the school.)

These eggs didn't weigh enough to be dangerous, and even if you cracked one right on somebody's head, the shell crumbled quite nicely. Although other schools we knew had carnivals, none of them had our wonderful confetti eggs.

Best of all, no one tried to stop us from throwing them. Teachers, parents, even the principal not only allowed it, but encouraged it! Try as I might, though, I never did figure out exactly what confetti eggs had to do with celebrating Halloween.

—*Christopher Squyres*
Orange, California

GOING IN CIRCLES. Dorothy Allen of Midland, Michigan remembers the day her brother Cecil "volunteered" to teach her how to row a boat. Despite her best efforts, the boat kept going in circles—and Cecil began laughing so hard he nearly fell overboard. "That's when I finally figured out he had the anchor down on his end of the boat!" laughs Dorothy. "Would you believe such an angelic-looking boy would treat his sister that way?"

Sisters Had Their Fair *Share* of Fun

SOME HARDSHIPS imposed by the Depression years actually made life richer. One of them was having to share.

My two sisters and I shared one bedroom, one dresser and one closet. But we also shared secrets, gossip, homework and giggles. Being sent to our room was never a punishment. We just took our camaraderie upstairs with us.

We knew all the lyrics to the songs on the Hit Parade and sang ourselves to sleep every night. Avid movie buffs,

LITTLE MIMICS. Jean Chmurski, her twin, Jan, and their sister, Joy, often entertained themselves by impersonating teachers, friends and relatives. This "theatrical" moment was captured in 1934.

SISTERS AND FRIENDS. Jean says she and her sisters never minded sharing a room as youngsters. The experience only brought them closer, she remembers. From left are Joy, Jean and her twin, Jan.

we wrote fan letters to our favorite stars, convinced we'd become gorgeous actresses and marry Clark Gable, Don Ameche and Roy Rogers.

We made up scary stories and told them to each other, and when headlights flashed from wall to wall like ghosts as cars came down our street, I was grateful I could pull the covers overhead and hold onto my twin.

Midnight shadows made our clothes hanging over the bedroom chair look like Dracula ready to pounce on me, but I knew I could awaken my sisters and the three of us would pounce right back.

On the small radio in our room, we secretly listened to *Lights Out* every Friday night. Trembling as a sinister voice ordered, "Lights out, everybody", we huddled under the covers, daring each other to turn on the lights.

There were no commercial breaks to bring relief from the sustained suspense, so often one of us *did* bolt across the room to turn on the switch and bathe our room in the security of light.

In our shared room, we each had one drawer in the dresser, and if one of us was mad at the other, she'd dump out that sister's bureau drawer. If we were really mad, one would pull the other's clothes from the closet hangers. Really, *really* mad? Simple! We'd dump out the drawer, pull the clothes from the hangers and jump up and down on everything.

Truthfully, sharing a room with my sisters was never a hardship. It taught us companionship, loyalty and humor.
—*Jean Chmurski, Seminole, Florida*

Poem Helped Them Finish Evening Chore

EVERY EVENING, when it was time for my sister, Ruby, and me to do the dishes, we stalled and argued until our mother's patience was exhausted. Once she even taped our mouths with Scotch tape and said "no more nonsense".

One day, Mother clipped a poem out of the newspaper and told us we had to memorize it and learn to get along better. Here's how it went:

Sunday, Monday, Tuesday, every day of the week,
Breakfast, dinner, supper, wouldn't it be sweet,
If dishes washed and dried and did themselves
And placed on proper shelves?
But since they do not do this

And since it must be done,
Bring on the sparkling soapsuds
And let's pretend it's fun.

That was quite a few years ago, but at age 70, I'm thankful I can look back and remember the times we recited that poem.
—*Virginia Katula*
Glendale, Arizona

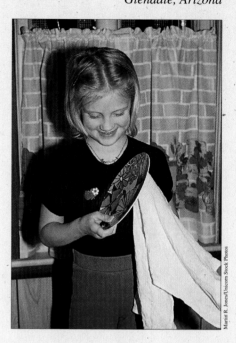

Faith in Big Brother Kept Her on Steady Path

I IDOLIZED my big brother, Louis, and trusted him implicitly. Having hoped for a baby brother, he may have been mildly disappointed when he got another sister, but he never let on. (Maybe that's why when he got his first paycheck at age 16, he used part of it to buy me a toy fire engine!)

When I got my first bike at age 6, I was so terrified of falling I never rode it. Louis was determined that I learn to ride and patiently ran me back and forth on the sidewalk, holding my bike straight as I tried to balance. But every time he let go and I realized he wasn't there, I lost my balance and fell.

Finally, Louis brought out a ball of string and tied the end to the back of the seat. "As long as I hold onto this string," he assured me, "your bike won't tip." How naive I was—and how trusting.

Off we went, with Louis holding the bike as usual. I can still hear him yelling, "Pedal, pedal fast!" Believing in him with all my heart, I pedaled furiously—but he had let go.

When I looked back, he was holding the ball of string and yelling, "Keep

BIG BROTHER. Theresa Blydenburgh adored Louis, who was 15 years older. When she was learning to ride a bike, his support made all the difference.

going—I've got you!" So I kept going.

Then I looked back again. I can still see him doubled up with laughter, and the unwinding ball of string trailing along the sidewalk behind me. It was only then that I realized how dumb I had been.

I turned the bike around and pedaled indignantly back to Louis. When he managed to stop laughing, he hugged me and said, "I *knew* you could do it. Don't ever be afraid to try new things. If you fall, just pick yourself up and try again."

Louis encouraged and supported me in all my endeavors over the years, and his words inspired and helped me through many a rough spot in life.
—*Theresa Blydenburgh, Islip, New York*

Woods and the River Left Lasting Legacy

EVERY SPRING when the river and lowlands behind our house flooded, my brothers built a raft from Dad's discarded lumber.

They went out every day after school and on weekends, rowing and pushing with long poles through the woods. My

RAFTING ADVENTURES were a rite of spring for Marion Prange's brothers. Every year, they built a raft to explore floodwaters near their home. Photo at right of Bobby and Carl was taken in 1950.

sisters and I watched, frightened they'd be washed overboard any minute.

On the other side of the river was Sugar Hill. Grandpa told us the Indians once grew sugarcane there and wild rice in the lowlands. We believed him, because we always found stone arrowheads after spring plowing.

The hill also provided a place for us to sled in winter. We visited the river often, too, for ice skating in winter and swimming in summer.

Every other weekend, Dad took us for walks in the woods, identifying the new plants and trees. We found mounds that looked like graves—probably for the livestock. No matter what we found, Dad always had a story to tell us about it.

There were 10 of us children, but we had more "riches" than many wealthy families. We had a hill, a river and walks with a wonderful father.
—*Marion Prange*
Howards Grove, Wisconsin

Moonlight Rides Brought Young People Together

IN THE small village of English, Texas, there wasn't much entertainment, so young people were ingenious in devising ways to get together.

My mother recalls picnics, candy pulls, spelling bees, charades and play parties. The latter were just like square dances, with the music provided by singers rather than musicians.

On moonlit nights, a young man who could muster two horses —one for him, one for his girl—would contact all his friends and ask them to do the same. They'd assemble at my grandmother's boardinghouse, then set off in pairs, girls riding sidesaddle in their Sunday best. There was enough space between couples for private conversation, but never so much that any pair was out of the others' sight. —*Mary Jane Lowry*
Blossom, Texas

Best Friends Make the Best Fun

By Joanne Peck
Schenectady, New York

JEAN WAS, and is, my best friend in the world. She told me the facts of life, beat up a boy who punched me, took me to church and made me understand the meaning of the word "friend". Because of her, my childhood was a very happy one.

Jean's mother and mine were sisters as well as best friends, so she's always been a part of my life. We spent many summer days just talking while we walked in the woods, sat in a tree or looked for a four-leaf clover.

Being 3 years younger, I sometimes got bored when Jean wanted to read *True Story* magazine or sit outside the kitchen window and eavesdrop on our mothers, but we usually ended up doing what she wanted.

Jean could always find something to do. Once we had a boxful of dollhouse furniture but no dollhouse. Jean took a piece of chalk, drew a floor plan on the brown tile floor of her bedroom and we played happily all afternoon.

Before anyone had heard of Barbie, Jean designed "gowns" for our dolls, using chiffon scarves held together with safety pins.

Because of her age, Jean could read

BUDDIES FOR LIFE. Joanne Peck (left) and her cousin Jean were the best of friends as children and remain close today. "She taught me the meaning of the word 'friend'," Joanne says.

books and see movies I didn't have access to, then she shared the stories with me afterward. When I saw the original *King Kong*, it paled in comparison to Jean's vivid description of it. She made everything better for me.

Even when Jean became a teenager in the '50s, she never abandoned me. She gave me a sense of self-worth.

I was jealous of her other friends. They shared a part of her world that I couldn't—junior high, boys, the softball league, wearing lipstick.

Once I tried to pick a fight with one of them, but Jean had rules: Everyone had to get along when they were with her. Some of her other friends couldn't stand each other, but in Jean's company they behaved like the best of pals.

My family moved away when I was 12, and Jean and I did our best to stay in touch. We spent most of our summers together, and she was always there where I needed her.

We grew up but not apart. We both got married, loved and hated jobs, wept with pain and pride for our children, lost our mothers and looked in wonder at the miracle of our grandchildren.

In short, we became average middle-aged women. And yet I'm *not* average. I'm blessed, for I have Jean in my life. I live in New York and she's in Florida, but we chat on the phone as often as we dare, (and does Ma Bell *love* us). Then every year or so we get together to just talk and remember.

After all these years, I will still do whatever it takes to be in Jean's company. She taught me the meaning of the word "friend" and I love her. ❧

THE VALUE OF A TRUE PAL has long been written about, and this quote from the Old Testament holds true today: "A faithful friend is a strong defence, and he that hath found such a one hath found a treasure."

Young "Skaters" Kept Waxed Floors Gleaming

IN OUR family, washing and waxing the floors wasn't a chore—it was a planned activity we looked forward to. Our friends begged to help, and those who weren't invited felt left out. That's because we kids were the floor polishers!

About three times a year, Mama would wash the floors and apply a thick coat of paste wax. Then we'd pull Dad's old wool socks over our shoes and skate around the rooms. Our efforts produced a high gloss that a machine could never duplicate.

The anticipation was almost unbearable as we waited for Mama to scrub, strip and rinse the floors. While they dried, we ate lunch—tuna sandwiches and hot cocoa. For us, that was real party fare.

Finally, Mama applied the wax… then it was time!

At first, paste wax is a bit stiff, but continued buffing makes it very slick, and for a couple of hours, we skated happily to music from the radio. It was like having our own mini-rink. Sometimes we tried to sneak in a game of "crack the whip", but Mama always put a damper on that.

The longer we skated, the slicker the floor got. When the falls started coming faster, Mama would call out a final "be sure you catch the corners", and it was time to quit. The babies and toddlers were pulled around on an old army blanket for the final buffing.

Mama's floors were the slickest and shiniest in town, the envy of all her friends who marveled at how she managed it with so many children and lousy Washington weather.

They would have really been surprised if they'd known just how those floors got so shiny! —*Arlee Johnson*
Mesa, Arizona

Bedtime Routine Called For Assembly Line

MY RECOLLECTIONS of the Depression aren't depressing, and the memories of our bath time routine still make me giggle!

When my father took a pay cut and my uncles were laid off, we all moved into Grandma's big three-story house. There were lots of bedrooms, but only one bathroom. To maintain order, we children got baths only when it was essential.

The youngest child would go first, with just enough water to cover the bottom of the tub. The next oldest went next, with another inch of hot water added to what was already in the tub, and so on, until we'd all had a bath.

My mother and aunts handled this as if they were on an assembly line, with one bathing, one drying and one helping with pajamas.

The situation might not have seemed funny at the time, but whenever my cousin and I talk about it now, we can't help giggling. Hearing our children and grandchildren groan, "Ugh! How gross!" just makes us laugh harder.

I have another special memory of our time at Grandma's. All the kids slept crosswise, three to a bed, in a single room. I thought I was special because I had my own "bed" in my parents' room—Mother's steamer trunk, padded with quilts.

Although I was separated from the other kids, I didn't feel left out. Mother made me feel like I had the very best spot. —*Toni Kohlstedt, Oxford, Ohio*

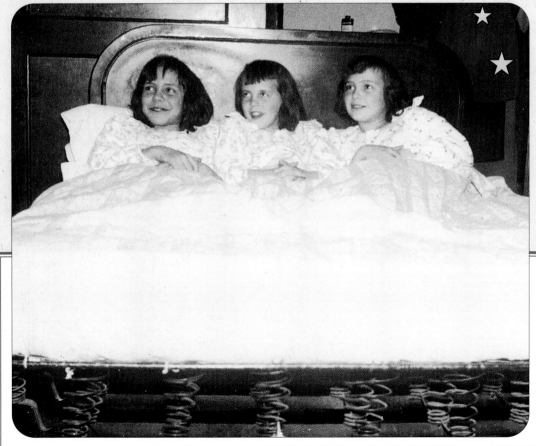

OVERNIGHTER. Her mother, Kathleen Shrake (left), and aunts, Sharon and Joanne, stayed over at a friend's apartment on Christmas 1950 and shared the Murphy bed, says Ann Follansbee of Milwaukee, Wisconsin.

NUTS OVER NUTS. There's nothing sweeter than the meat of a hickory nut, as these youngsters will discover in a few months when their cache is dry enough to crack.

Berry-Picking Was Simple Family Fun

I REMEMBER when a good mulberry tree was as important as a good apple tree. We knew exactly which would bear large, juicy plump berries, which were the male trees and which produced white mulberries.

When I was growing up in the '40s, my family had a row of them on the sand trail west of our Nebraska farm and a few more in the pasture. The biggest of them all, out in the front yard, had a rope swing.

Unfortunately, we could tell by the bird droppings when the mulberries were ripe. How Mother detested the mess they made on her freshly laundered sheets hanging on the line!

Picking mulberries was a family affair. We set out to shake the berries with a long-handled rake, an old bedspread, the canner and two milk buckets. We did this either early in the morning or in the evening, when there was little wind.

I preferred morning, when the meadowlarks sang and a turtledove answered with a mournful cry in the distance. There were always interesting wildflowers to observe on these excursions, and sometimes a hard-shelled turtle meandered by.

We spread the cloth out under the tree, then my brother hooked the rake on a big branch and shook it until the berries came tumbling down. Many landed on our heads or fell down our backs, leaving big purple blotches.

We would empty the cloth after each shake and move from tree to tree until we had enough. By then, our mouths were outlined in purple from "sampling".

Back home, we washed the berries, picking out all the sticks and leaves that had fallen with them.

Mother made jelly and jam, sauce to use on pancakes in winter, and many pies. But tastiest of all was a big bowl of just-picked mulberries with sugar and our own fresh cream.

—Vera Heithoff, Elgin, Nebraska

Winter Walnuts Taught Them About Life

HAVE YOU EVER watched a squirrel grab a large black walnut in his mouth and scurry away to find a secret hiding place? When the north winds howl and the ground is covered with snow, he'll retrieve the walnut and enjoy a winter feast. Our father taught us the same thrifty habit.

We gathered the green fruits in early fall, then Dad took our harvest to the basement and spread the nuts on paper to dry. It was quite a sight, as the shells oozed a black substance that would stain our hands and clothes if we dared to touch it.

When the nuts were dry, Dad put them in a basket on a shelf next to Mother's home-canned vegetables and fruits.

Winter limited our outdoor activities, and the nights seemed very long. When our spirits got low, Dad knew it was time to prepare a batch of walnuts.

He'd put the basket on the cellar floor and crack the hard shells with a hammer. We girls gathered the pieces in our laps and removed the nut meats with sharp picks—a tedious task. Since I was the youngest, it was extra hard for me. Dad helped when I needed it.

We placed the pieces in coffee cups, then took them to the kitchen. Dad warmed the nuts in hot water, then drained 'em and sprinkled 'em with salt. We ate these delicacies as we sat in a semicircle on the living room floor, listening to the radio. Each small morsel was a treat, and we savored every bite.

Those times taught us love and sharing—and that it takes work and effort to achieve something you really want. I'm grateful my father taught me those lessons in such a creative way.

—Deloris Cameron, Minerva, Ohio

Annual Chestnut Hunt Followed First Frost

WHEN I WAS 10 years old (*only* about 80 years ago), I looked forward to chestnut hunting with my grandfather every fall. We had to wait for a heavy frost, which would make the burrs fall and break open.

Each of us carried a cloth bag into the woods and checked the open burrs, revealing their treasure of nuts. When our bags were full, we hung them on a beam in the attic to keep the squirrels from getting to them first.

From time to time during winter, part of our cache would be brought down and boiled in salt water for a delicious treat.

—Anne Rapsher
Philadelphia, Pennsylvania

SHAGBARK SHAGGERS. The first step in proper nut gathering is...gathering.

Grandparents Shared Their Love of the Great Outdoors

By Beth Stefanek, Alma, Michigan

MY GRANDPARENTS' lives have always been centered around family and the woodlands and rivers of Michigan's Upper Peninsula. As their first grandchild, I got an early introduction to the great outdoors.

My grandparents began taking me trout fishing when I was 7 or 8. Grandpa would spend a whole day packing his rusty Ford truck with items we might need in "what if" situations—winches, two or three toolboxes, chains, axes and enough fresh water to last 3 to 5 days. It was his nature—cautious and ever-prepared.

The three of us started out early in the morning, traversing the county in a big circle and casting a line at every creek and river along the way. We prepared all of our meals in a large coffee can hung over a fire. To this day, I can picture the blackened sides of those red Folger's cans.

An Exciting Catch

One time, when we were on the Fence River, Grandma suggested I cast my line in a shady area upstream. After catching three or four chubs, I landed my first rainbow trout. I was thrilled, but Grandma was delighted!

I admired the fish's smooth pink belly and black speckles. Of course, I wanted to keep it. But when we measured it with the tackle box ruler, it was only

TREAT OF TROUT. Beth Stefanek's grandfather, Herb Sjostrom, is pictured cooking up a trout in 1927. He loved the outdoors and shared his zeal with her.

6-3/4 inches—1/4 inch short of legal. Mind you, my grandparents are DNR-respecting, law-abiding citizens, but this was their granddaughter's very first rainbow trout!

"Here," Grandma said. "I'll roll it up in my pant cuff and we'll put it through the wringer on the washing machine when we get home. That will stretch it out just enough."

She said it with a grin, and we both felt satisfied.

As we traveled the old logging roads, Grandma and Grandpa told me tales of their days in the woods. They had seen a rare albino buck—not once, but twice.

Good Hunters, Too

And Grandma and her two sisters often went deer hunting together. One day in 1950, all three of them shot a deer each while bow-hunting! That triple feat earned them stories in several area newspapers.

In fall, we'd drive and walk the logging roads, looking for woodcock and partridge. One day we spied a partridge doing a drumming dance on a log near the roadside. Grandma insisted we stop and roll down the window to watch and listen.

My grandparents are in their 80s now, but they still enjoy riding those roads, glimpsing the wildlife and reminiscing about the times they've spent in those woods. I no longer live in the woods, but thanks to my grandparents, the woods still live in me. ❧

Family Rose at Dawn for Day of Molasses Making

TO MAKE extra money and add food to the table in the early 1940s, my grandparents made molasses. My sister, two young uncles and I cut the sugarcane and brought it to the molasses mill. We started at sunrise, as molasses making was an all-day job that required many people.

I was only 5, but I remember feeding the cane into a press, which a horse turned by walking around the outside. The sap was cooked down until it became beautiful thick molasses. It took lots of wood to keep the fire going until the molasses was done.

My mouth still waters when I remember chewing sugarcane on a cool autumn morning, and eating molasses on a big country biscuit Grandma had just baked in her black wood-burning cookstove. —*Shelby Teaney Rocky Mount, Missouri*

Dining Table Was Hub of Activity

THE CENTER of many of our childhood activities was the old rectangular table in our dining room.

At dinnertime, all nine of us sat in our usual places on the long benches with heads bowed while Daddy said the blessing. Then the action began, with eating, conversation and ever-an-alert eye and hand to protect our glasses of milk from the grasp of a crafty sibling.

We each had to take a helping of everything served, and I recall taking one brussels sprout and secretly depositing it under the table on a little shelf made by a corner brace.

That table was more than just a place to eat meals, though. In the evenings, we gathered around to do our homework while Daddy worked on papers from the office.

On weekends, there always seemed to be a project in progress at the table. We worked on our stamp collections there, and in February, we gathered to make valentines. At Easter, we had a marvelous time decorating 7 dozen hard-boiled eggs.

April found us decorating old cottage cheese containers with crepe paper, paste and ribbons. Then on May Day, we filled these gorgeous baskets with blossoms and delivered them to our neighbors.

During summer, the kids worked at the table sealing jars with paraf-fin as Mom put up vegetables and made jelly and jam. In fall, we sat there to press and wax the colorful leaves we'd collected, making a marvelous preserved leaf collection.

December was a busy time. Cookie and candy making took weeks, and the delicious aroma wafting through the house was out of this world.

As Christmas neared, we gathered holly, greens and ribbon to make evergreen sprays to present to our neighbors with the cookies we'd custom-decorated.

Looking back, I wonder if my mother was giving the neighbors all those gifts for putting up with seven active, jubilant children!

—Barbara Kurz
Silver Spring, Maryland

Sunday Nights Were for Family

SUNDAY NIGHTS in the '30s and '40s were always "family night" at our house, and the only time our round tea cart was used.

We had a big meal at noon, so in the evening we had cut sandwiches with hot cocoa or ginger ale and homemade pie or cake for dessert.

When it was time to listen to *The Edgar Bergen and Charlie McCarthy Show* or *One Man's Family* on the radio, we munched away on big bowls of popcorn.

—Mary Elwood, Carlisle, New York

Lamp-Lit Nights Were "Like a Gift from God"

NOTHING brings back childhood memories like the aroma of a coal-oil lamp. Ours was saved for one special time that, to me, was like a gift from God—the nights the electricity went out.

We lived in an old farmhouse, with a windmill that pumped water from a well, and an old barn that hadn't seen a coat of paint since before I was born. We were surrounded by farmland and timber—the kind of country just made

GLOWING MEMORIES. That soft glow in the living room in the good old days wasn't a television, it was the warm and friendly lamp. Many a quiet night was spent basking in its light; reading, talking or maybe having a snack.

for a young boy, with plenty of wide-open spaces.

But the beautiful setting had its drawbacks, too—like frequent power outages. In our part of the country, they could last for days.

The electricity usually went out at night, during a storm. Then Dad would lower the magnificent glass lamp from the mantel. As he lit the wick, black smoke floated to the ceiling, and its aroma filled the air. When the globe was replaced, the light filled the room. The lamp cast dancing shadows as Dad carried it to the kitchen.

We all sat at the table while Mom dished out ice cream. The cartons weren't leak-proof then, and if the ice cream melted, it would make a mess. As much as you could possibly eat was the general rule.

With the only light from the yellow illumination of the lamp, we'd tell stories and eat ice cream until we couldn't swallow another bite. What more could a boy ask for?

Those days are long gone. Electricity is more reliable, refrigerators are better insulated and ice cream cartons are leak-proof. But I'll always have my memories of eating ice cream by the light of the coal-oil lamp on a stormy night.
—*Chuck Hughes, St. Joseph, Missouri*

Tending to Lamps Kept Little Hands Busy

IN THE good old days when I was a young girl on the farm, it was my task to keep the lamp chimneys polished. *Your hand is smaller...you can get it in the chimney, my dear.*

In a family of three boys and three girls, it took a number of lamps to keep all our rooms lighted.

The chimneys always seemed to attract soot, especially when a breeze entered the room on summer evenngs. But what *really* got me disgusted was when the moths flew into the chimney and fluttered around, making the inside very black. That meant taking newspaper to remove the worst soot, then wiping it with a damp cloth, followed by a lintless dry cloth.

The chimneys were quite narrow, although for one or two of our lamps we had a fancy wider chimney with white designs painted on. We hardly ever used the red ceramic lamp with the big roses and a matching globe. That was reserved for the parlor, which

STORY TIME. There was nothing Arthur Kightlinger Jr. liked better than having his dad read to him, and that's just what he was doing here in the late '20s. From these experiences come the pleasant memories of the close times we shared at home, nestled on Mom or Dad's lap. Arthur's wife, Louella, of Erie, Pennsylvania shared the photo.

we used only for guests. (I wish I had that lamp now...I don't remember what became of it.)

When I was a bigger girl, we got the newfangled Aladdin lamp, which had a very tall thin chimney and a mantle in it that gave out a bright white light. But oh, how careful you had to be, or that mantle would shatter.

Chimneys weren't the only part needing attention. The wicks had to be trimmed or they'd smoke. That was a smelly dirty task. The burned-off part of the wick had to be cut off with scissors.

Then the bowl of the lamp had to have enough kerosene in it to last the evening. How dangerous it must have been to carry those burning lamps from room to room, with a draft as you passed the open windows.

How privileged we are now. All we have to do to light up a room is touch a button—and when we no longer need the light, we don't have to lean over the lamp and huff and puff. Still, my memories of family times by lamplight are some of the brightest.
—*Katherine Penner, Inman, Kansas*

COOL CUSTOMERS. Skating tots look like they're getting ready to give the kid on the end a good ride of "crack the whip" on the neighborhood pond.

Burning Leaves Cooked The Perfect Potato

WHEN I WAS a boy in Connecticut, fall was my favorite time of year. By October, the sun was still bright, but the crisp winds off Long Island Sound hinted that winter's cold was just around the corner.

All the yards in my neighborhood had huge old maple and hickory trees. When the wind blew, thousands of brightly colored leaves rained down on us. This was long before the days of recycling and mulching, so my father would simply rake the leaves into a gigantic pile at the curb and light it.

I know this wasn't good for the air-quality index—a term that didn't exist then—but burning leaves was one of the highlights of fall. The children would circle around the fires for warmth, watching in amazement as the leaves quickly caught fire and burned, giving off a wonderful aroma and crackling sounds.

My mother would give each child a large raw potato to throw into the burning leaves. Then we'd search the neighborhood for the longest sticks we could find, and use them to periodically pull the potatoes out of the fire to check their progress.

After what seemed like forever, the pile of leaves was reduced to a fine ash and our potatoes were done. We held them in gloved hands

SNOW PANTS. "It looked like we spent more time on our knees than on our blades," says Joseph Donnelly (left) of Auburn, New York. Joseph was with his cousins Mary Kay Reich and Donald Binns at Hoopes Park in Auburn in 1940.

as we brushed off the blackened skin. I can still taste that first delicious bite!

Over the years, I've eaten in some of the finest restaurants in the country, and I often order a baked potato with my meal. But I've never had one that tasted as good as those I ate as a child, while a cold October wind blew a million leaves through the air.
—*Gregory Farrell*
Basking Ridge, New Jersey

Family Savored "Icy" Fishing, Skating Trips

ONE OF MY favorite family excursions was ice fishing at the ponds around our home in Great Pond, Maine.

When the ponds froze over, Dad cut holes in the ice with a chisel, and we dropped lines baited with the tiny silver "shiners" into each hole. Attached to each line was a stick with a red flag—the flag would rise when a fish nibbled at the bait. I always felt sorry for the shiners, but I watched the flags pop up just as eagerly as my three brothers did.

When we tired of watching the fishing holes, my brothers and I skated. Dad would build a fire near the shore and Mama made hot cocoa. When we returned, ravenous and rosy-cheeked, we roasted hot dogs and marshmallows on sticks. Nothing tasted better than food cooked over an open fire and eaten in the evergreen-scented air of the woods!

Sometimes we skated in the moonlight. The cool air made our faces tingle, but it wasn't unpleasant. The dense woods surrounding the pond provided so much shelter from the wind that it was kind of like being in a large room.

If we got too cold, we'd go back to the little fire to warm our hands and feet. The night breezes rustled through the forest around us. Sometimes we'd hear the skittering feet of a small animal or the clomping steps of a larger one. How still and peaceful the woods and crackling fire were!

Later, as the fire died down, we regretfully doused it with water from one of the fishing holes and headed for home. If we'd come in the sleigh pulled by "Silver", our big workhorse, we sang our way home over the powdery snow.

Many of our neighbors literally went to bed "with the chickens", and I'm sure our singing woke some of them, but they never complained. Perhaps the old sleigh brought back memories for them and rolled back the years for a moment—just as this memory does for me.
—*Elizabeth Nash*
Bradford, Massachusetts

CLEAN START. Back in Sidell, Illinois in the '30s, kids took to the streets when it snowed, relates Earl Cox of Albuquerque, New Mexico. A couple of kids would grab the bumper of the Illinois Dry Cleaner truck (above), then hook their toes to sleds behind them, and the whole gang would get pulled six blocks to the edge of town.

me to the Cadillac of sledding hills, a road leading to an abandoned mine. It was the steepest road I'd ever seen, leading straight up the mountain.

Father promised that if we could make it up the road, we'd be in for an unbelievable ride to the bottom. With his encouragement, I managed to make it to the top. I was tired but happy, looking forward to the ride down.

After catching our breath, we climbed on the Flyer. I sat in front, with Father's strong arms wrapped around me. He told me to hang on tight, and away we went.

We seemed to fly down the road, with Father skillfully steering around the corners. As the cold wind hit my face, I found myself laughing, yelling and screaming—and hoping it would never end. It was the greatest sledding memory of my life.

From then on, the Flexible Flyer was a big part of my childhood. It accompanied us on many outings and was the only ingredient we needed for fun. The Flyer seemed to have a special power—it was the fastest sled on the hill.

And it was tough, too. Whenever there was a crash, we ended up scraped and bruised, but the sled always came through unscathed, ready to fly again.

—Kenneth Dey
Spokane, Washington

Flyer Gave 5-Year-Old The Ride of His Life

MY OLD Flexible Flyer sled still hangs on the wall of my parents' shed. The years have taken their toll—the wood is faded, and the metal is rusted and bent. But there's no way we'd ever throw it away. Just looking at it brings back many memories of my Montana childhood.

Mom received the sled for Christmas when she was 6, so it was already over 20 years old when it entered my life, doubling as my winter stroller.

Family pictures show me in a wooden box lashed to the top, all bundled up and ready for another woodland excursion with my father.

My earliest memory of the sled is when I was about 5. On a beautiful winter day, Father took

COLD COMFORT. Even as a baby, Kenneth Dey was comfortable in his Flexible Flyer. With a wooden box lashed to the top, it doubled as his winter stroller!

BURNING LEAVES bring back many happy memories for readers who reveled in this favorite of autumn scents.

Julie Habel

Certain Scents Signaled Arrival of Fall

FALL EVOKES the unique scent of burning leaves. When the trees' bright plumage fell to the ground, we gathered around bonfires in our backyards for wienie roasts. Our toasted marshmallows usually caught fire, charring the outside and melting the center into a luscious, tantalizing morsel.

I remember other fall aromas, too, like newly threshed wheat. And when someone made apple butter, they could perfume an entire block.

—*Norman Maroney, Reno, Nevada*

Autumn Leaves Gave Children Days of Fun

IN AUTUMN, after all the leaves fell, we children were allowed a few weeks to play in them.

First we'd rake them into "leaf houses", with neat piles representing the walls. We'd put our dolls and play furniture in the rooms and play house for days. Each evening before bed, we'd pray a windstorm wouldn't come up overnight and scatter our walls.

After we tired of that game, we'd rake all our walls into a gigantic pile, get a stepladder and jump from it into the leaves. They were soft, smelled wonderful and kept us happy for days.

At last, some of the leaves were taken to our gardens and spaded into the soil. The men in the neighborhood gathered the leftover leaves and burned them in the alley. How we loved that wonderful aroma in the crisp air.

We now knew Halloween was right around the corner, and Old Man Winter close behind. —*Helen Swanson Houston, Texas*

Attic Was a Santuary of Fun

ONE OF MY most pleasant childhood memories is of the stormy days we spent in the attic of our eight-room farmhouse. A window at either end provided light, and there were two large racks made of two-by-fours.

One held ears of seed corn with the husks pulled back, drying to use for spring planting. The other held an old buffalo robe and my father's ankle-length fur coat. These were used on cold bobsled rides into town.

Beside a large wooden barrel of black walnuts were boxes of outdated clothing—shoes with buttons on the sides, an old hat we often borrowed for our "talent shows", and a white parasol edged with eyelet embroidery and lace. We often used these things to dress up and "play house". —*Norma Doser Dubuque, Iowa*

ATTIC ATTIRE. Dressing up in old clothes found in the attic was fun, recalls Norma Doser.

Rainy Days Brought Farm Family Together

WHENEVER we had a dry spell on the farm, everyone would talk about how badly the crops needed rain, and I still remember the feeling of joy when the warm summer rains finally came.

The whole family would stand on the long farmhouse porch, just watching the rain come down and talking about how thankful we were.

I remember running out into the yard, feeling the wet grass on my bare feet, dancing, singing and opening my mouth while looking skyward to catch the warm drops. My mother put out pans to catch the rainwater, which she used to wash our hair.

There was another reason I liked rainy days—my father couldn't work outside! He stayed in the house then and we'd pop corn or make fudge and play games. My mother confessed that she "didn't get any housework done when George is in the house".

What a wise woman she was to put the really important things—spending quality time with her family—ahead of routine chores. Even now, rainy days put me in the mood for family togetherness.

—*Georgia Whiteford*
Ottawa, Kansas

Dish from Box of Oats Held Precious Memories

ONE childhood memory from the '30s is still very real to me. Daddy was coming home in the wagon, kicking up dust and carrying a big box of cereal.

"Oh, Mama," I cried. "Can I open the box that Daddy's bringing?"

You see, one of the highlights of my youth was the suspense of opening the Mother's Oats box to see what kind of premium was inside. It was always a dish of some kind—a jelly dish, a pink plate or cookie jar, a blue Shirley Temple pitcher or a white teacup and saucer. On this particular day, it was an orange jelly dish shaped like a little riverboat.

"Can I keep this dish for my very own?" I pleaded.

On my 65 birthday, I happened to open a cabinet that held that very dish. What a wonderful warm feeling...that dish took me back to Mama's kitchen, to a time when I felt so loved and secure. I can feel the same love now, 60 years later and 600 miles away.

—*Martha Query, Maroa, Illinois*

STUBBORN AS MULES. When Evelyn Corzine and her cousins got together, they couldn't wait to ride the family donkeys—so two or three kids would pile on at a time. Evelyn is standing, holding one of her cousins.

Donkey Outsmarted Impatient Riders

RIDING my family's donkeys was one of our favorite things to do when our cousins visited. When we got impatient at waiting our turn, we sometimes sped things up by piling on three at a time.

One donkey, "Jenny", didn't seem to appreciate that. When one rider got on, that was okay, and two she could tolerate.

But after a third child climbed aboard, she'd head straight for a tree with a low-hanging branch...just the right height to knock all the riders off!

—*Evelyn Corzine*
New Port Richey, Florida

GIRL'S BEST FRIEND. In this case, it was "Tuffy", the Boston terrier, says Rosalee Sternhagen of Avon, South Dakota. He was her mother's special pet when she was 16. The photo was taken in 1926 next to the cistern pump in the family's backyard.

H. Armstrong Roberts

A Simple Catalog Took Them to Another World

By Magdeline Boyd, Purvis, Mississippi

MY SISTER and I were raised in the cotton fields of the Mississippi Delta. That was over 70 years ago, when the Sears Roebuck catalog was our only contact with the outside world.

That catalog had a special place in our home, on an old table alongside the Bible and the Baptist hymnbook Mama and Daddy brought with them as we moved from plantation to plantation, seeking a better life.

Just as fall was beginning to cool the scorched earth, our catalog came. We could hear the mail rider a mile away, blowing the horn of his old Model A, and ran the half mile from the fields to meet him (he always greeted us with a big smile and a piece of Wrigley's gum).

This was a special time for us, and we tenderly tucked the catalog in its spe-

cial place until dusk, when chores were done. Only then could we take it down, giggling expectantly as we stretched out on our bellies before the fire.

The catalog took us to a different world, where pretty ladies wore lovely dresses and silk panties—something we'd never seen. Mama made *our* panties from cotton flour sacks (she got the letters off by rubbing the sack with lye soap, letting it stand for a day, then boiling it in the big washpot outside).

Once I got a pair of black satin shoes and black silk stockings from the catalog. Not rayon, not nylon, but silk! Daddy measured my foot by placing it on the catalog page and drawing around it. When I wore those shoes and stock-

ings, I felt just like the beautiful ladies in the catalog.

After most of the cotton was picked, we'd ride the wagon with Daddy to the gin. If there was enough money, he'd ask for the Sears catalog and place an order for groceries—a hoop of cheese, a gallon of peanut butter, a 5-gallon can of oil sausage and a 24-pound bag of flour.

In about a week, we'd hear the welcome *ah-ooo-gah* of the Model A. Daddy would hitch the mule to our handmade sled and rush down to meet the mail carrier. Sister and I ran behind, excited that "Mr. Sears Roebuck" had gotten Daddy's letter and we'd have special treats throughout the winter.

With spring came a new catalog… and, of course, you already know where the old catalog went! ❧

Just Headin' Out to Eat Was a Big Treat

LET'S GET "SPAGHET". Her college friends were on their way to "Joe's Spaghetti Place" in Oneonta, New York when she snapped the photo at right in 1939, says Carol Anderson of Maple Springs, New York. Look out, Joe—they look mighty hungry!

IT'S ON THE HOUSE. Going out to eat didn't take much for her daughters Adrienne and Nadine (right), says Mildred Guertin (left in photo) of Westchester, Illinois. Back in 1950, they owned "Nips Hamburgers" in Chicago and lived in an apartment in back. The girls had their breakfast each day in the restaurant.

THEY'RE STILL GOING OUT! Fred and Jan Scheel of Las Vegas, Nevada (in the backseat in 1958 photo below and on left in photo below right) are still double-dating with Mahlon and Carolyn Blumenshine of Washington, Illinois after 37 years. Bet Mahlon wishes he still had that '55 Olds.

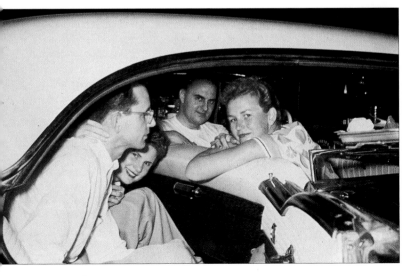

Barn Dances Let Families Kick Up Their Heels

By Helen Oakley, New Milford, Pennsylvania

WHEN I WAS a teenager in the late 1930s and early '40s in rural New York State, there was a "round and square" barn dance almost every Saturday night. Those were the most exciting times of my teenage years.

An entire family could have an evening of fun for a few pennies. The ladies brought all the refreshments, and the hat was passed to pay for the coffee and root beer.

Small children, youngsters and tiny babies sat along the sidelines with the older folks, watching the dancers and keeping time to the music. It was quite natural to attend social events with the family, and I truly believe most teenagers enjoyed having fun with the grown-ups there. I know *I* did.

All Gussied Up

It was wonderful to gaze upon the beautiful ladies and handsome gentlemen promenading around the halls to the music. The ladies wore full, rustling skirts and petticoats; the men wore clean white shirts, ties and dress pants. And most were kind and considerate to the children and teenagers who were just learning the dances.

Barn dances always had three squares, then round dance music with waltzes, polkas and a new dance called the jitterbug. "Grab yer pardners" would send the fellows scurrying to find a partner for the squares.

The teenagers mingled freely, dancing with many partners. Many met their future spouses at those dances—including me. My husband-to-be was so handsome, and older. But he didn't seem to notice me until a straight pin holding my blouse cuff together popped off and pricked him during a square dance!

"Rounds and squares" gave us a wealth of good times and pleasant memories of sharing happiness as a family. Back then, parents seemed to have a firm grip on teenagers, and young people looked to their folks for guidance as they felt their way into the grown-up world.

"It must have been terrible to grow up when you were young," the grandchildren often say when they hear how strict our parents were. I assure them my teen years were among the most wonderful of my life. I feel sad that today's teens don't have "round and square" dances. What happy times they were! ♪

SWING YOUR PARTNER. Round or square, dancing was great fun.

J.C. Allen and Son

"Pound Parties" Welcomed Servicemen on Furlough

DURING World War II, "pound parties" were very popular for neighborhood servicemen home on furlough. The man's family usually hosted the party, and each guest brought a pound of something—everything from fresh-butchered liver to divinity fudge.

More people squeezed into old farmhouses than you could imagine, and it was standing room only except for the older generation. Later, we played yard games in the moonlight, with a few kerosene lanterns hung around.

Preparing for these parties took time and planning. The house had to be thoroughly cleaned. The rugs were swept and shaken, the walls wiped down and the lamps filled and cleaned.

Feed was set out at the hitch rail for the guests' horses, and extra wood was carried to the back porch for fuel. And, of course, the outhouse had to be scrubbed and swept, and a fresh catalog supplied if necessary.

These parties were somewhat bittersweet, however, because while we were happy to see the man on furlough, we knew he'd be going back in a few days…and there were always missing friends who hadn't made it back.

—*Louise Evans, Hidalgo, Illinois*

HAIL, HAIL, the gang was all there at a 40th birthday party for George Hackbarth in 1934. Photo, from Myrtle Frederick of Brookfield, Wisconsin, was taken in the hall at Holy Ghost Church in Milwaukee, Wisconsin.

"Planting" Red Ears Kept Husking Bees Lively

HUSKING CORN was time-consuming, but the husking bees held in our neighborhood in the northern Berkshires of Massachusetts made it fun.

Neighbors and friends gathered in the barn around a big pile of unhusked corn, sitting on stools or pails, usually by lantern light. To keep things interesting, a few ears of red corn were "planted" in the pile. If a lady found one, she was kissed by all the boys and men. If a male found one, he could go around and kiss the girls.

Sometimes there were objections, resulting in a game of "catch me if you can" or good-natured wrestling in the husks. Any bashful young fellows who didn't even try to kiss the girls found themselves being chased—usually by the married women!

When the kissing was finished, the red ears had to be turned in or confiscated, as some enterprising young fellow or girl was likely to use them over again.

Around 10:30 p.m. or so, the host family served coffee or cider and doughnuts. If someone had his fiddle or banjo, there'd be a few rounds of a Virginia reel, money musk, Portland fancy or other square dance right there in the barn.

Afterward, everyone went home satisfied, knowing a good job had been done. I'm 76 now and still remember being one of those bashful young men who liked to be chased!

—Lloyd Copeland
Suffern, New York

AW, SHUCKS. Husking corn on a small farm in the good old days kept folks together, as this family shows. Looks like they've got a "fer piece" to go!

After-Dinner Postcards Kept Relatives in Touch

MY WIFE liked having guests for dinner, and our house often ended up filled with 20 to 25 relatives, many of them children. We never had a bit of trouble with any of them, though.

After dinner, I'd bring out a stack of postcards addressed to a loved one who

NICELY NESTLED. Old-time postcards, like this one from Marian Kuenzie of Desert Hot Springs, California, hatched some colorful memories.

was away at college or in the military, and each guest would write a few lines. Even the babies "wrote" messages (with some help from the adults).

We did this for years, and many of our relatives still talk about what fun it was to receive those cards.

One Christmas right after World War II ended, we all wrote to a nephew serving in Tokyo. He still hasn't forgotten the thrill of answering mail call that day and getting *30* postcards!
—*William Eskilson, Visalia, California*

Bonfire, Slide Show Made Election Night Festive

By Hilda Kraus, Westport, Connecticut

ELECTION NIGHT was one of the best and most exciting times on 79th Street in New York City. The big boys would gather wood all day from various sources—wooden crates, old kitchen chairs, anything that would burn—to make a great big fire in the middle of the gutter.

The street was closed off to traffic at both ends. A huge white cloth was strung up on the facade of the Democratic Club, where election results would be shown on slides projected from a window of the Republican Club across the street.

As soon as it got dark enough and there were some results from the precincts, the slide show would begin and a crowd started to gather in the street to watch. The boys would light the bonfire, which was away from the crowds, and the little kids were sent off to gather potatoes from home for roasting.

Somehow, nothing tasted quite so good as a charcoal-blackened potato with its inside soft and white, and much too hot to eat right away. These were called "mickeys". If you were lucky, you might even get a "sweet mickey"—a yam or sweet potato.

The excitement lasted late into the night and the following morning, until all the precincts had reported. However, the bonfire usually burned out by about 10 o'clock. By then, the children had long been gathered and put to bed. ❧

"Tacky" Was Fashionable At This Party

NO ONE in our small community had much money, so my parents tried to think of inexpensive ways to get people together.

To everyone's delight, they held a "tacky party". Guests were told to wear their tackiest clothing and come with messy hair. We had a wiener roast, ate cookies and played games.

The idea caught on, and other "play parties" followed. With each family bringing something to eat or drink, the evening wasn't costly and no one needed baby-sitters.

Perhaps if today's families got together like this, our children wouldn't get into trouble looking for "something to do". Wouldn't it be great to turn off the TV for just one night?
—*Zula Shenk, Robstown, Texas*

HATS OFF, PLEASE! They might have looked silly, but it sure was fun dressing in zany get-ups for a theme party, as Zula Shenk recalls at right.

Church Lemon Socials Made Sweet Memories

DURING THE 1930s, money was hard to come by and most social affairs were church-related. The one I remember best was the "lemon social". Here's how it worked:

Each teenager took a lemon and paid 2¢ for each seed it contained. The money paid for ice and sugar for lemonade (our mothers took turn baking the cookies). Those *really* were the good old days. —*Bonnie Baumgardner*
Sylva, North Carolina

Pie Suppers Helped Buy Playground Equipment

AT MY country grade school, we had a pie supper or box supper every fall to raise money. To prepare for this event, the girls helped the teacher decorate an elaborate pie box with different colors of crepe paper.

First there was a children's program. Then a man in the crowd would auction off the delicious homemade pies one at a time. No one knew whose pie was in the box, and the winning bidder would later eat his pie with whoever had made it.

We also raised money by having "elections" at a penny a vote. For instance, the woman voted worst housekeeper might receive a child's broom as a prize...the man with the dirtiest feet could win a bar of soap ...and the "most lovesick couple" won a jar of pickles.

The money raised was put to good use— it bought new playground equipment, which was always in short supply.
—*Della Whitesell*
El Dorado Springs, Missouri

Feather-Stripping Parties Tickled Their Fancy

I'LL NEVER FORGET winter "feather-stripping parties" in northern Michigan.

After word-of-mouth invitations were passed along on the school bus, about a dozen teenagers would gather in the kitchen of a neighbor's home.

We'd sit around a long wooden table with a mound of white goose feathers in the middle. A kerosene lamp lit the scene as we stripped the down from the shaft.

The soft down was used for stuffing pillows. All the stories and jokes we told made it difficult not to laugh too hard or sneeze— which would have been disastrous!

After an hour or two of "stripping", the hostess would take the feathers away and bring on some tasty dessert and hot chocolate to reward us for such "hard work". Our fun evening ended with a walk home in the moonlight through cold, crunchy snow.
—*Cecilia Meyer, Fort Collins, Colorado*

IF THE WORLD hands you lemons, just make a lemon pie. Pie suppers and bake sales, like the one below, provided needed funds and satisfied many a sweet tooth.

Sleepless Night Took Him Home

By C. Basil Coleman, Indianapolis, Indiana

ONE NIGHT not long ago, I was having a hard time sleeping. I finally began flipping through all the TV channels until I punched the "off" button and settled back into the pillows.

Closing my eyes, I saw a little boy—me—stretched out in his father's lap, listening to him sing and holding onto a crooked right thumb. Dad had injured it in the coal mines when he was 16. Not receiving proper medical treatment, it had healed crooked and stiff, but when I held onto that familiar thumb and heard his songs, everything was right with the world.

Suddenly I was back in western Kentucky, in the old three-room house where Mom had delivered me in the summer of 1930. (I was told later that after the delivery, I was temporarily placed in a drawer of the old chest that stood in the corner. Someone had closed the drawer to make more room, so for a few minutes, I was lost until someone remembered what they'd done with the baby!)

In my memory, I saw Mom sewing and patching our clothes. As she folded and put away the pillowcases and sheets, I smelled the homemade lye soap and watched her smile when Dad forgot the next line in one of his songs—*Comin' 'Round the Mountain, Barbara Allen, My Old Kentucky Home, Let the Rest of the World Go By, Streets of Laredo* and *Whipping That Old TB.*

Jimmy Rodgers was Dad's favorite singer, and my favorite song that Dad sang was *Casey Jones,* about a train engineer killed in a wreck because he tried to make up lost time.

My next choice for entertainment was listening to our neighbor, Mr. Garrett, tell stories from his youth. All the kids would sit in a semicircle around his fireplace, staring at the yellow and blue flames as the coal burned in the grate.

My heart would pound when he got to the exciting parts—especially during ghost stories.

End of an Era

Then one summer afternoon, a salesman drove into our yard. When he left, he had 50¢ in his pocket and four or five of Mom's hens—the down payment on a Philco battery radio!

Mom listened to beautiful gospel music on Sunday mornings, and I learned lots of hymns by listening with her.

I recall all of us going outside to search the sky for "death rays" when Orson Welles broadcast *War of the Worlds* on Halloween.

I remember friends and relatives visiting us to listen to the fights, and Dad listening to Sunday baseball games, sticking his ear close to the speaker when storms interfered with the reception. I believe his favorite team was the St. Louis Browns.

As I look back, it seems Dad's songs stopped after that radio came along—unless the battery was "down". Mr. Garrett's stories ended then, too. *How I missed them.*

And as I remembered those days, I suddenly realized how much was lost. I wanted to go back to an old cane-bottomed rocking chair, holding onto a crooked thumb while Dad sang *Wednesday Night Waltz.* I wanted to see Mom sitting there with us, putting a half-sole on an old pair of shoes or doing one of her many chores by the firelight, smiling as she cast proud glances over her little world.

I wanted to see that beautiful room with newspapered walls to help keep out the winter wind…the chipped but polished mantel over the fireplace…a doily embroidered with red roses, its crocheted edges carefully stiffened with sugar water…the security of the oil lamp smoldering with a yellow glow.

Bring back my little rubber cars to drive across the cracks and knots in the old wood floors, scrubbed clean with a stiff brush and strong soap.

Bring back familiar faces of friends and neighbors, Grandmas and Grandpas who gave me that "look" when I misbehaved. Bring back my father's face, his skin imbedded with black marks from the coal chipped by his sharp pick over the years.

Bring back the hot burning smell of goldenrod in August, of tarred cross ties on the railroad track I walked over on the way to school. Bring back the breeze that cooled my sweaty face and carried the scents of summer days long past, never to be appreciated by anyone ever again.

I didn't sleep much that "night not long ago", but I relived my love of life as a child before radio and television. *Please, God, give me another sleepless night to go back home again.* ☙

KEEPING THE HOME FIRES BURNING. Making a rag rug was simple entertainment…the best kind.

Ewing Galloway